D1213345

From the Library

Gordon L. Harding

Lucid Interval

For Isabel and Ronald Lumgair,
the Good Mother and Good Father

Lucid Interval

Subjective writing and madness in history

George MacLennan

Rutherford • Madison • Teaneck
Fairleigh Dickinson University Press

1-17-07

Associated University Presses
440 Forsgate Drive
Cranbury, NJ 08512

Library of Congress Cataloging-in-Publication Data

MacLennan, George.
    Lucid interval : subjective writing and madness in history /
George MacLennan.
      p.   cm.
    "First published in Great Britain in 1992 by Leicester University
Press (a division of Pinter Publishers Limited)" – T.p. verso.
    Includes bibliographical references and index.
    ISBN 0-8386-3505-9 (alk. paper)
    1. English literature – History and criticism. 2. Nerval, Gérard
de. 1808–1855 – Criticism and interpretation. 3. Mentally ill,
Writings of the – History and criticism. 4. Literature and mental
illness. 5. Mentally ill in literature. 6. Authors – Mental health.
I. Title.
PR120.M47M33 1992
820.9'353-dc20
                                      92-2590
                                       CIP

PR
120
,M47
M33
1992

Contents

Acknowledgements

John Dixon Hunt, Victor Sage and Roger Sales read sections of the book in draft: I am indebted to them for comments and suggestions which were often invaluable. Thanks are also due to an anonymous reader for Leicester University Press: comments on various points in the draft led to a number of fruitful revisions. I owe a long-term debt of gratitude to Clive Scott who supervised my doctoral thesis on Nerval, and who has encouraged my subsequent efforts to develop it. The direction of these efforts was influenced by numerous conversations I enjoyed with Lee Garner: I have also benefited from conversations with Wieslaw Kuhn, who shares my interest in the history of madness. Sharon Sage checked through my translations from Tasso's prose, and spared me some howlers: those which remain are entirely my own responsibility. Dee Reynolds, Cristina Ruffini, George Hyde and Michael Hollington all contributed help on specific points. Rachel Spence and Elred Fernandez assisted me in compiling an index. Finally, thanks once more to Rachel, also to Professor Jack Spence, who were instrumental in helping the orphan manuscript find a home.

Introduction

I

This book examines the ways in which the experience of madness
becomes available in literature for the production and expression of
subjective meaning. Autobiographical and subjective prose and
poetry mediate the experience of madness in ways that are determined by the situation of the individual writer, while this situation
is itself determined in various ways – biographically, medically,
culturally and historically. With these concerns in mind, I have
focused on eight writers: Thomas Hoccleve, Torquato Tasso, James
Carkesse, John Bunyan, George Trosse, William Cowper, John
Clare and Gérard de Nerval. With the exception of Bunyan, all of
these were, in their own lifetimes, viewed or treated as madmen.

They were not, however, necessarily mad when they wrote, and
my enquiry is at least as much concerned with conditions of
recovery as of madness. Discourses of madness and recovery
provide, under tellingly extreme conditions, instances of how
subjective identity is constituted in any given period. In examining
these writings, I have hazarded an overarching hypothesis about
relationships between madness and subjective experience in the long
period under review. Briefly stated, my argument is that an
interiorisation of madness occurs between the medieval and modern
periods: this, moreover, determines the eventual emergence of a
'creative' writing which, in the nineteenth century, occurs within
the experience of madness itself.

This argument lays no claim to novelty. The historian of ideas,
Georges Gusdorf, referring to Hölderlin and Nerval among others,
has noted that 'the Romantic mentality attains a new experience of
illness in the perspective of interiority.'[1] Gusdorf's remark is in
turn an unacknowledged echo of Michel Foucault's writings on the
madness of the artist – of Hölderlin in particular. Nevertheless the

phenomenon which Foucault and Gusdorf draw attention to remains in need of further critical attention: at the same time, its extensive 'prehistory' has, to my knowledge, been completely ignored.

The first of the following two sections of this introduction outlines in greater detail the scope and concerns of the study. The second provides definitions of the categories of 'discourse' which I have employed.

II

In 1690, the nonconformist priest George Trosse wrote an auto-biographical account of the episode of insanity he had suffered in the 1640s. Trosse, like the autobiographers of madness who preceded him (Otloh of St Emmeram, Margery Kempe), is an unduly neglected writer, but unlike them he does not stand in isola-tion. His *Life* was preceded by Richard Norwood's *Confessions* (1639–40) and Bunyan's *Grace abounding* (1666); it was succeeded in the eighteenth century by William Cowper's *Memoir* (1765). All of these Protestant spiritual autobiographies recount psychical ordeals of varying degrees of acuteness.

By the seventeenth century, an increasingly self-conscious and psychologically self-aware culture was in the process of emerging in Western Europe: as part of this phenomenon, the self-examining discourses of Puritanism were alert to the evidence of inner crisis as a condition of spiritual rebirth. It is in this context that effectively psychological discriminations of inner crisis become increasingly available.

If autobiographical discourses provide one indicator of the paradigms which affect how certain individuals experienced madness, another is provided by the genres of poetry. The nexus which links poetry, inspiration, possession and madness is older than Plato, while the writings of Plato and Aristotle have provided influential sources for the association of poetry, madness and melancholia. After Torquato Tasso's emotional instability resulted in his being detained in the hospital of Sant'Anna, he admitted to melancholia while denying that his carefully crafted poetry was the product of 'enthusiasm.' Conversely, James Carkesse, confined in New Bedlam in 1679, justified his mad verse as *furor poeticus*.

Towards the end of the eighteenth century, inspiration came to be understood as an inner, creative dynamic. Romanticism revitalised a notion which had decayed to a cursory formula in the Age of Reason. It is around this moment that an unprecedented cluster of mad poets congregrate: at an early moment, Christopher Smart, then Friedrich Hölderlin, John Clare and Gérard de Nerval.

In his discussions of Hölderlin, Michel Foucault has sought to comprehend the extent of this phenomenon. According to Foucault, Hölderlin confronted the absence of the gods as an absolute, epochal crisis. In the disruption occasioned by this crisis, a 'nondiscursive' (noncommunicative) language is thrown back on its own interiority, initiating a transgressive rupture at the interior of language itself. It is under these conditions that the 'unthinkable' convergence of madness and poetry occurs: 'This state can no longer be understood as a Platonic ecstasy which protects [the artist] from illusion and exposes him to the radiant light of the gods, but as a subterranean relationship in which the work and what it is not construct their exteriority within the language of dark interiority.'[2] Through Hölderlin's madness, lyric poetry is constituted as a nondiscursive practice: 'a revelation that no language could have expressed outside the abyss that engulfs it.'[3] Throughout the 1960s Foucault was concerned with the limits of dialectics and philosophical reason, and found in Hölderlin the poet whose madness not only marked the end of *l'âge classique*, but also (by way of Hölderlin's versions of *The Death of Empedocles*) provided the precondition for Nietzsche, the mad philosopher. In this sense, then, Hölderlin, as poet, inaugurates madness as the utterance of the impossibility of utterance.

Foucault's discussion of Hölderlin provides a benchmark for my own enquiry into the relationship between madness and subjective writing. Nevertheless I find his formulations at least as unsatisfactory as they are illuminating. This, then, is an appropriate point at which to measure my own concerns against those of Foucault.

In *Madness and civilization*, Foucault showed that, from about 1650, madness came to be excluded from the community of reason. He investigated the discourses and practices which organised this internment, but his analysis was distinguished by a subversive concern with the integrity of madness itself. For Foucault, the silencing of madness by the agencies of reason was the precondition of their discourses on madness: 'The language of psychiatry, which is a monologue of reason *about* madness, has been established only on the basis of such a silence. I have not tried to write the history

of that language, but rather the archeology of that silence."[4] In the
brief essay which concluded *Madness and civilization*, Foucault
attempted to address madness on its own problematic ground.

If Classical Reason had interned and silenced madness, then it fell
to a new practice of writing which, towards the end of the eighteenth century, emerged at the outer limits of the orders of
discourse to articulate the silence of madness. This, according to
Foucault, is 'literature' (a term which only comes into general usage
at this moment): Hölderlin, more than any other writer, is its practitioner. Madness subsists in Hölderlin's writing as a radicalisation
of that very silence to which Reason had confined it, thus madness
is constituted in literature not as an *oeuvre*, but, in Foucault's
talismanic phrase, as the absence of an *oeuvre* – *l'absence d'oeuvre*.

In implying that Hölderlin's 'nondiscursive' poetry emerges in and
through the very absence of productive discourse, articulating the
silent obverse of reason itself, Foucault revealed the desire of his
own writing to exceed the academic constraints of a discourse of
knowledge. Inasmuch as he posited madness as that critical rupture
which never ceases to interrogate the discourse of knowledge, then
Hölderlin provides its necessary *terminus ad quem*. With the advent
of this poet, madness, at length, expresses its own self-emptying
essence as *absence d'oeuvre*. To put this in other terms, in
Hölderlin's lyric nondiscourse, the silence of madness, held in
suspension during the Age of Reason, is at length precipitated.

The extent of my indebtedness to Foucault's thought is evident
in every chapter of this book, nevertheless I find some of his
assumptions questionable. In his writings, madness is posited as an
incommunicable 'truth,' beyond knowledge, to which the non-mad
have related in various ways through the ages. The moment at
which the artist reveals the dark luminosity this truth – the
moment of Goya and Sade no less than Hölderlin – is constituted
as an absolute epistemological divide. On the far side stand Tasso,
Swift and Rousseau, who (although differentiated under the respective headings of madness, melancholy and delirium) are producers
of *oeuvres*: on the near side are Hölderlin, Nerval and Artaud, all
artists whose madness is manifested as an *absence d'oeuvre*.

While the end of the eighteenth century undoubtedly marks a
crucial juncture, a number of subjective writings which reflect on
or express experiences of madness, from Otloh's in the eleventh
century down to the present day, reveal (as one might in fact
expect) a picture which is both less clear-cut and less metaphysically
heroic than the one which Foucault proposes. When read from an

historical and critical perspective, these writings suggest that madness is a culture-bound phenomenon, if not in its origins then in its manifestations and self-representations. In approaching a number of such writings I have attempted a provisional reconstruction of how experiences of madness are culturally and historically constituted.

It should immediately be said that this amounts to considerably less than an history of madness. If there is a self-representing 'culture of madness' at any given time, it is usually a privileged one. The very notion of a subjective, self-representing mode of experience, where it does not derive from a relatively privileged social position, is arguably a product of literate self-consciousness.[5] When this becomes available to members of non-privileged groups who have usually been denied the cultural status of an individual self-identity, it does so under conditions of far-reaching social and cultural change.[6] The ironies of this development become spectacular in the case of John Clare. In the first half of the nineteenth century, Clare, a largely self-educated rural labourer, experienced madness under conditions which must be objectively described as 'privileged.' In terms of this study, Clare is a rule-proving exception. In his writings, he gains access to the meanings of his madness, but, by a further turn of the screw, those meanings effectively negate his subjective experience. In Clare's writings of 1841, as in Nerval's writings of 1853-4, there is a problematisation of subjective identity, but in the case of Clare this further reacts with contradictions which derive from his class position.

Madness may be projected in discourses in very different ways. Writers who seek to express the meanings of their experiences of madness need *not* do so in terms of subjective interiority: James Carkesse did not. In Carkesse's poems, not only does madness not implicate an interiorised condition of subjectivity, but Carkesse reacts against such a 'dark' interiorisation, naming it as 'lunacy' and distinguishing it from his own public and diurnal madness. The notion that madness is necessarily manifested in inward or psychological terms must be discounted in an historical perspective. Yet there is no doubt that, by the late eighteenth and nineteenth centuries, the relevant writings of Cowper, Clare and Nerval do in fact express an interiorised madness. In the cases of Cowper and Nerval, this form of madness is increasingly consonant with psychoanalytic postulates. A number of critics have recognised that the figures of the father and the mother are central to the

subjective themes of Nerval's writings. The same cannot be said of
Clare, but he is again atypical in ways which are revealing. If
Clare's actual father and mother seem unproblematic in the
perspective of his life and work, this is because the meanings they
represent for him are not interiorised, and so lack the subjective
implications that abound in Nerval's writings. This difference again
seems to me to be attributable less to different national cultures
than to the different social and class positions of the two writers.
It is as an adult and not as a child that Clare enters into
ambivalent and ultimately hostile relationships with authority
figures who belong to the middle and upper classes, including his
first asylum keeper, Matthew Allen. But these figures play no part
in his later subjective poetry. By contrast, Emile Blanche, who
treated Nerval during his later crises, is, for Nerval, positioned
'internally' as well as externally, by way of the writer's relationship
with his own doctor-father. In contrast with the autobiographical
inspiration of Nerval's later writings, Clare's later poetry expresses
an existence which has been drained of autobiographical meaning.
If an interiorisation of madness occurs in history, then a comparison of Nerval and Clare demonstrates that this is not a uniform
phenomenon (the historically late instance of Carkesse's *Lucida
intervalla* also indicates that it is not invariable).

What are the conditions under which such a process of interiorisation occurs in Western European culture? In attempting to answer
this question I have drawn on a range of analyses of subjective
interiorisation.[7] A brief review of these (in reverse order – going
back from the later period to the earlier one) will indicate their
relevance to a number of the writings discussed in this book.

   Theodore Adorno's critique of subjectivity as an epistemological
category, exemplified in Søren Kierkegaard's philosophy, offers a
definition of 'bourgeois subjectivity' which also prefaces other more
directly socio-historical approaches to the notion of interiorisation.
In his study of Kierkegaard, Adorno confronted subjectivity with its
historical and material substratum in the bourgeois domestic
interior. In Kant's philosophy, subjective autonomy is established
over and against the object world, but for Adorno, the object
world is not an absolute datum. Only through the furnishing of
reality in terms of commodification does it come to be set in apposi-
tion to subjective self-consciousness. 'Objective reality' is not objective reality as such, but the commodity form of bourgeois reality.
Subjectivity, in this view, is historically produced by the material

forms of bourgeois existence. More specifically, subjective interiority is an historical manifestation of the bourgeois domestic *intérieur*. Kierkegaard's philosophy may direct its attention away from outer reality to concern itself exclusively with the inner concerns of the subject; however Adorno, drawing on a metaphor supplied by Kierkegaard himself, demonstrates that this inward orientation is dependent on the material context which situates it:

> Images of interiors are at the center of the early Kierkegaard's philosophical constructions. These images are indeed produced by the philosophy, by the stratum of the subject–object relation in the work, but they point beyond this stratum by the strength of the things that they record. Just as in the metaphysical *intérieur* the intentions of Kierkegaard's philosophy intertwine, so the *intérieur* is also the real space that sets free the categories of philosophy.[8]

Adorno's exclusively philosophical definition of subjectivity disregards the psychological dimension of the *intérieur*, but it is in this direction I would wish to push Adorno's insights. Psychoanalysis, for example, finds its point of application in the interior of Berggasse 19. Adorno and his colleagues of the Frankfurt School were not at all unaware that psychoanalytic theory and practice were 'rooted in the concrete historical situation,'[9] however it was the social theorist Norbert Elias who most radically suggested the extent to which the social and class context of psychoanalysis was also responsible for producing the psychological material it analysed. Elias sought to trace the psychodynamics of superego, repression and infantile neurosis back to what he called 'the civilising process,' namely the evolution of middle- and upper-class moral and social codes, and their concern with self-regulation.

Elias's speculative reflections on the psychodynamic role of bourgeois forms of life as they develop in history find a more orthodox socio-historical counterpart in investigations of the bourgeois private and public spheres.[10] In the eighteenth century, the middle-class domestic interior acquired specifically psychological coloration through being distinguished from a rational (Enlightenment) public sphere. Articulated in the contrasting terms of intimacy and emotionality, the private sphere is exemplified for us by the domestic environment which William Cowper managed to create for himself between 1766 and 1773. Cowper's first encounter with madness in 1763 was brought on by public circumstances which he felt utterly incapable of managing. He decisively rejected the values of the public sphere, yet his consequent turn to domestic

Evangelicalism was to prove no less fateful. In 1773, his God pronounced his doom through the medium of a dream: in its interiorised mutation, his depressive madness, voicing as it were the very inner privacy of the subject, became an endemic condition. Of the 'literary' writers discussed in this study, none of those who preceded Cowper seems to have died mad, whereas none of those who succeeded him died sane.

In this respect, Cowper can be contrasted with the medieval poet, Thomas Hoccleve. Cowper's private sphere, thoroughly subjectivised, is a protective extension of an acutely vulnerable self (his poem, 'The Snail', provides an apt metaphor: 'He and his house are so combined'). In the aftermath of madness, Hoccleve too retreats to the privacy of his home. But Hoccleve's private environment is not yet a strictly demarcated space, and he relearns self-integrity through a series of relationships which bring him back into equilibrium with a non-alienated public world. In the modern period, by contrast, Cowper's recovery from his crisis of 1763–4 is inner-directed, and for that very reason, fatally flawed: the inner world in which the self seeks re-enclosure is unstable because founded in terms of an interiorised subjectivity.

A constant feature of the literature of madness and crisis is its proximity to religious experience: Otloh of St Emmeram, Margery Kempe, John Bunyan, George Trosse, William Cowper – all of these writers reveal their crises in the context of spiritual autobiographies. Confessional writings are intrinsically attuned to introspective reflection on inner experience. Within this generalisation, however, different autobiographies, written at different times, maintain distinct characteristics. Cowper's Evangelical God, peculiarly unstable because comprehended in private psychological terms, was preceded by the phenomenon of the Puritan internalised conscience. George Trosse experienced supernatural forces which announced themselves as visitations from God, but he came to understand that these phenomena were the work of the Devil in the guise of God. The chimerical irrationality which lurks within is literally devilish, while God prevails as an authorised norm of responsibility and rational understanding. While both Trosse's God and his Devil proceed from within, Trosse's culture enabled him to distinguish the 'true' voice of the conscience from the deceitful voice of disorder. Trosse's gradual recovery is a learning of self-regulation in Elias's sense.

Going back, finally, to the earliest autobiography of madness,

Otloh of St Emmeram's (also one of the earliest Western auto-biographies)[11] it is not fortuitous that Otloh was a monk. The long-term process of interiorisation which occurs in Western culture begins in the monasteries: the skill of silent reading was developed there. St Augustine, the first autobiographer, was the first to report on this phenomenon. Augustine also celebrated the inner and spiritual nature of the scriptural Logos, as distinct from the pagan art of rhetorical eloquence.[12] This conception of liturgy as an interiorised, 'metadiscursive' logos resonates in later writings of madness. Tasso's sonnet to the Duke of Mantua, pleading for release from the hospital of Sant'Anna, departs from conventional literary rhetoric: cast in the form of a prayer, it expresses a spiritual urgency which identifies it as a product of the Catholic Counter-Reformation. In the eighteenth century, Christopher Smart's *Jubilate agno* breaking with neoclassical conceptions of poetic procedure, is directly modelled on the poetry of the Scriptures. It is, I would suggest, this interiorised, transcendental conception of logos (transformed in ways which Foucault has suggested) which lies behind Hölderlin's 'nondiscourse': a number of Hölderlin's lyrics are grouped as 'Hymns'.

In summarising, we may return back along the chronological span. A process of interiorisation unfolds in the religious sphere before being eventually integrated into a secular and psychological one.[13] Spiritualised or religiously inspired conceptions of interiority are gradually transformed: by the end of the eighteenth century, they become Romantic or idealistic conceptions of the subjective self – for example, Kant's autonomous subject, which Adorno sought to demystify by identifying it critically in terms of the bourgeois milieu. This process is relevant to the experience of madness as mediated in subjective writings. A gradual interiorisation of madness, occurring between the medieval and modern periods, accelerates after 1640, culminating between 1750 and 1850 in a 'creative' writing of madness.

My study concludes with an extended discussion of Nerval's *Aurélia*, focusing largely on contexts and relationships relevant to the nineteenth-century French culture of madness – the asylum, the doctors, the fellow madman etc. *Aurélia*, however, is a work of more than psychohistorical interest. A heterodox spiritual autobiography, it also incorporates poetic lyricism in a text in which the concerns of dream, vision, madness and cure are inter-woven in patterns of extraordinary complexity.

Foucault remarks that 'Since Hölderlin and Nerval, the number of writers, painters and musicians who have "foundered" in madness has multiplied.'[14] In my concluding pages, I have pressed *Aurélia* for further information on the topics of madness, art and modernity. But if the text has kept its secrets, this is only appropriate: 'By way of the madness which interrupts it, a work opens up a void, a period of silence, a question without answer; it provokes a rupture without reconciliation whereby the world is required to question itself.'[15]

III

In discussing formal aspects of subjective writings which portray crises of identity, there remains the problem of how the terms 'identity' and 'subjectivity' are to be defined in the perspective of discourse. Two theorists, the critic Karlheinz Stierle and the linguist Emile Benveniste, have outlined definitions that are relevant to these terms. A comparative discussion of their analyses will enable us to arrive at a working classification of autobiographical and lyrical writings of madness.

Foucault, as we have seen, describes Hölderlin's poetry as 'non-discourse.' Karlheinz Stierle has developed this term into a concept of 'anti-discourse.'[16] Stierle's analysis is formalistic – in referring to Hölderlin and Nerval he never directly alludes to their madness. Nevertheless his analysis remains pertinent to a discussion which takes their madness into account.

Stierle defines 'discourse' as a language act which is sanctioned as communicative utterance by an institutionalised discursive 'schema,' underlying and regulating all particular discursive utterances.[17] Following this, he proposes that any instance of discourse possesses its own formal identity. This 'identity of discourse' derives from the prior identity of the speaker, while at the same time conforming to the set of norms which define the schema.[18] 'Identity of discourse' thus functions as a mode of constraint, reducing a multiplicity of possible semantic contexts and bringing about that measure of cohesion and continuity ('linearity') necessary for efficient communication. This constraining degree of formal identification in turn bears down on the prior identity of the subject, determining it in his or her discourse as a discursive role. Thus identity *in* discourse (defined here as discursive role), no less than identity *of* discourse, is a specifically ideological mode, constituted in the normative terms of stability and coherence.

Emile Benveniste has proposed his own distinctive definition of 'discourse' (*discours*) which, in counterpoint with Stierle's general thesis, addresses those utterances whereby speakers directly pose their subjective identity.[19] Benveniste (who shifts easily between oral and textual utterances – Stierle does so too) understands *discours* as the subjective dimension of language, embodied in the category of first and second person utterances (this category is contrasted with a non-subjective dimension involving third person utterances, which Benveniste labels *histoire*).[20] In first-person utterances, the subjective act of uttering is included in the statement itself. 'I' and 'you,' Benveniste notes, possess a uniqueness of reference in instances of discourse. They have no objectivity of reference inasmuch as they are realised only in the act of utterance. In positing an 'I' (and a 'you' which is not 'I') speakers posit themselves linguistically as individual subjects: 'There is (. . .) a combined double instance in this process: the instance of *I* as referent, and the instance of discourse containing *I* as referee. The definition can now be stated precisely as: *I* is "the individual who utters the present instance of discourse containing the linguistic instance *I*."'[21]

This is not a definition of what subjectivity is in language; rather it outlines the formal precondition of how subjectivity fills up the empty signifier 'I' when particular subjects refer to themselves as 'I' in particular instances of discourse:

> 'subjectivity' (. . .) is defined (. . .) as the psychic unity that transcends the totality of the actual experiences that it assembles and that makes the permanence of consciousness. Now we hold that 'subjectivity,' whether it is placed in phenomenology or psychology, as one may wish, is only the emergence in the being of a fundamental property of language. 'Ego' is he who *says* 'ego.'[22]

Benveniste characterises subjectivity not in terms of language, but as a potentiality of language ('language is (. . .) the possibility of subjectivity'), but even so, these statements are unsatisfactory. They treat the chimerical notion of subjectivity as a plenitude, fully equivalent to 'permanence of consciousness.' In the light of Stierle's argument we may assert that what Benveniste in fact defines through the attributes of unity and continuity ('permanence') is the function of identity.

Benveniste's analysis may be reconsidered from this point of view. When subjects say 'I' in instances of discourse, then their subject-hood (i.e. the condition of their being subjects) is contracted to a signifying order which mediates their experiential universe. The contractual 'I' of signification is then realised as a contextual 'I' whose univocal meaning must be 'legally' manifested in instances of discourse. That is to say, the enunciated 'I' is constituted as a mode of coherence according to the discursive terms of unity and continuity. These co-ordinates are the conditions according to which subjects locate and identify themselves in discourse. The 'self' of the subject is established in discourse as an identity. In first-person discourses, identity, much more than a discursive role (*qua* Stierle) is a performative mode of coherence which is articulated in and through the first- and second-person pronouns. Thus any discourse involving the first-person pronoun is determined as a discourse of identity. I would, then, suggest that Benveniste's category of *discours* be understood (with specific reference to texts) as 'discourse of identity.'

The concept of 'discourse of identity' is categorical, but not at all abstract. The formal category classifies any number of discursive practices involving first-person utterances. For the purpose of this book however, the notion is particularly instructive in considering those autobiographical accounts of madness which feature a crisis of personal identity. The autobiographies of madness discussed here are written from stated or assumed positions of reintegrated identity. With the ambiguous exception of Nerval's *Aurélia*, these discourses are formally normative: they implement stability and cohesion at the level of form as well as content through constituting themselves as discourses of identity. Thus, in considering autobiographies of madness, the general category of 'discourse of identity' situates those specific discursive projections of identity which are not only subject to the pressure of particular cultural and ideological determinations, but which themselves reproduce, with a greater or lesser degree of tension, the formal characteristics of identity.

These specifications of identity and discourse leave out of account the more amorphous matter of 'subjectivity.' This is a concept which is clearly not exhausted by subjective identity and which may well be taken to include not merely the extent of individual consciousness, but states which exceed consciousness – dream, intoxication and madness. At this point we may return to Stierle's analysis, which goes on to argue for a 'transgressive' category of anti-discourse.

With reference to Hölderlin (also to Nerval), Stierle argues that lyric poetry is a special case of discourse. By abolishing discursive linearity and simultaneously multiplying the semantic contexts which dispose meaning-potential, the lyric poem tends to transgress the constraining norms of identification. This tendency, pronounced in European poetry since Petrarch, is offset in pre-modern lyric discourse by various factors: Stierle notes the role of verse form; more importantly he suggests that the multiple semantic contexts which tend to open the poem out in an endlessly receding horizon of meaning are, in effect, co-ordinated by the lyric subject.[23] However, the resulting degree of identity is precarious, and when the lyric subject radically suspends the communicative function of the utterance (we might think, for example, of Mallarmé), then discursive role is crucially undermined, along with identity of discourse.

Such a thesis carries implications for the status of subjective identity as enacted in texts. Where this is not framed in discourse as a role then it can only articulate itself as a problematised identity through the medium of a problematised discourse. Thus the transgressive character of the lyric unavoidably entails the problematisation of the lyric subject,[24] a circumstance realised in Hölderlin's writing: 'In Hölderlin's practice of poetry, lyric discourse and the lyric subject approach ever closer to the threshold of a bursting open [rupture] of the tension inherent in an identity which is a tissue of contradictions.'[25]

In reserving the category of anti-discourse for 'transgressive' lyric poetry, Stierle argues an absolute opposition between normative discourses and transgressive anti-discourses, which are invariably lyric poems. Such a dualism is somewhat reductive. In considering particular autobiographical discourses of identity, pre-Hölderlinian lyrical poetry, and Nerval's late prose, a more modulated view is required, one which enables us to see how the discursive articulation of identity is variously ratified, displaced, subverted or fragmented, regardless of genre.

A further point: these analyses state or imply that subjective identity is articulated through discourse at the same time as formal identity is implemented.[26] Thus where identity is transgressed or exceeded in discourse, this is not a purely formal concern: Stierle's remark on Hölderlin implies as much.

For my purposes, the notion of a discourse of identity, taking effect at the levels of both form and content, must be supplemented by a concern with how such discourses come to be problematised within the diachronic dimension of interiorisation. Where discourses of subjective identity are exceeded in madness, as I will argue is the case in the nineteenth century with the writings of Clare and Nerval, then we approach Foucault's 'nondiscourse' and Stierle's 'anti-discourse.' I remain uncomfortable with these terms however, and propose, for the sake of economy, to differentiate, wherever possible, between implicitly normative discourses of identity and implicitly excessive (or transgressive) discourses of subjectivity.

These classificatory concepts – 'discourse of identity,' 'discourse of subjectivity' – are the main ones I shall deploy in discussing subjective writings of madness in the pages that follow. Briefly, I shall argue that an historical development is evident as we trace the succession of these writings. The writer's experience of madness, first conveyed through a discourse of identity, is increasingly articulated through a (problematic) discourse of subjectivity, a process which culminates in the nineteenth century in the writings of Hölderlin and, the two writers considered here, Clare and Nerval.

1 Tasso and Hoccleve:
The Poet as Madman

I

The status of Tasso's madness isn't easily determined.[1] His letters
of the 1580s bear witness to a mental disorder, but not one which
affected his coherence of expression or thought. In *Il messagiero*, one
of the *Dialoghi*, he states 'I do not deny being mad,' but at the same
time he insists that his powers of reason remain unimpaired. In
1581, he complains of the disturbances to which he is prey:

> these are of two kinds; human and diabolical. The ones which are
> human are cries of men and, in particular, women and young girls, and
> laughter full of scorn, and various animal noises which are stirred up by
> men to cause me disquiet, and a tumult of inanimate things, prompted
> by human hands. The ones which are diabolical are spells and charms;
> and although I am not altogether sure of the enchantments for the
> reason that the mice, of which the room is full, and which seem to me
> to be possessed by demons, could yet be making that uproar naturally,
> not only on account of enchantment; and some other noises which I
> hear could be attributed to human artifice as to their cause; nonetheless
> it seems to me certain enough that I have been bewitched: and the
> operations of the spells are very powerful, because when I pick up a
> book to study it, or a pen, I hear certain voices sounding in my ear,
> among which I distinguish the names of Pavolo, of Giacomo, of
> Girolamo, of Francesco, of Fulvio, and others, which are perhaps malig-
> nant and jealous of my tranquillity (. . .). Many vapours still rise up to
> my head, more now than ever before, though I frequently write before
> eating, so that the phantasms are quite perturbed (. . .). And if it
> happens that these internal impediments coincide with the external ones,
> as so often happens, I am moved to great rage; and many times I do not
> finish the letters but tear them up, then recommence writing them; as
> I have done with this one, so that I have torn up and recommenced
> many copies.[2]

He believes himself persecuted by 'external' supernatural agents, but is also ready to contemplate more rational, organic explanations, which he classifies as 'internal.' This is not untypical of Renaissance accounts of mental illness. When the painter Hugo van der Goes suffered a fit of madness a century earlier, his physician saw no contradiction between natural and supernatural explanations: 'certain people talked of a peculiar case of *frenesia magna*, the great frenzy of the brain. Others however believed him to be possessed of an evil spirit. There were in fact symptoms of both unfortunate diseases present in him.'[3] In another letter, Tasso recounts both the physical and mental symptoms from which he suffered:

> whatever might be the reason for my illness, the effects are these: gnawing of the intestines, with some few fluxions of blood: ringing in the ears and the head, sometimes so strong that it seems to me I have one of those pendulum clocks inside it; continued imagining of various things, all of them unpleasant; which perturbs me in such a way that I cannot apply my mind to my studies even for a sixteenth part of an hour; and the more I force myself to keep my mind concentrated on my studies, the more I am distracted by various imaginings, and sometimes by great anger, these moving in me according to the various fantasies which arise in me. Apart from this my head always fumes inordinately after I have eaten, and greatly heats up. Always I go inventing human voices with my imagination, in such a way that it seems to me very often that inanimate objects speak.[4]

Tasso's self-observation is in line with medical opinion of the day: Riolan, a contemporary physician, 'explained enthusiasm, or possession by a deity, as due to the effect of melancholic vapours on phantasy, and went on to point out that "it is not necessary for us to have recourse to a demon as the last refuge of ignorance, since we have a natural cause."'[5]

The letters quoted above were written in the hospital of Sant'Anna, where Tasso's patron, Alfonso d'Este, the Duke of Ferrara, had him detained from 1579 to 1586. In the years before 1579, the poet's behaviour had become increasingly neurotic. 1577 had been a year of crisis: he attacked a servant with a knife while in the apartment of Alfonso's sister Lucrezia, imagining him to be a spy. At this point a number of Tasso's contemporaries already believed him to be a madman: Alfonso placed him under surveillance, but he

managed to escape. He spent much of the next two years restlessly
wandering from court to court. Alfonso had kept possession of
Tasso's manuscript of the *Gerusalemme liberata*, the epic poem
which occupied him for much of his life. Drawn by this, the poet
returned to Ferrara in 1579, promising to be on his best behaviour.
Unfortunately the court was occupied with preparation for
Alfonso's forthcoming marriage with Margherita Gonzaga. Tasso
felt neglected: his frustration climaxed in an emotional breakdown:
'in an outburst of anger he shouted his denunciation of the Duke
and the Este family, and rushed off to the castle to demand his
rights. The attempts to restrain him provoked further outbursts,
until he was arrested, carried off to the hospital of St Anna close
by, and chained in a cell as a raving madman.'[6]

C.P. Brand remarks that Tasso's sequestration in Sant'Anna
brought about a worsening of his mental condition.[7] He was soon
lodged in relatively comfortable quarters where he was able to read,
write and receive visitors, but the hallucinations and bouts of
delirium which he records in his letters date from this period, when
there was little to distract him from brooding over his mental and
physical condition. Nevertheless he retained a sense of his own
identity. As his self-diagnoses demonstrate, his madness was
manifested through objectively observed symptoms of illness and
mental debilitation rather than as a shattering of an inner self.

For Michel Foucault, Tasso belongs to a period in which madness
and the work of art are exterior to each other: 'language which was
delirium was not a work of art. And conversely, delirium was
robbed of its meagre truth as madness if it was called a work of art.'
Thus the writer's madness, where it does not result in a merely
pathological 'babble of words,' bears witness to the 'truth' of the
work of art.[8] It was with this 'truth' that Tasso reassured himself
when, after some six years of confinement, he addressed the
problem of his madness. The dialogue *Il messagiero* tells how the
poet is visited by a winged creature which will not reveal its name.
The poet wonders

> whether it is possible that this is the imagining not of a man who is
> sleeping, but of a wakeful man who is in the grip of phantasy. The forces
> of the imaginative faculty are incredible: (. . .) it sometimes comes about
> that it overpowers the senses with violent efficacy and tricks them in
> such a manner that these do not distinguish actual objects.[9]

He goes on to cite instances of the inspired imagination in

precedents provided by Petrarch, Virgil, Horace and Dante. He
then considers his own case:

> Certainly it cannot be denied that there is some mental alienation, that,
> whether an infirmity of madness, like that of Orestes or Pentheus, or a
> divine frenzy, like that of those who have been captured by Bacchus or
> Amor, is such that it can, no less than dreams do, represent the false
> things for real; moreover it seems to have the more power to do so
> inasmuch as in dreams only the sensibilities are involved, but in frenzy
> the mind is obstructed; wherefore I would very much doubt, if that
> which is commonly said of my madness were true, that my vision is
> similar to that of Pentheus or Orestes. But because I am conscious to
> myself that it is in no way similar to that of Orestes or Pentheus, as I
> do not deny that I am mad, it suits me at least to believe that this new
> kind of madness has another cause. Perhaps it is an excessive melan-
> choly, and melancholics, as Aristotle affirms, have shown a distinct
> genius in studying philosophy, and in governing the republic, and in
> composing verses.[10]

The doctrine of the poet's divine *furor* offered a version of non-
conscious inspiration, but Tasso rejected any such notion: 'However
it may be, I can assure you of two things, one that I am not one
of those poets who do not understand the things written by them;
the other that I write with great effort, something not usually
endured by those who compose when moved by poetic frenzy.'[11]
Instead he diagnosed his condition as one of Aristotelian melancholy: the melancholic poet retains his intellectual powers and exercises conscious control of his craft.

Aristotle's analysis of the melancholy of 'all truly outstanding
men' was revived in the Renaissance: 'The Florentine Neo-Platonists
were quick to perceive that this Aristotelian doctrine supplied a
scientific basis for Plato's theory of "divine frenzy" (. . .). Thus the
expression *furor melancholicus* came to be synonymous with *furor
divinus*. What had been a calamity and, in its mildest form, a
handicap became a privilege, still dangerous but all the more
exalted: the privilege of genius.'[12] In this light, Tasso's self-
diagnosis admits to a grave mental affliction, but one which does
not disable his identity as poet and writer. Unlike Platonic *furor*,
furor melancholicus is an intellectually respectable affliction which
does not cast doubt on the poet's intelligence and conscious art.

In concluding that he is suffering from melancholic madness, Tasso
bears comparison with the medieval English poet, Thomas Hoccleve

(c. 1368–1430). In two narrative poems, *Thomas Hocclive's Complaint* and *Dialogus cum amico*, Hoccleve left a seemingly autobiographical account of his experiences of madness and melancholia: 'He was a clerk in the privy seal office at Westminster, and for a time, so he says, his reason left him, returning on All Saints' Day 1416.'[13]

In the *Complaint*, Thomas (as the poet names himself in the poems) tells how he was suddenly struck by an attack of madness. The derangement passes, but his acquaintances are reluctant to accept that he has recovered: their continuing suspicions leave him in a state of despair – his madness has abated only to be replaced by the 'thowghtfull maladye,' melancholy. He then reads a book of philosophical consolation wherein a discourse of reason vanquishes melancholic brooding. This reconciles him to his situation and signals his recovery.

In the medieval world, the disaster of madness was unmitigated. Hoccleve depicts it as a degrading loss of common humanity: 'Men seyden, I loked / as a wilde steere' (120).[14] There is no reference to *furor*, and no suggestion that madness or melancholy might be related to the practice of poetry. Notions of *enthousiasmos* were known to the Middle Ages by way of Horace, Seneca and others, but, according to E.R. Curtius, knowledge of the topoi of inspiration had no bearing on the status of poetry, which was not privileged over other forms of discourse.[15] Between Hoccleve's medieval culture and Tasso's Renaissance culture there is a shift affecting relations between poetry and madness. Whereas, for Hoccleve, madness is a condition apart, Tasso finds that Neo-Platonic notions of poetic madness are uncomfortably relevant to his own situation. He dignifies his condition by finding melancholic and even lunatic types among the philosophers. In the *Complaint*, by contrast, Thomas turns to philosophy for an antidote to melancholy. In a dialogue between a 'wofull man' and Reason, the commonsensical 'speche of Reason' completes a course in disintoxication. Reason's moralistic arguments provide the beleaguered poet with a model which enables him to write his *Complaint* as a discourse of recovered identity.

For both Tasso and Hoccleve an alienating experience of melancholy is related to the situation of solitude. In *Il messagiero*, Tasso fears the melancholic effects of solitude. He cites Petrarch's sonnet *Solo e pensoso*, relating it to its 'symptomatic' subtexts in Homer and Cicero: 'It is also possible to number Aiace and Bellerophon among the melancholics: one of whom in fact became mad, the other would often wander in deserted places.'[16] He anticipates Dr

Johnson's fear of the desocialised and ungoverned imagination: 'The
forces of the imaginative faculty are incredible: and it well seems that
it is more powerful then when the soul, not occupied in exercising
the exterior senses, retires into itself.'[17]

The relationship between solitude and melancholy is very
differently situated in Hoccleve, whose writings are more revealing
as discourses of healing than of crisis. Thomas experiences derangement as a loss of self: 'the substaunce / of my memory / went to
pley / as for a certayne space' (50–1). The crisis is glimpsed through
the eyes of acquaintances: 'A-nother spake / and of me seide also,
/ my feete weren aye wavynge to and fro / whane that I stonde
shulde' (131–3). Such exhibitions of madness are all the more
shameful for occurring outdoors or in public places. Thomas
recovers, but his contemporaries remain suspicious. Dejected and
feeling unable to reply, he withdraws into domestic privacy: here he
studies himself in a mirror:

> And in my chamber at home when I was
> my selfe alone / I in this wyse wrowght:
> I streite unto my myrrowr / and my glas,
> to loke how that me / of my chere thowght[e]
> yf any [other] were it than it owght[e];
> for fayne wolde I / yf it had not be right,
> amendyd it / to my kunynge and myght.
>
> Many a sawte made I to this myrrowre,
> thinkynge, yf that I loke in this manere
> amonge folke / as I do now, none errowr
> of suspecte loke / may in my face appere
>   (155–65)

This is not an act of introspection. Physical signs and symptoms
were taken as direct proof of madness in the medieval period,[18] so
it is important for Thomas to compose his features. Nevertheless the
scene is a properly psychological one. The psychological dimension
is implied by the contrast between an outdoors scene where the poet
is viewed by others, and an indoors scene where he views himself.
In studying his features in the glass, he checks on his ability to
control them. This provides a graphic image of a struggle for self-
control which, occurring indoors, is literally an interior struggle. His
'wylde infirmytie' has, as it were, evicted him from himself – 'me owt
of my selfe / cast and threw.' By contrast, his solitary self-
examination in the mirror demonstrates a self-awareness which is
heightened by his knowledge that the taint of madness excludes him

from the public consensus of 'them that have / conseytes resonable,'

> for ofte whan I / in westmynster hall[e],
> and eke in london / among the prese went[e],
> I se the chere / abaten and appalle
> of them that weren wonte for me to calle
> to companye
>
> (72–6)

Unable to take self-possession for granted, Thomas retreats into privacy in order to nurse an invalid sense of self. In Western culture, psychological awareness of subjective interiority coincides with the occupation of a private environment. Petrarch, in his rural retreat at Vaucluse, and Montaigne in his tower are key figures in an emerging culture of introspective self-awareness, one wherein the medieval monastic ideal of a secluded *vita contemplativa* is transformed in secular and implicitly psychological terms. Hoccleve stands in an oblique but revealing relationship to this development. The mirror into which he repeatedly gazes is more an agent of self-reconstruction than an instrument of self-reflection. Apropos of Kierkegaard's portrayal of the nineteenth-century bourgeois *intérieur*, Adorno remarks, 'melancholy appears in the symbol of the mirror.'[19] But the mirror into which Thomas gazes does not reflect a private self: by the same token, the interior space which the mirror reflects is not already constituted as a psychological space. The psychology that underlies Thomas's therapeutic interaction with the mirror objectivises self rather than subjectivising it: it is this process which determines Hoccleve's mirror as an antidote to melancholy, rather than as its emblem. This mirror is not yet an object which is commodified in relation to Thomas: it stands for him in the place of the world rather than as its replacement, therefore it functions as an objective interlocutor of the self, rather than as the reflector of an 'isolated privacy.'[20]

The self-loss of madness is the precondition of Thomas's act of self-inspection – his image in the mirror will (or will not) confirm that he is in possession of himself. Further, the pressure of a public consensus from which he feels himself excluded defines his isolation as a form of self-exclusion and self-incarceration. Under these negative conditions, the mirror begins to reconstruct the poet's interior as a space of self-reflexivity, but one to which the world bears witness through the objective character of his reflected self-image. Functioning as an intermediary between public and private, the mirror demarcates a space within which a new sense of self can

come into being. 'Many a sawte made I to this myrrowre': Thomas's
frequent returns to the mirror suggest that the episode involves a
stade du miroir – a determinate stage in a process not merely of self-
recovery but of self-discovery.

The mirror episode is succeeded by Thomas's reading of the
philosophical book of consolation. This is reproduced in the poem
as a dialogue between Reason and a 'wofull man,' identified as
'Thomas' in the margin of Hoccleve's manuscript. Self-confrontation
is recast in the form of an objectivised discourse:

> Than spake Reason / 'what menythe all this fare?
> thowghe welthe be not frindly to the yet,
> out of thyn herte / voyde wo and care!'
> 'by what skyll / how / and by what rede and wit,'
> seyd[e] this wofull man / 'myght I done it?'
> 'wrastle', quode Reason / 'a-gayne hevynesses
> of the worlde / troubles, suffering and duresses.'
>
> (337–42)

The poet's concern with checking and controlling his features now
recurs as an inner struggle, with Reason counselling the 'wofull man'
to 'wrastle' with himself. But inasmuch as this is externalised and
formalised through the dialogue itself, the poet remains balanced
between inner and outer contexts of selfhood.

The process of recovery is completed in a subsequent stage which
takes us beyond the introspective concerns of the *Complaint* itself.
As an appendix to this, Hoccleve wrote a subsequent poem entitled
Dialogus cum amico. Here he tells how he reads the *Complaint* to a
friend who visits him just as he has finished writing the poem. The
two then engage in a debate: the friend persistently casts doubt on
both the soundness of the poet's judgement and the extent of his
recovery, while Thomas forcefully defends both his recovered sanity
and his poem. His arguments eventually convince the friend, who
now reveals the purpose of his inquisition:

> Now, Thomas / by the feith I to god owe,
> Had I nat taastid [tested] thee / as that I now
> Doon have / it had been hard, maad me to trowe
> The good plyt / which I feele wel that thow
> Art in / I woot wel thow art wel ynow,
> What-so men of thee ymagine or clappe
>
> (484–9)

This dialogue resumes both the self-confrontation in the mirror and the dialogue between the 'wofull man' and Reason. Each confrontation occurs in private, but as self-questioning gives way first to an ideal then to a 'real' interlocutor, the poet tests his renewed self-identity in progressively externalised contexts, so that he is finally ready to re-emerge into public life. The *Dialogus cum amico*, which completes the sequence, recalls the reason Thomas gives for viewing himself in the mirror, '. . . yf that I loke in this manere / amonge folke / as I do now, none errowr / of suspecte loke / may in my face appere.' If Thomas is acutely vulnerable here, he is able, in the *Dialogus cum amico*, to assert with a new conviction the integrity of his self-presentation in public, an assertion which is enacted by the autobiographical form of the writings themselves.

There is nothing psychological about Thomas's madness in the *Complaint*, nevertheless the crisis of madness promotes psychology as its consequence. In coming to terms with his catastrophe, Thomas arrives at an increased awareness of selfhood in relation to its inner and outer contexts. A pattern of 'doubling' is realised not in schizophrenic but in remedial terms: through a process of balanced objectivisation, a disabled self-identity is reconstructed from the inside out. R.D. Laing entitled his study of schizophrenia *The divided self*, but the evidence provided first by Hoccleve, later by Trosse and Pepys, is that the divided self is a balanced one before it is an unbalanced one.

II

Hoccleve's *Complaint* is a performative statement of recovery, but Tasso confronts the alarming prospect that his madness is confirmed precisely because he is a poet. The English poet withdraws into privacy in order to recuperate, but, under conditions of solitary introspection, the Italian poet's imaginative faculty is prone to morbid hypertrophy. Alert to the danger, Tasso turns away from dangerous topoi of frenzied inspiration and embraces instead a conception of melancholia which was attributed to Aristotle by way of the *Problemata*.

This defensive strategy is, to some extent, repeated in Tasso's critical writings on poetry. In the sixteenth century, epic poetry was subjected to the discipline of Aristotelian logic: accordingly Tasso's discourses on heroic poetry not only omit any reference to *furor*, they specifically provide him with a stable point of reference as poet; he declared that his *Discorsi dell'arte poetica* were exercises in self-discipline ('scrissi i miei discorsi per ammaestramento di me stesso').[21]

The theme of inspiration is reserved for a self-referential sonnet, 'L'arme e'l duce cantai' ('Arms and the leader I sang'). This refers to his epic composition, the *Gerusalemme liberata*,

> . . .alcun detto
> del ciel spirommi o musa od altra diva:
> deh! spiri or sempre e di sé m'empia il petto.
>
> (869)[22]

(some heavenly utterance inspired me, whether muse or other goddess; Ah! breathe forever and so fill my breast)

In the context of the sonnet, these lines suggest that inspiration is more appropriate to the subjective voice of lyric poetry (i.e. to the sonnet itself) than to the impersonal voice of epic poetry, and it is in his commentary on the lyric poems that we find a reference to the inspired poet: 'poets are light winged creatures [cosa volatile] as Socrates says in the *Ion*.'[23] Given an implied contrast between the 'logical' discourse of heroic poetry and the 'inspirational' discourse of lyric poetry how does inspiration affect the lyric voice as a specifically subjective voice? We may address this question by way of one of Tasso's most noted lyrics:

> Tacciono i boschi e i fiumi
> e'l mare senza onda giace,
> ne le spelonche i venti han tregua e pace,
> e ne la notte bruna
> alta silenzio fa la bianca luna:
> e noi tegnamo ascose
> le dolcezze amorose.
> Amor non parli o spiri,
> Sien muti i baci e muti i miei sospiri.
>
> (790–1)

(Silent are the woodlands and the streams, and the sea, without waves, reposes; in the caves the winds are at truce, at peace; and in the dark night the white moon holds a high silence: and we keep in secret Love's sweetness: Love speak not, breathe not, quiet be our kisses and quiet my sighs.)

In this celebrated madrigal, the lyric subject is dissolved into the open spaces of the night, asserting his presence only in a dying breath which is the poem's closing word. The pathos of evanescence and the surrender to silence ensures the reader's identification with a voice which is not vocalised.

The 'silencing' of the subjective voice of lyricism was a relatively new circumstance in Western poetry, dating back no further than Petrarch. Yet the voice of Tasso's madrigal, unlike that of Petrarch's *Solo e pensoso*, is neither introspective nor melancholic. In *Tacciono i boschi*, the interiorised voice remains unidentified, therefore free from any spiritual or psychological problems which would threaten to undermine the poet's identity. The madrigals offer a near-ideal version of subjectivity, one which is free from the confines of the self and its concerns: the poet is precisely *cosa volatile*.

The musicality which is such a distinctive feature of Tasso's *Rime* is no less impressive for being a formally deliberate achievement: 'characteristic of the amorous lyrics (. . .) is the fluent, harmonious line of the *forma temperata*, marked in Tasso's words by *le dolcezze del numero, la sceltezza delle parole, la vaghezza e lo splendore dell'elocuzione* etc. Hence a large number of the lines slide smoothly from the lips so that the sound caresses the ear, and the mind barely grasps the meaning.'[24] In their brevity, ease and immersion in the commonplaces of pastoral love, these lyrics permit a measure of relaxation from the Aristotelian concerns of epic poetry. Moreover the pastoral themes and images, conventional though they are, open onto a more heterodox and sensual realm: a natural environment wherein the poetic imagination is liberated. 'Tasso,' writes Judith Kates, 'almost compulsively associates the language of dream and magic, of imagination and poetry, with love, beauty, sensual temptation (. . .). What Tasso's morality here condemns also powerfully attracts him as a creator of poetry.' Discussing the figure of Tancredi in the *Gerusalemme liberata*, she remarks that Tasso 'identifies love with dream and with the power of the undisciplined imagination.'[25] In the atmosphere of self-questioning promoted by the Counter-Reformation, the tension between sensual imagination and moral orthodoxy haunted Tasso, and he rewrote his epic poem in a chastened, 'morally correct' version, the *Gerusalemme conquistata*. The madrigals and lyrics are free from such tensions. Given the sheer quantity of the *rime amorose*, their formal slightness, and the rhetorical conventionality of so many of them, they bypass the poet's conscious need to curb his own heterodox tendencies. Thus in a number of the lyrics, the play of poetic imagination is projected in terms of a spontaneous lyric subjectivity which suspends or dissolves identity.

The concerns of identity, volatilised in the lyrics, are precipitated in the encomiastic poems – verse-addresses to named individuals.

Tasso wrote a number of these in Sant'Anna, including various petitions for release. Here, the poet reasserts an identity which has been
called into question by the circumstances of his confinement. He
speaks his grievances aloud and identifies himself in an autobiographical role as Tasso the much-wronged poet. These are poems of
enclosure in more than one sense: an awareness of the closed
environment of Sant'Anna returns the poet to the confines of the
self. By contrast, the madrigals, often set in an open space of nature,
are free from formal modes of address:

> Ecco mormorar l'onde
> e tremolar le fronde
> a l'aura mattutina e gli arboscelli,
> e sovra i verdi rami i vaghi augelli
> cantar soavemente
> e rider l'oriente
>
> (740)

(Now the waves murmur and leaves and bushes tremble in the morning
breeze, and above the green branches enamoured birds sing softly and the
east smiles) (tr. George Kay).

Expansive vowel sounds celebrate the character of the scene itself:
openness of both sound and scene delineate a felicitous space of non-
confinement and non-identity. Where, however, the poet laments
his confinement he asserts his identity through the medium of a
formal rhetorical diction:

> Da' nipoti d'Adamo,
> Ohimè! chi mi divide?
> O qual Circe mi spinge infra le gregge?
> Ohimè!
>
> (836)

(Ah woe! From Adam's stock who separates me? Oh what Circe thrusts me
amid the flock? Alas!)

The lines express a fear of dehumanisation which must have been
real enough, and which call to mind the images of animality which
convey Hoccleve's madness. Nevertheless, in a poem which is
entitled 'A le signore Principesse di Ferrara', Tasso's mannered
formality is determined by his aristocratic addressees. These lines
locate the poet in the role of court tragedian, staging his private
drama through an externalised, public persona. Their rhetoric,
intended for a particular audience, enables him to posit his identity
in terms of a given role.

Even one of the most movingly direct of the Sant'Anna poems, 'A la Signora Duchessa di Ferrara', is rhetorically constructed:

> Sposa regal, già la stagion ne viene
> che gli accorti amatori a' balli invita,
> e ch'essi a' rai di luce alma gradita
> vegghian le notti gelide e serena.
> Del suo fedel già le secrete pene
> ne' casti orecchi è di racôrre ardita
> la verginella, e lui tra morte e vita
> soave inforsa e'n dolce guerra il tiene.
> Suonano i gran palagi e i tetti adorni
> di canto; io sol di pianto il carcer tetro
> fo risonar. Questa è la data fede?
> Son questi i miei bramati alti ritorni?
> Lasso! dunque prigion, dunque feretro
> chiamate voi pietà, Donna e mercede?
>
> (844-5)

(Royal bride, now the season is coming round which invites attentive lovers to dance, and in which they charm the chill, clear nights in the rays of kindly, pleasing light. The young virgin dares to tell now the secret pangs of her lover to chaste ears, and softly leaves him doubtful between life and death and keeps him in sweet warfare.
The great palaces, the ornamented roofs resound with song; alone I make this dark prison echo with weeping. Is this the faith you plighted? Are these my longed-for, high deserts? Alas! then, Lady, you call a prison, pity, a coffin, then, recompense?) (tr. George Kay).

The possibility that the poet might not be heard by the addressee is not contemplated here, thus verbal decorum is called for. This prevents the poet from exploring his actual situation, and his plight is introduced in the second quatrain by the picture of a lover who is made to suffer by his lady's coyness. The poet's hope that his plea will be heard by Margherita in her palace implies the grim alternative that it will echo unheard in the dungeon. But the surrogate image of a lover languishing between life and death allows as much for hope that the plea will be heard ('vita') as for despair that it will not ('morte'). In the formal architecture of the sonnet, the palace is situated directly above the prison, and the two locations communicate through the enjambement which links the first line of the sestet ('gran palagi') with the second line ('carcer tetro'). Thus song and sigh occupy the same line, divided only by a semi-colon across which they might conceivably impinge on each other: it would, we understand, require only a small reversal to transform sigh into song, dungeon into palace. This link between the higher and lower worlds permits the rhetorical ambiguity of the poem's closing lines wherein the poet's real situation of imprisonment can easily be read as a metaphor of a lover's complaint to his cruel mistress. The role-playing quality of the petition confirms the poet as discursive identity: he is not required to turn inwards and confront the situation in terms of his own subjective situation. Imprisonment is not allowed to denote a space of interiority. Tasso, in these poems, refuses the option of melancholic introspection and so avoids the imponderables of a poetic discourse which would involve a subjective realisation of his situation.

All this tends to confirm Foucault's estimate of Tasso. However, one of the encomiastic poems stands apart, and by itself reopens the question of the relationship between poetry and madness. In the sonnet *Signor, nel precipizio ove mi spinse*, addressed to Guglielmo Gonzaga, Duke of Mantua, the topics of solitude and melancholy receive urgent expression as the poet confronts the possibility that his voice might not be heard and that his identity might therefore collapse.

> Signor, nel precipizio ove mi spinse
> Fortuna, ognor più caggio in ver' gli abissi,
> né quinci ancora alcun mio prego udissi,
> né volto di pietà per me si pinse.
> Ben veggio il sol, ma qual talora il cinse
> oscuro velo in tenebroso eclissi;
> e veggio in ciel i lumi erranti i fissi:
> ma chi d'atro pallor così li tinse?
> Or dal profondo oscuro a te mi volgo
> e grido: – A me, nel mio gran caso indegno,
> dammi, che puoi, la destra e mi solleva:
> ed a quel peso vil che sì l'aggreva
> sotraggi l'ale del veloce ingegno,
> e volar mi vedrai lunge dal volgo.
>
>   (851)

(Sir, down the precipice over which Fortune thrusts me, I fall and deeper fall towards the abyss, nor has anyone hearkened to my prayer up till now, nor has a face coloured with pity for me. Indeed I see the sun, but as he is when a dark veil wraps him in shadowy eclipse; and I see the fixed and wandering stars in heaven: but who has stained them like that with gloomy pallor?

Now from the dark depths I turn to you and cry: Give me, you who can, your right hand in my great unworthy plight, and raise me; and draw the wings of swift invention from under the vile weight that crushes it, and you will see me fly far from the crowd.) (tr. George Kay)

The sonnet unfolds in a dim limbo, with the octave elaborating a sequence around the themes of fall, darkness and loss. The initial metaphors present a state of inner crisis, which negates referentiality: the solid ground gives way underfoot, the sun turns dark, shrouding the object-world and immersing the subject in a state of psychical interiority.

Although the entire sonnet is addressed to the Duke of Mantua, and commences by apostrophising him, the addressee is effectively absent from the octave, wherein the poet laments the isolation which has prevented his voice from being heard: 'nor has anyone hearkened to my prayer up till now.' In *Tacciono i boschi* an intimate, expressive silence is celebrated, but in *Signor, nel precipizio*, where the poet is enclosed and unheard, silence is profoundly alienating. Gone are the expansive vowel sounds characteristically associated with the alfresco lyrics – 'a,' 'e,' 'o' (*Ecco mormorar l'onde*): in their place is a concentration of 'i' vowels. These restrict the tonal palette of the poem, as though formally enacting the draining away of colour into darkness which predominates in the imagery ('dark veil'; 'gloomy pallor'). The timbre of the octave is at once integrated and constricted so that voice becomes an echo of itself, heard only in the abyss towards which the poet falls. Virtuoso rhyming further turns the octave in on itself. All the rhymes rely on the combination of sibilants with 'i' sounds, staining all the vowels of the 'abbaabba' rhyme pattern. The steep pattern of mutually echoing rhyme words suggests the precipitously vertical nature of the poet's descent, with 'abissi' and 'eclissi' functioning as key terms both in the octave's sound pattern and its semantic organisation. Thus both sound and sense express vertiginous inwardness and loss: the very intention of the poem as verse message addressed to a named individual is subverted as a self-reflexive, 'abyssal' recession of voice sucks the subject inwards, potentially away from hearing and help. This cataclysmic loss of identity is the closest Tasso's writing comes to a crisis of identity.

But the poet refuses to consent to this catastrophe, and the sestet seeks to break the claustrophobic pattern. 'A te mi volgo e grido'. This cry of desperation is open-mouthed as 'o' vowels replace the pattern of 'i' vowels, formally enacting a voice which seeks to be heard outside itself. The volto or turn which characterises the sestet becomes the means by which the subject's voice, in seeking to be heard by another, resituates itself referentially. The communication of a heard voice stabilises a slippage of referentiality: the poet appeals for physical assistance: 'Give me, you who can, your right hand.'

'I see the sun, but as he is when a dark veil wraps him in shadowy
eclipse.' This image of cosmic reversal can be traced back to
Archilocus. 'The eclipse of the sun on April 6, 648 BC, would seem
to have given him [Archilocus] the idea that nothing was any longer
impossible now that Zeus had darkened the sun; no-one need be
surprised if the beasts of the field changed their food for that of
dolphins.'[26] The 'stringing together of impossibilities' became a
topos, or commonplace theme in the Middle Ages – 'the world
upside down.' E.R. Curtius suggests that 'in the twilight of a
distracted mind the "world upside down" can express horror.' At
what point, then, does the commonplace topic become
psychologically or existentially motivated? Curtius cites some lines
by the early seventeenth century French poet Théophile de Viau:

> Le feu brusle dedans la glace;
> Le soleil est devenu noir;
> Je voy la lune qui va cheoir;
> Cet arbre est sorty de sa place.

(fire burns in ice; the sun has turned black; I see the moon about to fall;
this tree has left its place).

However, there is no evidence that Viau's troubles provoked a
psychological crisis.[27] Even supposing that this were the case, these
entirely conventional images of reversal would remain impersonal.
Compare Nerval's *Aurélia*: 'I thought I saw a black sun in the
deserted sky and a blood-red globe above the Tuileries.' Nerval
probably derives his black sun from Dürer, but, in the context of a
report on a delirious perception of reality, it acquires a new
specificity and significance. Tasso's dark sun is neither Viau's
commonplace nor Nerval's autobiographical report: the appeal to
Guglielmo Gonzaga is directly referential, but the figures deployed in
the sonnet are not intended to relate to actual experiences (e.g.
hallucinations). The darkness which emanates from Tasso's eclipsed
sun, far from being autobiographical, conjures up the threat that
autobiographical reference itself will be swallowed by the precipice
which opens up before the poet: the collapse of identity is, simultaneously, the end of history and, by implication, the absence of
God from a disordered universe. The extremity of this situation
transforms the 'world upside down' commonplace: in a crucially
inwards shift, Tasso's poem abandons classical rhetoric, to engage
instead with Christian eschatology.
This is evident in sonnet's sestet: 'Or dal profondo oscuro a te me

volgo e grido'. The penitential psalms provide a text rather than a subtext: 'Out of the deep I cry to thee o Lord' (Psalm 130). The poet addresses Gonzaga as a sinner would address God, requesting salvation – hitherto no one has heard his prayer ('mio prego'). This extraordinary procedure is warranted by the gravity of the situation: only an extraordinary power can hear a voice which is being swallowed up in silence. The imagery of the octet is insistently delirious, while the liturgical allusion of the sestet implies that this depth is spiritually null. The abyss opens up as the threat of a descent into hell.

The urgency both of the poet's desperation and of his call for help find adequate expression via the religious subtext. For Tasso, caught up in the throes of the Counter-Reformation, and obsessively concerned with the condition of his soul, the religious dimension underscores a sense of seriousness which the courtly appeal to the Duchess of Ferrara cannot match. In *Sposa regal, già la stagion ne viene*, the poet does not seriously contemplate the possibility that his voice will not be heard, but in the sonnet to Guglielmo, this has become a distinct possibility.

The abyssal silence of the Guglielmo sonnet is different, too, from the idyllic openness celebrated in the madrigal *Tacciono i boschi*, where a mutual silence is the medium of intimacy and transparency. In the state of solitary enclosure which is the precondition of the sonnet, silence is a negative sign of self-collapse. It is in these circumstances that the poet calls on an 'inner speech' which, transcending rhetoric, is modelled on prayer – a call for assistance or intervention which is nevertheless uttered in silence or solitude.

Signor, nel precipizio reveals a crisis which is experienced subjectively. This is not the non-subjective madness which, in his letters, Tasso attributes to supernatural possession or else organic humours. Neither are Platonist or Aristotelian conceptions of *furor* an issue here: rather the relevant context is provided by the Counter-Reformational emphasis on inwardness. In promoting a heightened degree of introspective inwardness, the Counter-Reformation was instrumental in inducing much of Tasso's oppressive sense of religious guilt, but it also put him in touch with an inner-directed tradition which reached back to Augustine. In *Signor, nel precipizio*, this provided him with a means not only of poetically expressing an inner crisis, but of poetically coming to terms with it.

'Draw the wings of swift invention from under the vile weight that crushes it.' The plea to Guglielmo suggests that poetry itself is at

stake in this crisis. The dislocated cosmos of the sonnet expresses a
slippage of meaning. The precipice towards which the poet is
propelled fissures the ordered surface of rhetorical discourse itself,
threatening the collapse not only of an identity, but of the discourse
which mediates that identity – what is the use of a formal address
if the poet's voice cannot be heard? It is only in trespassing the
bounds of propriety and in addressing Guglielmo in terms of a
'religious sublime' that the poet-speaker can re-establish a means of
communication. The sestet thus seeks to return to stability in formal
as well as referential terms, reconfirming the threatened status of the
sonnet as encomiastic poem.

In the sonnet to Margherita, the upper world of the palace from
which the speaker is excluded and the lower world of the dungeon
to which he is confined become, in the sonnet's octave and sestet,
two wings of a single structure: Tasso's rhetorical strategy maintains
communication between the two domains. The abyss of the
Guglielmo sonnet, by contrast, is a non-location, and initiates a
process rather than a structure. The poet's unlocated voice is in
movement. If the octave expresses the encroachment of an inner
catastrophe then the sestet seeks to avert this impending threat;
there is a dynamic tension between the two units, with the latter
seeking to redefine the terms of the former. In this way the poem
expresses a sense of urgency absent from the sonnet to Margherita.
In signalling a new proximity between a subjective experience and
the discourse which emerges from that experience, it defines itself as
a discourse of subjectivity.

Nevertheless the depth which opens up in the poem is offset by
both the historical moment and the society to which the poet
belongs. The moment is that of the Counter-Reformation, the
society that of the Italian courts and their despotic rulers: these
enable the poet to find a form of language which can defuse the
dangerously excessive nature of the crisis. In the concluding section
of this chapter I shall attempt to assess what bearing the poet's socio-
cultural situation might have on his psychological situation.

III

Tasso, alert to his own standing as a poet, resented courtly
patronage, but was, at the same time, inescapably bound up with it.
The ambivalence of this situation is an underlying factor in one of
his most admired lyrics, the *Canzone al Metauro*. This is a poem

which, like other celebrated works (the *Aminta*, the *Gerusalemme liberata*) is determined by the culture of the Italian courts. But it also departs significantly from that culture.

The three stanzas of the poem (which remains unfinished) were written in 1577, before the dramatic incident in Lucrezia d'Este's apartment. In the opening stanza the poet arrives at the banks of the Metaurus, seeking refuge at Urbino, represented here by an 'alta Quercia', a tall oak – the crest of Francesco della Rovere, duke of Urbino. The poet is harried by 'quella cruda e cieca dea', the cruel, blind goddess Fortuna. Tasso goes on to depict a pattern of misfortune – a family life which is unable to provide any semblance of continuity or stability, the beloved mother soon dead, the father forced into a life of wandering, with his children following in his wake.

The presentation of family circumstances emerges oddly in the context of an encomiastic petition to the Duke of Urbino. In a despotic society such as that of sixteenth-century Ferrara there was no clear dividing line between the domestic sphere and the non-domestic sphere of court and state. Francis Barker has argued that such a social formation has direct consequences for the construction of subjectivity: 'Pre-bourgeois subjection does not properly involve subjectivity at all, but a condition of dependent membership in which place and articulation are defined, not by an interiorised self-recognition (. . .) but by incorporation in the body politic which is the king's body, in its social form.'[28] Philippe Ariès has argued that the pre-bourgeois family 'assured the transmission of life, property and name, but it didn't penetrate very deeply into human sensibility.'[29] The bourgeois family, by contrast, fosters a network of intensely private relationships through new ties of sentiment and emotion: in this way it differentiates itself from the larger community.

It would follow from this that the terms of an individualistic psychology, rooted in a private sphere, are irrelevant to Tasso. However the *Canzone al Metauro* does not altogether confirm such a conclusion. In the opening stanza Tasso petitions the Duke of Urbino, through the emblem of the Oak, to provide him with refuge:

> L'ombra sacra, ospital, ch'altrui non niega
> al suo fresco gentil riposo e sede,
> entro al più denso mi raccoglia e chiuda
> (813–14)

(The sacred, hospitable shade, which denies no-one rest and repose in its gentle coolness, I enter at its thickest, gather and enfold me)

In the following stanza the poet evokes the sanctuary which has been lost to him through the death of his mother: his image suggests that the infant has been torn from the womb itself:

> me dal sen de la madre empia fortuna
> pargoletto divelse. Ah! di quei baci
> ch'ella bagnò di lagrime dolenti,
> con sospir mi rimembra e de gli ardenti
> preghi che se 'n portâr l'aure fugaci:
> Ch'io non dovea giunger piu volto a volto
> fra quelle braccia accolto
> con nodi così stretti e sì tenaci.

(814)

(From my mother's breast cruel fortune tore me while still a child. Ah! I remember with sighs those kisses which she bathed with sorrowful tears, and the ardent prayers which the fleeting wind carries away; for never again can I, face to face, attain those arms embracing [me] in such close and strong bonds.)

The juxtaposition of the 'enfolding' oak with the lost maternal embrace might well seem logical for the modern reader: in requesting of Francesco the refuge which he has not been allowed to enjoy in the bosom of his own family, the poet seeks compensation for the deprivation he suffered as a child. This reading is, however, a problematic one. The encomiastic genre and the courtly context are both resistant to psychological thematisation: the emblematic character of the Oak externalises and conventionalises the very content which it represents, and even at the level of 'deep' implication it hardly seems likely that the poet is asking Francesco della Rovere to stand for him as a mother-substitute. Rather than retrospectively psychologising the first stanza, it makes more sense to read the lines on the poet's mother as a compelling rhetorical display of emotion, intended to exact a maximum of sympathy from the auditor. This is certainly how the passage commences, with its dramatic evocation of 'cruel fortune.' But at this point the poet switches his mode of address: in opening up the perspective of memory, he turns introspectively inwards ('con sospir mi rimembra'). As the bravura performance of emotion is converted into an intimate expression of personal grief, the poem's auditor must also shift position. From auditioning a formal appeal, he is now required to

respond to the enacted distress of a private voice. Such a development does not necessarily exceed the bounds of the formal occasion,
but here it does in fact do so, and Tasso goes on to strain his
encomiastic intention to the point of dislocating it. The maternal
sanctuary is, so the poet says, unrecoverably lost – 'ch'io non dovea
giunger piu'. The intensity of this assertion is scandalous, given the
poem's premise: having asked Francesco for sanctuary, Tasso forgets
himself and states that so great was his loss, nothing can compensate
for it. The thematic link between the Oak and the mother as images
of sanctuary merely serves to highlight their real discontinuity, as
the latter reveals the inadequacy and superficiality of the former.

In the succeeding lines on his father, Tasso shifts register yet again:
the family drama is now projected into an heroic dimension, invok-
ing a Virgilian precedent for his fate: 'Lasso! e seguii con mal sicure
piante, / qual Ascanio o Camilla, il padre errante.' / (Alas! and with
feeble steps I followed, like Ascanius or Camilla, my wandering
father.) Given these successive displacements, it is hardly surprising
that the poem was left unfinished.

Foucault notes that 'the psychological dimension in our culture is
the negation of epic perceptions.'[30] Tasso seems caught on the
horns of this transition. The lines on the mother, with their intermingling of memory and emotion, touch on a mode of utterance
which will later define the properly bourgeois style of Rousseau and
Cowper. In the eighteenth century it is the mother who, at the
centre of the domestic private sphere, is instrumental in fostering a
specifically bourgeois sense of subjectivity.[31] In this light, Tasso's
portrayal of the mother–son relationship may be said to point in the
direction of an 'interior self-recognition,' one which is alternative to
the mode of self-presentation associated with father or ruler. Thus,
in the Canzone al Metauro, the subjective affect of the maternal
instance is in tension with the two paternal instances that accompany it – the patronage and protection requested of Francesco della
Rovere, and the subsequent reference to the poet's actual father,
Bernardo Tasso.

For all Tasso's undoubted love and esteem for his father, his depiction of their relationship externalises it both formally (in terms of
epic) and literally (it is situated outside, not inside). In his dual
career as courtier and epic poet (author of the Amadigi), Bernardo
moved in the world of the Italian courts, and the mixed fortunes of
both father and son are attributable to the problems and uncertain-
ties of dependence on courtly patronage. The family home in
Sorrento, where Tasso spent his childhood with his mother, may

well have remained for him an idealised alternative to the non-domestic nature of court life. There is no direct evidence for this, but when Tasso escaped from surveillance in 1577 it was to the house of his sister Cornelia in Sorrento that he fled: it must have seemed like a homecoming.[32]

Looked at in another light, the father–son relationship of the *Canzone* reverses the claustrophobic overtones of the mother–child relationship. The Virgilian reference tacitly acknowledges that the son, as well as following the father, also apprenticed himself to his craft, the writing of epic poetry. Appropriately then, the father–son relationship is devoid of subjective implications (as is the ideal prince–poet relationship sought in the opening stanza). The objective situation which results is not without its positive aspect: instability is given not in inward or emotional terms, but simply through restlessness of movement as son follows father.

The relationship between instability and restlessness is a constant factor in succeeding centuries. Hölderlin, Clare and Nerval use movement in space as a means of offsetting psychological instability. Each of them undertakes an extensive journey at a time of crisis. Psychological instability is, it would seem, externalised through spatial movement. Conversely it is when these writers are immobilised and held in one place that an inner confrontation with subjective crisis becomes unavoidable. For the later writers, the pattern of movement away from or towards a place of asylum seems to involve the problem of what constitutes home, thus Clare's *Journey out of Essex* is at once a movement of escape from a wrong 'home' and a quest for the true one. Tasso's flight to Sorrento in 1577 may involve a comparable initiative. Conversely, the hospital of Sant'Anna, where he was held at the behest of a prince, constitutes a negative and parodic home, one which is psychologically damaging.

In the sonnet *Signor, nel precipizio ove mi spinse*, Tasso appeals to another prince with whom he hopes to form an alternative relationship, thus replacing a 'bad father' with a 'good' one. The psychologistic implication of these terms may not be justified, nevertheless the sonnet to Guglielmo Gonzaga is invested with an intensity lacking in the earlier address to Francesco della Rovere. It is conceivable that, in broaching a non-rhetorical language of religious sublimity, the appeal to Guglielmo begins to interiorise and psychologise the figure of the prince, just as, according to psychological theory, the infant 'at home' interiorises the figure of the father. In so doing, the sonnet provides a potent if ambivalent expression of a father–son relationship of a type which may be said to 'advance on' those evoked in the *Canzone al Metauro*. If the sonnet foresees the elements of a properly psychological configuration then Tasso's actual experience of confinement is integral to this development, inducing a disturbing experience of inwardness. The space of confinement, opening up an inner precipice, confronts the poet with an interiorised unreason which is potentially limitless in its extent. This foreshadows the later phenomenon, in literature, of a madness which is both fully interiorised and terminal.

But this was not Tasso's fate.[33] If a psychological dynamic is at work in *Signor, nel precipizio*, this must be balanced against the given circumstances which predetermine its scenario. Thus the interiorised precipice returns to the interior of Sant'Anna and the hypothetically interiorised *Signor* to the actual Duke of Mantua. This imposes limits on a possible psychoanalytic reading of the poem. We may, for example, locate in the sestet the Oedipal function of a paternal surrogate who stabilises a signifier which is sliding towards delirious non-meaning. But in the absence of any real evidence of infantile residues, then this 'underlying' meaning lacks explanatory force and is no more than a translation into psychological and formal terms of what is explicitly given in the socio-historical dimension – thus it was Guglielmo's son Vincenzo who actually did secure Tasso's release from Sant'Anna in 1586. The evidence requisite to a psychoanalytic reading is in short supply in Tasso's case because it is in short supply in his culture.

At the same time, the potential psychological reading cannot simply be discarded. In the *Canzone al Metauro*, the poet does point tantalisingly if inconclusively towards his childhood and its literally inner meaning. What is at issue here is whether madness is interiorised in terms of a subject-centred psychology or whether it is exteriorised in terms which depsychologise the available meanings of madness. Tasso is alone among the writers of madness in being difficult to place with respect to these alternatives. Typically, he exteriorises his situation in terms of the politics of his confinement or the Aristotelian pathology of his self-diagnosis. But the few writings in which we witness an inward turn are of great significance precisely because of Tasso's situation. The sonnet, *Signor, nel precipizio ove mi spinse* admits a subjective crisis to the process of discourse in a way that remains unprecedented for a further two centuries.

On the whole, the society and culture of late Renaissance Ferrara enabled Tasso to cling to a saving sense of identity. He glimpses what later poets and writers will experience as an interiorisation of madness: if, however, he manages to hold this 'existential' breakdown at bay, then it is an achievement which surely deserves congratulation.

2 James Carkesse: The Madman as Poet

I

In 1679 a slim volume was published in London, *Lucida intervalla*, 'Containing divers Miscellaneous Poems, written at Finsbury and Bethlem by the Doctor's Patient.'[1] Not a great deal is known about James Carkesse, the author of these Bedlam verses, but the biographical traces he has left behind reveal an intriguing figure.[2]

Aside from *Lucida intervalla*, Carkesse is known to us through Pepys's Diary. The two men were colleagues in the Navy Office where Carkesse worked as a clerk in the Ticket Office. Pepys initially formed a good opinion of him, but he came to believe that Carkesse was using his position to line his own pocket, and, in 1667, was instrumental in bringing about his dismissal. Carkesse fought back: he succeeded in having his case heard by the Privy Council, which cleared his name. He was restored to his post but eventually lost it once more. We next hear of him in 1678 when, following an onset of religious mania, he was committed first to Finsbury madhouse, then to New Bethlem, where he remained for six months before being discharged.

Michael V. Deporte remarks that *Lucida intervalla* 'must be the first collection of verse ever published in English by the inmate of an asylum.'[3] Its publication coincides with what Michel Foucault has called 'the great confinement,' i.e. the large-scale removal of responsibility for mad people from the family and community to private or state-run institutions. Confinement is a phenomenon of the Age of Reason and can be dated from the second half of the seventeenth century: in the context of France, Foucault takes 1656 – the founding of the Hôpital Général in Paris – as the landmark date.[4] In England the age of confinement has more modest

beginnings and a more gradual evolution; however Carkesse's
experiences of both Finsbury and Bethlem can be said to mark a
point of departure. Private madhouses, such as the establishment at
Finsbury, became a marked feature of the social landscape after
1660, while in 1676 Bethlem Hospital, the only state-run institution
for the insane, was reopened on a new site after a fire had destroyed
the old premises. New Bethlem was considerably enlarged: it now
contained some 140 inmates as against Old Bethlem's 44 in 1642 (27
in 1632). In 1678 Carkesse joined their number.

He was, no doubt, diagnosed as a case of mania. Convinced that
he had a mission 'to reduce Dissenters unto the CHURCH,' he set
about disrupting Dissenter meetings, an activity which led to his
committal. During the Privy Council hearings Pepys had already
concluded that Carkesse was 'distracted.' He appears to have been
a contrary and quarrelsome individual: in *Lucida intervalla* he refers
to himself as 'hot-headed' and attacks his enemies, notably his physician, Dr Allen, with energy.

Allen shares a name with John Clare's first asylum keeper,
Matthew Allen. In contrast with his nineteenth-century namesake,
Carkesse's doctor saw verse writing as an unhealthy symptom. It
seems too that Carkesse's attacks on the treatment he received in
the asylum did not leave the physician indifferent: the poems
provide vivid glimpses of the confrontation between the two men:

> Desiring his Imprison'd *Muse* t'enlarge,
> The *Poet*, *Mad-Quack* mov'd for his *discharge*.
> He angry answer'd, *Parson*, 'tis too soon,
> As yet I have not Cur'd you of *Lampoon*;
>   (51)

Carkesse's doggerel verse gains its edge from being written in
rebellion: it anticipates the anger and insurrectionary energy of
Clare's *Don Juan*. But *Lucida intervalla* is more than a document of
protest. In his poems, Carkesse undertakes an ingenious justification
of his behaviour and his situation. Seventeenth-century medical
opinion distinguished between mania and melancholy as dual but
related disorders.[5] Adopting this classification for his own purposes,
Carkesse distinguishes between the influence of Luna, the moon,
which is suffered passively by the lunatic, and the more active
agency of Phoebus, the sun. He himself is free from Luna's morbid
nocturnal influence:

For though at *Bedlam* Wits ebb and flow,
As wandring Stars move swift or slow;
My Brains not rul'd by the Pale Moon,
Nor keeps the Sphears my soul in Tune;
But she observes, and changes notes
With th'azure of sky-couloured Coats.

(34)

While repudiating Luna, Carkesse does not deny that he is mad. Indeed, his invocation of Phoebus involves an attempt to redefine the condition of madness in terms of the integrity of his own identity. His 'New Distinction', summed up in the contrasting titles of two poems, 'Poets are Mad' and 'Poet no Lunatic', does not (as one commentator has supposed) involve a contradiction. Madness is governed by the sun, lunacy by the moon, thus the melancholic lunatic lives out his existence in a cold, sad obscurity, a sleep of the faculties of reason. Not so the witty madman, who quickens to vital, energetic activity.

Two sorts of patient *Quack* in *Bedlam* has
The one that *witty* is; t'other that was
Mad both (. . .)

By contraries to Cure, thus *Doc* takes pains,
Our much, *with different heat*, distemper'd *brains*.
But howso'ere the *Moon* he may controll,
By *Muses* he's defy'd, and by their *Droll*.

(28)

In 'The Doctor's Advice', the doctor attempts to persuade his patient to 'leave off the *Poet* and *Lampoon*,' on the grounds that Phoebus, who is Carkesse's mentor, cannot be separated from Luna, for '*Phoebus* and *Luna*, Sister are and brother'; to be influenced by one is to be influenced by both: 'Then *Wit* forswear, and like me prove but *Dunce*, / The *Sun* and Moon will quit you both at once' (27). The doctor's argument is in line with the medical opinion of the day: 'I call that kind of melancholy Madness, where men rave in an extravagant Manner, Lunacy; because it is only the same Disease, improved in a hot Biliose Constitution.'[6] Carkesse will have none of this. *Lucida intervalla* is a product of daylight consciousness: its language, lacking in emotional or imaginative depths, allows no scope for introspection. Lunatic melancholy would, for Carkesse, preclude the assertion of an identity which does not rely on a sense of inwardness. His 'new Madness' is a

phenomenon of clarity. It is hot in its anger and proclaims its condition unabashedly in daylight: it is, in a word, inspired:

> Prophets and Poets Mad are (in a sense)
> And Sober grow, as they their gift dispense:
> One vents his Rage by words in open Air,
> By Ink on Paper He drops his with care
>
> (36)

Poets have been associated with madness from time immemorial,
but Carkesse self-consciously reverses the association: he is mad
therefore he is a poet. His self-proclamation as poet responds directly
to the circumstances in which he finds himself: 'Others,' he declares
to his physician,

> . . . your *Physick* cures, but I complain
> It works with me the clean contrary way,
> And makes me *Poet*, who are *Mad* they say.
>
> (32)

He invokes the Platonic tradition of *numine afflatur*: 'Phoebus (. . .)
does inspire / My breast with breath of a diviner fire.' In making this
claim, Carkesse turns the ancient association between poetry and
madness on its head. In Plato's *Phaedrus*, poetic enthusiasm, possession by a god, is a 'privileged' condition, visited upon 'the favoured
prophet, philosopher or poet.'[7] Carkesse's *furor*, however, denotes
real rage: 'This is not Lunacy in any kind: / But naturally flow hence
(as I do think) / Poetick Rage, sharp Pen, and Gall in Ink.' Such a
literalisation of the Platonic *furor* serves to justify the kind of manic
behaviour which caused Carkesse's committal in the first place, and
in this way he comes to exemplify the definition of madness given
some twenty years earlier by Hobbes in the *Leviathan* (1651): 'Pride
subjecteth a man to anger, the excess whereof, is the madness called
Rage and *Fury*.'[8] Hobbes's pre-Enlightenment secularism dispenses
with the inheritance of Plato and Aristotle: notions of divine inspiration and demoniacal possession are both rejected, making way for a
sceptically rationalistic understanding of madness.[9] Such a
desublimation of Platonic *furor* as manic fury marks a shift away from
the Renaissance and its Neoplatonistic conceptions of an ideal poetic
madness. Hobbes's anti-idealist philosophy presents Carkesse's
pretentions in an unflattering light, yet in the dawning age of the
Enlightenment Carkesse emerges from the pages of *Lucida intervalla*
as the Hobbesian madman *par excellence*.

Jürgen Habermas has identified a new dimension of social existence which was emerging in late seventeenth-century London, namely a 'public sphere': 'By "the public sphere" we mean first of all a realm of our social life where something approaching public opinion can be formed (. . .). Citizens behave as a public body when they confer in an unrestricted fashion – that is, with the guarantee of freedom of assembly and association and the freedom to express and publish their opinions – about matters of general interest.'[10] In *Lucida intervalla* the argumentative loudness of the poems is appropriate to a public occasion:

> *Henry* the Eighth this Hospital Erected,
> *Madmen* to Cure, with *Lunacy* Infected:
> But *Anger*, a short *Madness* call'd, and *Passion*
> Here to arraign was ne're th'intent nor *Fashion*:
> (63)

Carkesse, it is true, addresses many poems to particular individuals, but he doesn't necessarily know them personally, and the poems are sometimes formal petitions to titular personages ('To the Duke, General of the Artillery, Overlook't by Finnes-burrough Mad-House, Where I was confined'). Still others resemble topical pamphlets, pronouncing on particular issues ('On the Doctor's telling him, that 'till he left off making Verses, he was not fit to be Discharg'd'). Clamouring for an immediate hearing, they are, for the most part, intended for an assembled audience.

Habermas understands the Enlightenment public sphere to be a specifically bourgeois phenomenon. Richard Sennett's related notion of public life modifies this proposition in ways which are relevant to Carkesse. Sennett argues that civic public life emerges towards the end of the seventeenth century as a phenomenon of *ancien régime* society as defined by Tocqueville, i.e. one which features a mixture of feudal privileges, mercantile opportunities and administrative bureaucracy.[11] These conditions prevail during the Restoration period. The years following 1660 saw a vast increase in mercantile trade, and, in an urban society where the coffee houses assumed a new importance in the dissemination of political opinion, it was the gentry and the educated and monied class which came to constitute the 'public', in advance of the Glorious Revolution of 1688.

Klaus Doerner argues that the formation of public opinion in London around this time creates a space in which unreason becomes first visible, then fascinating: 'Insanity in that era must unquestionably be seen as a political issue in the broadest sense of the word, and contemporary medical approaches and practitioners were strongly influenced by the concepts of the emergent bourgeoisie.'[12] Madness was a topic of conversation in the coffee houses, and a number of key figures in the dissemination of public opinion and debate, Locke and Mandeville, Defoe and Swift, took a close interest in the issue of insanity and how it was dealt with (Locke and Mandeville were themselves physicians).[13] The public exhibition of lunacy also served to focus public attention on the insane. After the reopening of Bethlem in 1676, visiting the insane was resumed and became a fashionable pastime.[14] The titles of Carkesse's poems record frequent visits, and also let us know that his visitors were far from unwelcome: 'The Duke of Grafton, Looking into his Cloyster, And kindly asking him; How he did'; 'To a Lady, who was very kind to him in the place'; 'To Mr Stackhouse, Presenting me with a PERIWIG'. There is no evidence that he was mocked (he is sufficiently belligerent and sensitive to let us know). Deporte is no doubt correct in suggesting that as a gentleman and practising versifier Carkesse received a better class of attention than the average inmate, nevertheless the absence of any sign of impatience or annoyance with visitors is noteworthy. Carkesse clearly valued the visits not only for the gifts and the attention he received but also as an extension of a public space in which his verse thrived.

If *Lucida intervalla* bears witness to an emerging public sphere, there is no doubt either that it is a product of the *ancien régime* culture of the Restoration. Carkesse compliments his visitors with laboured conceits which are histrionic and unconcerned with sincerity: aristocratic visitors bring out in him a strain of magniloquence to which he is more than usually ill-suited. These *ancien régime* features do not contradict the impression he gives of being at home in a contemporary public arena. The first poem in the volume is dedicated 'To the King's Majesty', but this is a public address and not a personal petition: the poet assumes his right to be heard as a loyal citizen speaking on public issues (namely the recent Titus Oates affair). When he addresses poems to the public at large, his language is less bombastic, but there is no essential difference of tone.

His use of theatre as a point of reference similarly implicates both court and city. 'In London the Restoration brought into being a theater less dependent upon royal or aristocratic patronage, more able to sustain itself (. . .) by public subscription.'[15] In 1667, Pepys tells how he saw a play entitled *The coffee house* in the presence of the King and the Duke of York; meanwhile his wife complained to him of the impudence of her lady companion Deborah Willett 'in sitting cheek by jowl with us' (October 15, 1667). When *Lucida inter-valla* shows its author receiving visits variously from the young Duke of Grafton, 'a Tinman's Wife'; the Lady Sheriffesse Beckford, and a Mrs Moniments from Charing Cross ('in such a *Tomb* I chuse to lie / And yield up *Ghost* before I *Die*'), it reproduces the social juxtapositions which, according to Sennett, characterise Enlightenment public life.

For Sennett it is the theatre more than the coffee house which determines the essential character of *ancien régime* metropolis.[16] Carkesse repeatedly represents the public space of New Bethlem as a theatre:

> *Poets* and *Players*, now pack up your *Awls*,
> To *Bedlam* you aloud, *Fop Mad-Quack* calls;
> And 'till he cures you of *Poetick Rage*,
> Our *Galleries* you must fill, quit *Pit* and *Stage*.
> (50)

The Theatre Royal and Bethlem were rebuilt on new premises within two years of each other (in 1674 and 1676 respectively). Both figured prominently among the entertainments of the metropolis: 'Bedlam is a pleasant place (. . .) and abounds with amusement' one wit commented in 1700.[17] Roy Porter suggests that the inmates of New Bethlem were alert to the theatrical possibilities of their situation: 'in *ancien régime* Bedlam (. . .) surely the Bedlamites themselves played to the gallery, putting on a "show" in return for attention, ha'pence and food.'[18] 'nor am I *Mad*,' Carkesse claims, 'but with design for certain: / Acting the Part' (45). This is opportunistic, but 'Madness in Mascarade' doesn't necessarily contradict the simultaneous assertion of a 'new sort of Madness.' After all, what is Bedlam if not a theatre where the witty madman acts his part? Carkesse's acting of madness is not to be strictly distinguished from the writing of witty poems:

> Thus as I lie, I Fancy I'm *Jack-Straw*.
> And to *Rebellious Bedlam* give the *Law*;
> Yet though a Prince, so low my *Fortune*'s sunk,
> That I do want, which you supply, the *Trunk*:
> And for my *Verses* writ on *Apricocks*,
> You kindly make *Jack-Straw*, *Jack-in-a-Box*.
> (44)

The ungainliness of this piece should not blind us to the

sophistication of its irony. As a 'mad' poem written in Bedlam, it begins by mimicking madness ('I Fancy I'm *Jack-Straw*') only to finish with a punning reversal which indicates the writer's self-conscious awareness of the mimicry ('You kindly make *Jack-Straw, Jack-in-a-Box*'). Carkesse is able to do this because the manifestation of such 'wit' shows that while he is mad, he is no more or less mad than are Rochester, Dryden or the players of the Restoration theatre. Carkesse depicts New Bethlem not in terms of the old commonplace of the world upside down but rather, in a new version of *theatrum mundi*, as the theatre upside down: 'Our *Galleries* you must fill, quit *Pit* and *Stage*.' The players are in the galleries, and yet on show: meanwhile, at another level of inversion, madness in masquerade becomes a literal play of self-representation, as a witty acting of madness encounters the witty madness of acting: '*Madness* and *Wit* act one part in the play' (21).

The wit of a non-lunatic madness consists precisely in its staging of itself; it is this ironic self-consciousness which distinguishes it from the self-loss of lunatic melancholy, which is incapable of representation. Thus Carkesse blames his doctor for failing to distinguish 'Betwixt a *Senseless* condition / And *Madness* in *Mascarade*' (10). For Foucault, such an ironic play of self-representation is typical of *l'âge classique*: 'it is the privileged age of *trompe l'oeil* painting, of the comic illusion, of the play that duplicates itself by representing another play.'[19] Roy Porter suggests that the display of madness as a spectacle for those visiting New Bethlem promoted a self-conscious and self-referring play of madness: '[the inmates of Bedlam] may well have "acted crazy" to establish a mocking rapport with the sane, turning all into a gallery of distorting mirrors.'[20]

In 1664 Richard Flecknoe complained of the emphasis on visual spectacle in the Restoration theatre: 'Now, for the difference betwixt our Theatres and those of former times, that which makes our stage the better makes our Playes the worse perhaps, they striving now to make them more for sight then hearing, whence that solid joy of the interior is lost.'[21] Carkesse's play of madness, too, lacks a 'solid interior.' He continually assumes roles. He acts them out in all seriousness, yet he cannot be said to be deluded inasmuch as these do not impinge on any deeper sense of self or subjectivity. He remains secure in his identity as James Carkesse (he is able to pun playfully on his own name), while the roles of parson, poet and player are so many personae which enable him to act in a play of real and feigned madness:

> My name is *James*, not *Nokes*, and yet an *Actor*;
> But now, *Mad Devil*, seek another *Factor*:
> I am a minister of God's holy *Word*,
> Have taken up the *Gown*, laid down the *Sword*:
>
> (5)

According to Sennett, identity in the *ancien régime* public domain is conceived in terms of acting.[22] Carkesse's various roles do not indicate a fragmented identity. He is able to shift position so easily because he has no interest in self-scrutiny or introspective self-questioning. Consistency of viewpoint is not a matter of concern: his successive changes of position displace each other strategically, as part of the public polemic which he stages. Dr Allen is the subject of Carkesse's whole-hearted abuse, but he is also a dramatis persona in Carkesse's staging of madness – 'Fop Mad-Quack,' a necessary foil to the poet's superior wit:

> . . . I, the *Scorn & Sport*
> Will make you, e're I've done of *Cit* and Court.
> Blush for your folly, *Fop*, or timely say,
> Revenge for my *Lampoons* has made the *Play*:
>
> (31)

II

It is Carkesse's exclusively public emphasis which, as much as anything else, sets him apart from Pepys, his rival and erstwhile colleague. 'By the end of the 17th Century, the opposition of "public" and "private" was shaded more like the terms are now used.'[23] The adjacency of the two domains is evident in Pepys's *Diary*. As Francis Barker comments, the fact that 'Pepys is now located as a private citizen in a domestic space, over against the world, is not (. . .) a natural fact.'[24] Pepys possesses a Janus-like ability to negotiate both public and private spheres. This involves a trade-off between private conscience and public behaviour of which Carkesse is seemingly incapable.

What surprised Pepys about Carkesse's self-defence during the Privy Council hearings was his inability to distinguish between friendly and unfriendly witnesses: 'He summons people without distinction – sure he is distracted' (August 17, 1667). Carkesse, it seems, lacks the psychological balance necessary for prudent self-management. Pepys's 'balance', however, presupposes a large measure of self-dividedness: 'The diary keeping that is so significant a symptom of the new type of character may be viewed as a kind of time-and-motion study by which the individual records and judges his output day by day. It is evidence of the separation between the behaving and the recording self.'[25] A split between instinct and conscience, one of the major forms taken by this inner division, is evident in the repeated excuses which Pepys provides in February 1668 for his buying and reading of *L'escholle des Filles*: 'a mighty lewd book, but yet not amiss for a sober man to read over to inform himself in the villainy of the world.' After relating how in the privacy of his chamber he masturbated over the book then burned it, he feels it necessary to repeat what is by now a patently duplicitous excuse: 'a lewd book, but what do no wrong once to read for information sake.' Pepys's 'good sense', the quality which so distinguishes him from Carkesse, is a good deal less psychologically straightforward than Carkesse's public mania.

The business of the pornographic book occurred at a time when Pepys was required to go before the Commission of Accounts to justify his involvement in goods overhastily taken as booty from captured Dutch vessels – a process which requires that his account books be inventoried. He resolves 'to conceal nothing but tell the truth,' believing that the affair poses no threat – 'yet I do find so poor a spirit within me, that it makes me almost out of my wits, and puts me to so much pain that I cannot think of anything, nor do anything but vex and fret and imagine myself undone' (February 5, 1668). The need to justify himself in public induces in him feelings of personal guilt, even though he requires no alibis. This counter-balances his self-conscious conjuring away of guilt in the private sphere where an alibi is not strictly required. Pepys's buying then burning of a scandalous and secret book directly follows the opening up of his account books to the Commission: this suggests that the two episodes are not unconnected. The pornographic book, burned so that it will not feature in the inventory of Pepys's library, is scapegoated. Between the public domain and the private interior, desire for self-gratification is relocated so that it can be consummated in intimate solitude: simultaneously the accompanying guilt is displaced onto a text which can be burned.[26]

If there is a balance between public and private in Pepys it is not a simple or harmonious one. The conflicting demands of the two spheres can only be resolved at the cost of a continual psychological tension between the public and the private self. Yet Pepys's success in the society and culture of Restoration London, in inverse ratio to

Carkesse's lack of success, consists precisely in his ability to balance the books. 'At each of the summaries he writes at the end of year or volume, the narrative is halted so that he may sum up the public and private events in turn, in much the same way as he makes up his monthly and annual accounts of expenses and savings.'[27] As Victor Sage suggests, the economic metaphor of credit and debit – of the balanced book – possesses in this period a psychological efficacy:[28] equilibrium is related to the management of outgoings and incomings.

By comparison, Carkesse is certainly unbalanced, but this term should not necessarily be understood in a psychological sense. Indeed, it can be argued that Carkesse's lack of balance precludes the degree of psychological complexity which underlies Pepys's balance. Unlike Pepys, Carkesse requires no alibis for a divided *Lebenswelt*: he functions exclusively in terms of a public sphere wherein inner psychological motivations are elided, and so he recognises no restraints on behaviour. His verse speaks out unselfconsciously, without shame or embarrassment, in the assumption that the reader will find the writer's arguments persuasive and accept his point of view. This assumption is, of course, erroneous, and reveals how out of touch Carkesse actually was with his contemporaries. He laments the contrast between his fate and Pepys's:

> (. . .) Mr. *Pepys*, who hath my *Rival* been
> For the *Dukes* favour, more than years *thirteen*:
> But I excluded, he High and Fortunate;
>
> (5)

The exclusion he complains of is unsurprising. In refusing to recognise the bounds of private behaviour and in justifying 'inspired' impulses as public acts, he simply confirms a diagnosis of mania.

III

Carkesse is nowhere more persuasive than in his protests against Dr Allen's regime: '*Purges, Vomits* and *Bleeding* / Are his method of Cure' (13). He was also deprived of his clothes and beaten (14). Allen, nevertheless, seems to have been a conscientious physician,[29] and what Carkesse experienced as a series of violent assaults was in conformity with the treatment recommended in 1672 by Thomas Willis for the cure of manic (as against melancholic) forms of madness:

Furious Mad-men are sooner, and more certainly cured by punishments, and hard usage, in a strait room, than by Physick or Medicines. But yet a course of Physick ought to be instituted besides, which may suppress or cast down Elation of the Corporeal Soul. Wherefore in the Disease, Bloodletting, Vomits, or very strong Purges, and boldly and rashly given, are the most convenient.[30]

Carkesse's emphasis on surfaces and his correlative repudiation of depths renders him particularly hostile to this kind of 'lowering' treatment. In *Lucida intervalla*, witty madness resists Allen's medical interventions: his 'sharp Pen' opposes the doctor's 'Lance' (lancet), while bleeding cannot prick his 'Poetick Vein.' These puns convert organic treatment of the body into incorporeal metaphors, thus demonstrating the mad poet's superiority over the dull doctor:

> So little *Wit*, so much of *Phlegm* and *Rheume*
> Our *Mad-Quack* has, that I may well *presume*
> Hither as *Patient* he'll ne're be prefer'd
>
> (31)

Carkesse usually exercises his wit through puns. When the physician himself speaks in 'The Poetical History of Finnesbury Mad-House,' his lack of wit is shown through the erroneous, or rather unwitting puns on which his method of treatment is based:

> I laid him in *Straw* for a Bed,
>   Lest *feather* should make him *light-headed*;
> . . .
> His *Diet* was most of it *Milk*,
>   To reduce him again to a *Child*.
>
> (13–14)

This regime is based on the old doctrine of sympathy. According to Hunter and Macalpine, this notion continued to evolve in the seventeenth century,[31] but Carkesse's experience suggests rather a survival of old-fashioned therapies.[32] Michel Foucault argues that, at about the beginning of the seventeenth century, medieval and Renaissance categories of resemblance and similitude were displaced by Classical categories of representation.[33] Carkesse's puns specifically play on the representational function of language as a characteristic which detaches it from the body and its corporality. It is no accident that the doctor's essential dullness is characterised in terms which are corporal and humoral – 'Phlegm and Rheume.'

Carkesse's most detailed and most sarcastic account of his treatment

is given in 'The Poetical History Of Finnesbury Mad-House': it is
here, not in Bethlem, that he is most vulnerable. There is a correla-
tion between the dark interior of Allen's private madhouse and the
offensive treatment to which the patient is subjected. In 'The
Poetical History', Carkesse triumphs over claustrophobic interiority
and depths. Even when the doctor shuts Carkesse away in a cell he
cannot lock him within himself. The doctor says,

> Moreover I him in the *Hole*,
>   As under a Bushel, confin'd;
> Lest God's Word, the Light of the Soul,
>   In my Mad-house should have Shin'd:
> Ne're the less into the *Dungeon*,
>   He let in the Rayes of the *Sun*,
> And i'th'Pit, where him I did plunge in,
>   Made Night and Day meet in one.
>   (12–13)

In Tasso's sonnet to Giuglielmo Gonzaga, a crisis which threatens
to engulf the poet is expressed through the eclipse of the sun.
Carkesse's 'Poetical History' reverses such negative images. The poet,
imprisoned, converts darkness to light and depths into surface.
Phoebus, unlike Luna, retains his bright identity: melancholic
lunacy is passive and vulnerable; it surrenders to non-identity, a
condition which is exemplified by the darkness of the madhouse. In
turning away from a dangerous subjective inwardness Carkesse is
able to depict himself as a hero triumphing over confinement. He
literally abolishes the prison of interiority in which he is held: '. . .
Fetters they were but *Straw*, / To the sinews of his Armes;/ And he
burst Bars and Doors . . .' (12)

These depths nevertheless leave their mark on the poem, if only
through the seriousness of its religious references. The 'Hole' or 'Pit'
in which the poet is confined is an image of hell. Transferred from
Finsbury, Carkesse is freed from the underworld. Quite literally he
is freed from the underworld of lunacy itself – from the dark interior
of the private madhouse to the public location of New Bethlem.

In a poem addressed to the president of Bethlem, Carkesse
confirms the eschatological implications of his account of the madhouse. Both Finsbury and Bethlem are, he states, purgatories, but of
the two Bethlem is to be preferred because 'To *Hell* that's nearer,
this to *Heavens* Gate.' Another poem, *The Mistake*, qualifies this
assertion: initially he found Bethlem an improvement on Finsbury
but he now realises his error. Nevertheless (his doctor excepted)

Carkesse does not rail out against Bethlem as he does against
Finsbury (one of the Bethlem poems shows him receiving a visit
'when he lay in Chains,' but the tone is droll and lacking in
animus). He seems to have found conditions in the newly reopened
Bethlem more congenial than those in the private madhouse. This
is not suprising: 'the new hospital built in 1676 was open and airy
in ways that impressed visitors.'[34] Cells with chains existed for
dangerous patients, but, as a contemporary visitor reports, 'Many
inoffensive madmen walk in the big gallery.'[35] Moreover Bethlem,
unlike the private madhouses, operated according to 'unimpeach-
able' statutes and regulations,[36] with inmates reviewed for
discharge after a year – Deporte tells us that Carkesse successfully
petitioned for his discharge after only six months of hospitalisation.
Everything, then, tends to indicate that the regime Carkesse found
in New Bethlem provided an exteriorised rather than interiorised
space of confinement, one which approximated a public sphere.

This points up the differences between New Bethlem and the
private madhouses which began to multiply in Carkesse's lifetime.
Dr Allen's was probably typical of these. The madhouses were
usually small: 'it is significant that the standard eighteenth century
term for such institutions was mad*house*, or just *house* (. . .) for most
indeed were integral or adjacent to the owner's residence.'[37] Such
establishments were shrouded in secrecy and obscurity: as Porter
neatly puts it, 'private madhouses had always been deeply
concerned to keep those who were out of their mind out of sight.'
The madhouses acquired some of the characteristics of the emerging private sphere: 'the asylum itself laid pretensions to be a home,
a mad*house*, endowed with its own surrogate family – while of
course it simultaneously separated the confined from his true
family.'[38] This proved to be beneficial for some. George Trosse,
treated in a madhouse in Glastonbury in the 1640s, recuperated
under the care and moral influence of the asylum keeper's wife. But
Carkesse (who viewed his wife as one of his enemies) would have
reacted badly to such a milieu. He does not identify Finsbury
madhouse in terms of a private sphere, but the given images of
darkness and confinement arguably constitute a negative insight
into the developing middle-class domestic regime.[39] Melancholic
lunatics, to whose condition Carkesse opposes his own, are
gendered in female terms. The female Luna, who presides over
lunacy, is contrasted with her brother Phoebus ('Yield *Luna* to your
Brothers more *powerful rays*'). Lack or loss of identity is thus directly
associated with a female sphere of influence: 'For though at

Bedlam Wits ebb and flow; / My Brains not ruled by the Pale Moon'
(34). In viewing intuitive interiority in terms of a female lack of identity Carkesse foreshadows a later shift in representations of madness
which, as Elaine Showalter has shown, come, from the end of the
eighteenth century, to be predominantly female in their imagery.[40]
Carkesse, in gendering 'safe' forms of social identity as male and
'unsafe' forms of non-identity and interiority as female, provides a
notably ambivalent anticipation of later developments. All in all, it
is appropriate that we know very little about his private or family
circumstances.

However, Carkesse's most determined resistance to the psychological forms of a nascent bourgeois culture emerge in the religious
sphere. His adoption of the roles of 'Parson' and 'minister' does not
bear witness to any very profound religious sensibility, and in this
instance he may again be contrasted with his contemporary, the
nonconformist minister George Trosse. Trosse experiences madness
as a spiritual crisis which brings him to God. Carkesse's acted calling
in Bedlam ('I am a minister of God's holy *Word*') contrasts with the
'authentic' (inner) nature of Trosse's conversion.

But to say that Carkesse's religious sense is superficial is not to say
that it is not serious – after all he was committed to Finsbury asylum
following his disruption of Dissenter meetings. After the turmoils of
the Civil War Carkesse, in his mission 'to reduce Dissenters unto the
CHURCH,' sides with Church and civil authority against nonconformist Protestant individualism. His religious role-playing, in its
very contingency, offers a strategic resistance to the Puritan emphasis
on direct spiritual experience. This in turn suggests that he resists a
psychical interiorisation of madness at the moment when this
process becomes evident in Trosse's spiritual autobiography. *The Life
of the Reverend Mr. George Trosse* is probably the first psychologistic
account of a full-blown episode of madness. Puritan theology is the
means whereby Trosse converts his experience of madness into an
inner drama.

In the era of the spiritual testimonies of Bunyan, Norwood, Trosse
and others, *Lucida intervalla* can be seen as an anti-confessional
writing, one which is, in effect, antithetical to Trosse's psychodrama.
In his references to Restoration theatre Carkesse plants an anti-
Puritanical touchstone at the heart of *Lucida intervalla*. The title
page clearly shows the market of curiosity seekers at which the
poems were aimed: 'Containing divers Miscellaneous Poems, written
at Finsbury and Bethlem by the Doctor's Patient. Extraordinary.'
The epithet is that of a playbill or public advertisement. The drama

of Carkesse's madness is a public spectacle – one which would be intolerably scandalous did not the public space of New Bethlem provide an appropriate stage for such a display.

3 Bunyan and Trosse: The Pathology of Puritanism

I

The seventeenth century, the heyday of English Puritanism, saw a profusion of autobiographical writings of the 'progress of the soul' type. Puritan spiritual autobiographies were not only more numerous than Catholic and Anglican counterparts but were also characterised by a greater degree of inwardness: 'spiritual experiences are no longer simple, objective events, but moments of intense emotional contact between God and the individual soul.'[1] The Protestant concerns of introspective self-scrutiny, the need to be spiritually reborn in God, and a requirement for '*experimental* Evidences of the work of *grace*,'[2] made the confessional autobiography an apt vehicle for Puritan writers.

The most famous work in this genre is Bunyan's *Grace abounding to the chief of sinners* (1666). Less well-known, but no less memorable, is *The Life of the Reverend Mr. George Trosse*, written by the nonconformist minister of that name in 1692–3. Both of these works tell stories of reprobate youth, spiritual crisis and conversion. In each case the crisis turns on pathological disturbance. Bunyan suffers a prolonged testing of his 'inner man' through extremes of obsession and despair. Trosse's crisis is still more traumatic: he recounts three successive episodes of insanity which he suffered in his mid-twenties. The experiences reported by Bunyan and Trosse are extreme, but neither of their discourses are generically atypical.[3] In comparing the two documents we see that Trosse's madness is different in degree but not in kind from the spiritual experiences of his Puritan contemporaries. Extreme as they are, the conversion experiences of both writers throw into relief significant elements of the psychological disposition of Lutheran and Calvinist Protestantism.

Puritan autobiography reproduces intensities of affective experience which result from the internalisation of conscience. For seventeenth-century Puritans, spiritual life – the inevitability of sin, the promise of salvation (predestined in the case of Calvinists), and an accompanying threat of damnation – became a matter of urgent concern as the self was required to monitor its own condition. Individuals became the keeper of their own consciences, rather than having them kept by the authority of the Catholic or Established churches. This explains the prominence in Puritan writings of the mysterious and unpardonable sin against against the Holy Ghost: 'members of the laity were probably little concerned with it, until the Puritan emphasis upon Scripture made Bible-reading a common practice among ordinary people. Many thereafter were troubled by the references to the sin against the Holy Ghost, and some developed a conviction that they were guilty of this offence.'[4] Bunyan and Trosse were haunted by this fear, as Cowper was to be in the 1760s.

Both Bunyan and Trosse survey the errors of their sinful past and the travails of spiritual awakening. Thus the 'I' of the autobiography distinguishes between the autobiographical narrator and a protagonist who struggles, through crisis, to become that narrator. The vantage point of a justified narrator implements narration as a discourse of identity. The identity in question, however, is a renewed one: it has been painfully regenerated out of the breakdown of a former self: intensity of regeneration is correlative to severity of breakdown.

The characteristic features of the inner drama of the Puritan conscience can be traced back to the figure of Luther himself. In *Young Man Luther*, Erik Erikson analysed the development of Luther's career in terms of identity crisis. Erikson takes into account a range of data in order to establish the historical scope of Luther's 'process of identity,' but doesn't specify how the psychology of identity formation is itself historically determined. When he suggests that Luther carried forward the 'incomplete' programme of the Renaissance 'by applying some of the individualistic principles immanent in the Renaissance to the Church's still highly fortified home ground – the conscience of ordinary man,'[5] he assumes that Luther's revolutionary position involves new inner and psychological co-ordinates of identity, but the implications of that assumption remain unexamined. Identity crisis may be, as Erikson suggests, a perennial factor in cultural history,[6] but it acquires in Luther a fresh dynamism which has very considerable consequences in succeeding centuries – particularly, so the evidence suggests, in England.

Christopher Hill has complained that 'Sociological and psychological historians have not got very far in explaining why there was so much despair in the late sixteenth and early seventeenth centuries, leading some to suicide, some to atheism, some to conversion.'[7] Evidently not all of this can be laid at the door of Luther; however, as Erikson makes clear, his questioning of papal authority and his resumption of inner-directed, Augustinian theological concerns emerge as a force in European culture alongside other factors with which they significantly coincide, most notably Gutenberg's invention of printing. Subsequently, Elizabeth Eisenstein has argued that the emergence of a print culture is a necessary precondition of the Reformation,[8] and Walter Ong has outlined the psychological scope of this development: 'Even apart from the expressed doctrine of private interpretation [of the Scriptures], the printed text throws the individual back on himself, away from the group or tribe. Psychological structures supporting the corporate sense of the Christian are weakened (. . .) when private reading of the Bible is moved to the centre of Christian life.'[9] Luther (initially at least) insisted that Christians should acquire the ability to read the Bible: literacy rates were higher in Protestant Northern Europe than Catholic Southern Europe in the seventeenth century, and penetrated further down the social hierarchy.[10] It is the general availability of the Scriptures which guarantees a direct, inner relationship with God. Reading and writing are the prerequisites of the internalised conscience: to put it another way, the internalised conscience is accompanied by the interiorisation of script. Bunyan provides an extraordinary account of the drama of literacy in a humble man born in the wake of Luther. The only reason he finds to mention his first wife is that she brings two godly books with her as dowry; his reading of other printed matter, including Luther's pamphlet on the Galatians, are important events. His immersion in the text of the Scriptures is so all-consuming that Biblical phrases and expressions assume for him a tangible, heard reality.[11]

Most of the cases of spiritual crisis that Christopher Hill lists in *The world turned upside down* occur among non-Anglicans,[12] and we know about many of them because of the collapse of censorship in 1641. Print, literacy, conscience and the break with absolutist political and ecclesiastical authority – these come together to form a potent constellation: 'Innumerable zealots took to the streets and market-places (. . .). The more literate among them called on the printers to aid the dissemination of the spiritual experiences which had been granted them. A vast pamphlet literature thus came into existence between 1649 and 1660, most of it more or less directly personal in tone.'[13] Hill notes that 'evidence [of personal crisis] increases as the revolutionary crisis deepened.'[14] Erikson is surely correct to suggest that Luther's identity crisis relates to 'the spiritual and political identity crisis of Northern Christendom in Luther's time.'[15] We need only go a little further in suggesting that Luther patented a particular form of identity crisis appropriate to his epoch, namely the internalisation of conscience.

Bunyan depicts his struggle with despair through images of personal subsidence: 'I now began to sink greatly in my soul' (26); 'I found myself as on a miry bog' (27); 'truly I did now feel myself to sink into a gulf' (62).[16] In the collapse of the old world where the recognised external authorities – Church, King, community – which have previously underpinned identity lose validity then the self must rediscover its own inner authority. But this is a process which is undertaken at great cost.[17] The autobiographies of Bunyan and Trosse testify that the internalisation of conscience which Luther bequeathed to the 'ordinary man' of the Protestant West is born from inner crisis – and that Luther's bequest includes his own experiences of melancholy and despair.

Crisis is almost a *sine qua non* of a self reborn in God: the soul becomes a battlefield of conflicting impulses, torn between the forces of the Devil and the force of God: 'The main point to be made here is Luther's new emphasis on man in *inner* conflict and his salvation through introspective perfection.'[18] In propounding a divorce between faith and works, Luther pronounced a break between the inner and outer man,[19] leaving the Christian conscience with the full burden of responsibility for its sinful nature, which faith alone could redeem. Guilt was a necessary product of this doctrine, and despair was a frequent byproduct. The inner pressures induced by notions of individual responsibility and a personal salvation guaranteed by faith alone could – and did – raise psychical tensions to breaking point. Religious melancholy was a widely recognised symptom in seventeenth-century England: Bunyan was merely one of many who read with terror *A relation of the fearful estate of Francis Spira*, Nathaniel Bacon's account of an Italian cleric who, in the climate of the Counter-Reformation, had recanted his Protestantism and died in despair of salvation ('The reading of Spira's case causeth or increaseth melancholy for many,' the Puritan divine Richard Baxter commented.[20]) Those who, like Bunyan and Trosse, had tempered themselves spiritually in the forge of religious crisis acquired considerable moral authority: 'emphasis falls on regeneration, on the regathering and strengthening of spiritual integrity, while never letting go the knowledge of guilt and terror once felt (. . .). Thus, far from being despised or even pitied, the melancholics who succesfully regather themselves may join the race of saints, as many believed Trosse had done.'[21]

As Christopher Hill remarks, the intensity of this drama was heightened by the context of the events of mid-century: 'In the widespread despair and atheism of the late 1640s and early 1650s we can sense the impact of the revolutionary crisis on the certainties of traditional Calvinism.'[22] The personal crises of Bunyan and Trosse both coincided with the turmoil of the 'Puritan Revolution' of 1640–60.

Stephen Greenblatt has contrasted the Puritan 'representation of inwardness' with a 'presentation of inwardness' found in sixteenth-century writings: 'In seventeenth century spiritual autobiography, the inner life is *represented* in outward discourse; that is, the reader encounters the record of events that have already transpired (. . .). In the early sixteenth century there is not yet so clearly a fluid, continuous inner voice.'[23] This assessment of Puritan writing is somewhat misleading. Puritan self-representation is not merely 'the record of events that have already transpired.' The 'justified' viewpoint asserts a spiritual victory which is never secure because always threatened by the felt reality of ungodly forces. In the 'Conclusion' of *Grace abounding*, Bunyan itemises 'abominations' which 'I continuallie see and feel, and am afflicted and oppressed with.' Yet they serve a good purpose – 'they show me the need I have to watch and be sober' (103). The Puritan conscience is required to subject itself to a process of continual self-monitoring, so Puritan autobiography reenacts the inner discourse of a subject whose self-examination is an ongoing concern: in this way it reproduces an immediate inner self-reflexivity.

What Greenblatt calls 'outward discourse' is closely linked to the inward reality which it relates. Bunyan draws attention to the functional style that his serious matter demands:

> I could also have stepped into a stile much higher than this in which I
> have here discoursed, and could have adorned all things more than here
> I have seemed to do: but I dare not: God did not play in convincing of
> me (. . .); neither did I play when I sunk as into a bottomless pit, *when*

the pangs of hell caught hold upon me: wherefore I may not play in my relating of them, but be plain and simple. (3)

Joan Webber has related the Anglican high style and the Puritan plain style to the respective versions of selfhood which they represent. The 'I' of the Anglican writer 'is obscure, ambiguous, many-sided because that is how he looks to himself, both in his use of such metaphysical figures as optical illusion, paradox, and word-play, and in stylistic shifts from one point to another in his prose. He is aware that "he" need not even be the same person from moment to moment.' The Puritan writer, by contrast, 'is active, timebound, as simple and visible as possible, desirous of being taken literally and seriously.'[24]

Bunyan's language of self-awareness, unlike that of Donne, does not derive from Renaissance humanism. He rejects humanistic rhetoric on religious grounds, but the rejection comes all the more easily inasmuch as 'I never went to school to Aristotle or Plato.'[25] The anti-rhetorical realism of *Grace abounding* is consistent with Bunyan's education and his unprivileged social position generally.[26] His moral pilgrimage begins with his first marriage: 'though we came together as poor as poor might be, (not having so much houshold-stuff as a Dish or Spoon betwixt us both), yet this she had for her part, *The plain mans path-way to heaven*' (8). Just as Bunyan the writer disdains the showy ornaments and decorations of the Anglican high style, so the young Bunyan, awakening to conscience in circumstances of relative scarcity, cannot afford the luxury of rhetorical self-projection. His circumstances at the time of his marriage mean that the spiritual value of *The plain mans path-way* cannot be dissociated from the material values of property.[27] Donne and other humanist writers come into possession of a privileged rhetoric of self-presentation: under these conditions, a perceived mutability of the self may be of concern to a 'melancholic' observer such as Montaigne ('Myself now and myself a while ago are indeed two'),[28] but is not experienced as a crisis of self-value. Bunyan, for his part, experiences God's Word as a material support for the self – 'this sentence stood like a Mill-post at my back' (60). The substantial Word, however, doesn't guarantee self-possession: on the contrary, 'all these fears of mine did arise from a stedfast belief that I had of the stability of the holy Word of God' (57). Bunyan's 'inner man' belongs to God, not to himself, and where his thoughts or behaviour leave salvation in doubt, then his inner reality, granted only under divine licence, begins to crumble: 'I had cut myself off by my transgressions, and left myself neither foot-hold, nor hand-hold amongst all the stayes and props in the precious word of Life. And truly I did now feel myself to sink into a gulf, as an house whose foundation is destroyed' (62).

Victor Sage, discussing the forms of Puritan psychology, draws our attention to a passage from *Grace abounding* in which Bunyan likens two opposed thoughts in his mind to a pair of oscillating scales – 'sometimes one end would be uppermost, and sometimes again the other' (65). Bunyan's narrational metaphor of balance controls the images of inner imbalance which it conveys: 'The power of this kind of metaphor,' Sage comments, 'prevents the language from shading over into psychopathology.'[29] Bunyan's art 'is not to let the "I" appear at all unstable,' while narrating the instability which the same 'I' has passed through. The metaphor of the scales derives from an inner economy of self-accounting: Sage quotes Calvin on 'the anxiety which fills the breasts of believers, who sincerely examine themselves. Every mind, therefore, would first begin to hesitate and at length to despair, while each determined for itself with how a great a load of debt it was still oppressed (. . .).'[30] Sage comments, 'The language of finance (. . .) in which the sincere deal with themselves supplies the most objective-seeming metaphor of all for mental-process: the account book. (. . .) The idea of debit and credit is somehow more "real": the "weight of debt" seems literally to drag the mind down.'[31] There is, then, nothing at all reassuring about this most objective of metaphors. Bunyan's image of the scales, in allying a metaphorical economy of the inner self with the subtext of real economic concerns, underscores the felt reality of the protagonist's tormenting fear that, like Esau, he has sold his birthright.[32] The economic metaphor may guarantee the stability of the narrational 'I', but it maintains, nevertheless, an underlying affinity with the real instability it so effectively expresses.

It seems to me that Bunyan's discourse is intrinsically related to the crisis it represents. Metaphors, by virtue of their very operative seriousness, can acquire a disturbingly hallucinatory potential in that cast of mind which seeks to validate images in terms of reality. When Freud suggests that the schizophrenic takes words for things,[33] his notion applies with particular force to the Puritan self. If madness comes frighteningly close to Bunyan it is because his perception and representation of reality are so utterly serious. Donne can afford to be referentially and metaphorically playful without summoning the threat of madness precisely because he is unconcerned with the

perception or representation in language of a material experience of
spiritual reality.

We may refer here to Roman Jakobson's celebrated distinction
between 'metaphoric' and 'metonymic' aspects of language. Jakobson
proposed that lyric poetry is metaphorical inasmuch as it embodies
a paradigmatic axis of substitution, whereas realist prose is
metonymic, primarily embodying a syntagmatic axis of combination.[34] Jakobson formulated this thesis in a paper on aphasic disturbance, and it was his analysis of the two general types of aphasia
which gave rise to his classificatory categories. In extending these to
literary genres, he avoided any implication of pathological disorder
– with, however, one intriguing exception. On the side of metonymy
he referred to a Russian realist writer, Gleb Uspenskij, who, according to Jakobson, suffered a mental disorder which affected his prose
style, resulting in an 'abnormal' overload of metonymic detail.[35]
Thus, in the case of referential realism, and only in this case, Jakobson allowed an implicit criterion distinguishing normal from abnormal or pathological referentiality. Realism, unlike figurative or lyric
writing, incorporates evidential norms, enabling judgmental perspec-
tives of norm and deviation which may operate from within the text
as well as from without. Where realism is above all a psychological
imperative, as it is in Bunyan and Trosse, then it implicates deviation as a psychological – which is to say psychopathological –
tendency. As a result Trosse directly recognises his deviant perception as madness, constituting that madness as a pathological fact. In
comparison, the Anglican poet Christopher Smart's subjective,
lyrical and prophetic asylum poem *Jubilate agno* has no truck with
realistic representation or evidential norms. Correspondingly it
includes no recognition or acknowledgement of madness. Smart's
celebratory mode of subjectivity is undespairing and free from the
pathological torments of Bunyan, Trosse and Cowper: 'For the sin
against the HOLY GHOST is INGRATITUDE.'[36]

Bunyan's 'house whose foundation is destroyed,' liable to collapse at
any moment, is the narrator's figure for a self in need of reconstruction, but it is more than that. The metaphor is prominently positioned in the Conclusion of *Grace abounding*, where it reveals its
scriptural origin:

> Of all the Temptations that I ever met with in my life, to question the
> being of God, and the truth of his Gospel, is the worst, and worst to be
> borne; when this temptation comes, it takes my girdle away from me, and

removeth the foundation from under me: O I have often thought of that Word, *Have your loyns girt about with truth*; and of that, *When the foundations are destroyed what can the righteous do?* (102)

Given its source, this is no mere rhetorical figure. The protagonist has experienced it as a literal force acting on his experience of reality. In the well-known bell-ringing episode, the young Bunyan, his conscience freshly awakened, feels compelled to abandon his guilty enjoyment of bell-ringing for fear that the church bell and church steeple will come tumbling down to crush him. The figurative instability of a Church without 'true' foundations acquires here the dimensions of pathological instability:

> Now you must know, that before that I had taken much delight in ringing, but my Conscience beginning to be tender, I thought that such a practice was but vain, and therefore forced my self to leave it, yet my mind hanckered, wherefore I should go to the Steeple house, and look on: though I durst not ring. But I thought this did not become Religion neither, yet I forced my self and would look on still; but quickly after, I began to think, How, if one of the Bells should fall: then I chose to stand under a main Beam that lay over thwart the Steeple from side to side, thinking there I might stand sure: But then I should think again, Should the Bell fall with a swing, it might first hit the Wall, and then rebounding upon me, might kill me for all this Beam; this made me stand in the Steeple door, and now, thought I, I am safe enough, for if a Bell should then fall, I can slip out behind these thick Walls, and so be preserved notwithstanding.
> So after this, I would yet go to see them ring, but would not go further than the Steeple door, but then it came into my head, how if the Steeple it self should fall, and this thought, (it may fall for ought I know) would when I stood and looked on, continually so shake my mind. that I durst not stand at the Steeple door any longer, but was forced to fly, for fear it should fall on my head. (13-14)

The psychological realism of this account should not blind us to its allegorical potential: added to the third edition of 1672, it arguably exemplifies the scriptural citation in the (already written) Conclusion, 'When the foundations are destroyed . . .'. The protagonist must exit from an unsound Church and its communal-festival activities, which threaten spiritual collapse and destruction: he must do so in order to undertake a putting-in-order of his own house. However, Bunyan does not open out this underlying allegorical implication: indeed he gives no indication of being aware of it. Allegory can only emerge outside the temporal narrative, as a

token of promised redemption. To impose it at this point would be
to abolish the immediate urgency of the historical narrative as it
conveys the protagonist's crisis-experience. Nevertheless the implication insists as a problem of meaning. As the threat of collapse takes
possession of the protagonist's mind, his guilt and fear seize on a
given particular – the bell, which might fall – but are unable to
contain it in this detail, and leap uncontrollably from bell to entire
steeple in a concatenating sequence. This can be traced back to
Calvin's analysis of the ramifying obsessions of the fearful conscience: 'When a man begins to doubt whether it is lawful for him
to use linen for sheets, shirts, napkins, and handkerchiefs, he will
long be secure as to hemp, and will at last have doubts as to
tow.'[37] The uneasy or guilty conscience falls victim to its own over-
literalistic perception of the meanings of reality. To use Jakobson's
terms of reference, a metaphorical meaning is pathologically grasped
in terms of a sequence of metonymic details: these progressively
contaminate each other as a perceived instability of reality itself. The
newly awakened conscience recognises that the edifice – the very
structure of meaning – which it had previously inhabited is unsound
and lacks foundation or support: a new meaning must be discovered,
without which the unsupported self will collapse: 'but now a Word,
a Word to lean a weary Soul upon, that I might not sink for ever!
'twas that I hunted for' (78). This acquires potentially hallucinatory
dimensions when projected by the guilty conscience as a literal
perception of reality.

However, literal meaning, felt negatively by the protagonist when
it acts on his perception of reality, is redeemed when converted into
the higher meaning of allegory.[38] In *Grace abounding*, explicit
allegory is restricted to a premonitory dream-vision of salvation:
Bunyan sees the elect of Bedford 'as if they were set on the sunny
side of some high Mountain.' He is separated from them by a wall
encircling the mountain, keeping him out in a wintry cold. He goes
round and round the wall, finding at length a 'narrow gap' through
which he succeeds in passing only with the greatest difficulty. The
meaning of the vision is then spelled out:

> the Mountain signified the Church of the living God; the Sun that shone
> thereon, the comfortable shining of his mercifull face on them that were
> therein: the wall I thought was the Word that did make separation
> between the Christians and the world: and the gap which was in this
> wall, I thought was Jesus Christ, who is the way to God the Father. (18)

Bunyan deploys here a full complement of conditionals ('methinks,' 'as it were') which indicate the non-reality of the vision. The literal exit from the church steeple is compensated by a non-literal but prophetic entry into the true Church – via a 'Word' founded in a concrete but non-literal image. The anticipated triumph of the narrative of self-regeneration is celebrated through the allegorisation of meaning, with *Pilgrim's progress* (1678) already in view. In *Pilgrim's progress*, meaning itself is regenerated and redeemed. Promising salvation, the positive meaning of allegory redresses the negative one of a pathological literality which threatens damnation. Both terms tend towards a visualisation and 'reification' of figural or symbolic modes of meaning, but if allegory is a positive instrument used by Bunyan the writer in ordering meaning, then pathological literality is negatively instrumental and acts on Bunyan as a passive, helpless protagonist.[39]

In the eighteenth century, Christopher Smart, for all that he acknowledges his situation and location, never considers the possibility of an aberrant madness. Because his transcendental Anglican God does not judge him, Smart does not judge himself. Bunyan's God is not a transcendental force: his operations are as real as they are mysterious. In relation to him, Bunyan may be either really saved or really damned: it is not a matter which lies within his choosing. Throughout his crisis, there is no active determination of meaning on his part: meaning must be solicited, awaited and received. So sustained and intense is Bunyan's concentration on Scripture that it acquires an autonomous reality: he is continually assailed by scriptural texts which bolt into his mind or sound in his ear. In this way meaning acquires the tangible dimension of reality while losing none of its spiritual efficacy. Whether it takes the form of diabolical literality or of godly allegory, this substantialisation of meaning relates to an historically specific self, projected through the formal realism of the autobiographical narrative. The psychology embodied in the autobiography is inseparable from the commitment which autobiographical discourse makes to realism as a mode of representation: autobiography, as history of an inner self, necessarily involves an acknowledgement of the given conditions wherein the self discovers and confirms its authenticity. Even in his allegorical dream-vision Bunyan must struggle with the unyielding materiality of a wall. By contrast, material obstacles provide no hindrance to Bunyan's contemporary, James Carkesse ('*Fetters* they were but *Straw*. . .).

Carkesse's 'witty' self-representation is playful where Bunyan's is not. The crises of Bunyan and Trosse remove them from Carkesse's non-psychological realm of play, spectacle and public exteriority. Bunyan receives his ominous call to grace 'in the midst of a game of Cat.' As we shall see, Trosse too is abruptly removed from a life of idle conviviality.

II

In *The Life of the Reverend Mr. George Trosse*, the Puritan internalisation of conscience coincides with an interiorised experience of madness. The collapse of self-identity in madness which threatens Bunyan in *Grace abounding* overtakes his contemporary, George Trosse.

The first twenty pages of Trosse's *Life* relate his early life – his education, his decision to become a merchant, and his sojourns in France and Portugal. At about the age of twenty he returns to his native Exeter where he remains for the next five years – a period of inaction passed over briefly in the narrative. Trosse suspends his narrative at this point to provide a fifteen-page summary of the various ways in which he has broken the Commandments. Only then does he resume his story: in this way he sums up and judges a closed chapter.

Before his crisis, Trosse seems to exist solely in terms of a limited area of surface consciousness: he depicts himself in the first phase of his life as lacking in any sense of inner or spiritual awareness. His youth unfolds against a backdrop of historical crisis – the Civil War, the execution of Charles I, and the Protectorate, but these events scarcely seem to affect him. He was, by his own account, anti-Parliamentarian before his madness, but not actively so: Cavalier attitudes were congenial to his youthful lack of seriousness. Otherwise it's difficult to assess the significance of national events to his state of mind. Yet the single, seemingly innocuous occurrence which precipitates his breakdown involves the religious and political tensions of the day. Trosse stands surety for a former major in the King's army, held on this account to be a 'suspected Person,' and thus required by the Sheriff 'to give Security in a *Bond*, of some Hundreds of Pounds, not to leave the city' (84).[40] This is an act of impulsive political enthusiasm: 'I was a *vain rash Young-Fellow*, thoroughly devoted to the *Interest* of the *Cavaliers*, and extreamly fond of *that Party*' (85). He then gets roaring drunk and goes home to sleep it off. Only on awakening to find himself beset by hallucinations and delusions does he become aware of the consequences for himself should the major default – but otherwise there is no obvious relationship between the given events and the descent into madness: this is abrupt, inexplicable and unmotivated. Just as Gregor Samsa awakens to find himself transformed into a beetle, so Trosse awakens to find himself mad.

As a flagrant non sequitur the episode underlines the arbitrary quality of the autobiographical narrative up to this point. The young Trosse's choice of career is motivated by selfish and opportunistic concerns: 'having a *Roving Fancy*, a *Desire* to get *Riches*, and to live *luxuriously* in the World, I was bent upon *Merchandize* and *Travelling* into *Foreign Parts*. But then in this I had no other Motive, but the Satisfying the Great Lords and Commanders of the *unregenerate World, the lusts of the Eyes, and the Pride of Life*' (48–9). On a day-to-day basis, this existence is largely contingent, and Trosse depicts his pre-crisis self as a thoughtless and conscienceless creature. Reverend Trosse reproaches his youthful self for neglecting private prayer: unconcerned with the obligation of private self-scrutiny, the young Trosse lacks moral awareness. He doesn't experience himself subjectively and so doesn't experience public events as factors of consequence in his own existence:

> As to the *Protector*, as *Oliver* was called, I hated and revil'd him, and wish'd his Ruine and Destruction, (not out of any Conscience towards God, because he had so horribly sinn'd against the *Fifth Command*, by putting the *King to Death*; and *usurping Authority*, but) *meerly* from a proud Fancy, and because he seem'd to favour those who were *religious* and *pious*. (79)

Trosse's madness, far from being the result of some psychological trauma, instigates psychological self-awareness. Whereas Reverend Trosse routinely condemns and rejects his pre-crisis self, his discourse acquires an urgency of involvement in narrating his madness.

The attraction travelling had held for Trosse contrasts with his reluctance, when mad, to move at all. Disrupting his superficial way of life, madness plunges him into the dimension of depths: 'I was resolv'd *not to move out of my Bed*; for I was perswaded that if I remov'd out of it, I should fall into *Hell*, and be plung'd into the *Depths of Misery*' (92). Spatial movement no longer occurs in terms of a horizontal surface but opens up vertically. His removal to Glastonbury and the private madhouse is experienced as a descent into hell: 'I was now perswaded that I was no longer *upon Earth*, but in the *Regions of Hell*. When we came to the Town, I thought I was in the *midst of Hell*' (93). This threatening descent plumbs the depths of a negative self: 'If I went out of my Chamber, every *Place, Person* and *Object* afforded Matter of *Terror and Confusion*; for I carry'd, as it were, my *Hell within* me, and therefore could see nothing *without* that was pleasing to me' (98).

Trosse's *descensus Averno* is no less psychological for occurring in terms of Christian eschatology. The Puritan self does not determine its own meanings, but incorporates those which the Bible and Providence make available.[41] Accordingly, alienated or negative forms of conscience are understood as manifestations of the Devil. As the Devil becomes a psychological reality, he loses his old magical attributes. If God is a positive measure of inner reality then the Devil is the agent of unreality or loss of reality, and Trosse credits him as the author of his delusions and hallucinations: 'I was dispos'd to believe every *Falsehood* that the *Father of Lies* might impose on me' (88).

Nevertheless madness is instrumental in revealing to Trosse the superficiality and unreliability of the world of appearances in which he has hitherto moved: only when insane is he exposed to the content of his experience and confronted with the need to interpret it: 'Walking up and down in the Room, in a miserable distracted, despairing Condition, I had a Suggestion and Temptation to *curse God and die*. Whatever was the Meaning of *those Words* in the Mouth of *Job's Wife*, I am sure, I *then apprehended them to be Literally meant*' (89). His interpretation is bad because, clinging to a shallow literalism, he fails to penetrate to an authentic depth of understanding. Even in the catastrophic breakdown of everyday reality, he remains subject to delusory surfaces and appearances, enabling the Devil to dupe him. Trosse must, eventually, confront the hallucinatory depths of the *Bottomless Pit* before learning that, for him, stability is founded in a moral relationship with the world. In Camus's *L'Etranger*, Meursault's relationship with his environment empties out the kind of moral relationship between character and milieu which obtains in Balzac or Dickens. But, in the seventeenth century, it is just this emptiness that Trosse must fill with meaning, otherwise the factitious world of surfaces he has inhabited up to now will fall to pieces. The course of his madness, which takes him down into the bowels of Glastonbury madhouse, is a process of death and rebirth through which he progresses towards a morally authenticated reality. From being a place of hallucinatory damnation, Glastonbury will become a scene of real recovery and enduring conversion.

When Trosse awakens to madness, the hallucinatory voice addresses to him the question '*Who art thou?*' Self-knowledge and identity are at issue here. Trosse, hallucinated, misrecognises his spiritual adversary because he does not know himself. Towards the end of his account he is able to answer this question: 'I am what I was not.' Trosse's discourse of identity, in replying to the hallucinatory question of identity, reveals the hell of his madness as the crucible in which an inadequate self is transmuted: 'I perceiv'd a *Voice*, (*I heard it plainly*) saying unto me, *Who art thou? Which, knowing it could be the Voice of no Mortal*, I concluded it was the *Voice of God*, and with Tears, as I remember, reply'd, *I am a very great Sinner, Lord!*' (86). The narrator retrospectively views this as a satanic ploy: 'Thus, pretending the *Worship of God*, I fell, in effect, to the *Worshipping* of the *Devil*.' However, Trosse's God and his Devil are doubles, and the moral force of the question of identity persists.

The ambivalent status of the voice – God or Devil? – corresponds to an implied duality of inner and outer: it is the 'good' voice of the internalised conscience, hitherto dormant, which returns, sounded externally as an aural hallucination. As the narrative continues, the voice, a grotesque parody of the self-punishing voice of awakened conscience, prompts Trosse to humiliate and abase himself. The passage, which climaxes with Trosse's realisation that the voice is bent on driving him to self-destruction, is worth quoting at length:

> while I was praying on my Knees, I heard a Voice, as I fancy'd, saying, as it were just behind me, *Yet more humble, Yet more humble*; with some Continuance. And not knowing the Meaning of the *Voice*, but undoubtedly concluding it came from God, I endeavour'd to comply with it. Considering that I kneel'd upon something, I remov'd it; and then I had some kind of Intimation given me, that that was what was requir'd. Thus I kneel'd upon the Ground: But the Voice still continu'd, *Yet more humble; Yet more humble*. In Compliance with it I proceeded to pluck down my *Stockings*, and to kneel upon my *bare Knees*: But the same *awful Voice* still sounding in my Ear, I proceeded to pull off my *Stockings*, and then my *Hose*, and my *Doublet*; and as I was thus uncloathing my self, I had a strong internal Impression, that all was well done, and a full Compliance with the Design of the *Voice*. In Answer likewise to this *Call*, I would *bow* my Body as *low as possibly I could*, with a great deal of Pain, & *this* I often repeated: But *all* I could do was not *low enough*, nor *humble enough*. At last, observing that there was an Hole in the Planking of the Room, I lay my self down flat upon the Ground, and thrust in my Head there as far as I could; but because I could not fully do it, I put my Hand into the Hole, and took out *Earth* and *Dust*, and sprinkled it on my *Head*; some *Scripture Expressions* at that Time offering themselves to my Mind,

I thought this was the *Lying down in Dust and Ashes* thereby prescrib'd. At length, standing up before the *Window*, I either *heard a Voice*, which bid me, *or had a strong Impulse*, which excited me, to *Cut off my Hair*; to which I reply'd, *I have no Scissars*. It was then hinted, that a *Knife would do it*; but I answer'd, *I have none*. Had I one I verily believe, this *Voice* would have gone from my *Hair* to my *Throat*, and commanded me to *cut it*: For I have all reason to conclude, that the *Voice* was the Voice of *Satan*, and that his Design was to *humble* me as low as *Hell*. (86-7)

The ramifying process of Trosse's self-abasement resembles a passage in Calvin's *Institutes* which we have already noted. Calvin cautions against overscrupulosity of conscience in regard to external observances: 'When a man begins to doubt whether it is lawful for him to use linen for sheets, shirts, napkins, and handkerchiefs, he will not long be secure as to hemp, and will at last have doubts as to tow (. . .). Here some must be by despair hurried into an abyss.'[42] Calvin confirms the rhetorical pattern of the above passage. The abyss towards which Trosse's self-chastising conscience is hurried acquires an hallucinatory literality as the voice prompts him to cut his hair. The direction of the admonition, which has just taken him down to the floor, makes all too credible the projection of a descending knife path from the cutting of hair to the cutting of the throat. But it is the degree of control whereby the narrator's voice retrospectively trumps the literal force of the hallucinatory voice which impresses in this passage. Rhetorical control at the formal level is inversely proportional to hallucinatory control at the level of content: 'his Design was to *humble* me as *low as Hell*.' In deciphering the underlying design, Reverend Trosse's discourse reasserts mastery: the demonic parody of the good voice of conscience, entrapping the self in a concatenation of guilt, is vanquished by the stable voice of the writer himself, retrospectively elucidating the true meaning of his earlier experiences. Madness both inverts and perverts meaning: 'applying my self to read in a Book I had taken up, I saw, as I apprehended, horrid *Blasphemies* in it' (100). But, through the writing of the *Life*, Reverend Trosse is able to recapitulate these negative meanings in a spiritually significant testament.

In therapeutically redoubling the negative voice of the alienated conscience, Trosse's discourse compensates for the psychopathological doubling of God and Devil. This doubling is a projection of the tensions that derive from Lutheran and Calvinistic theology. The Puritan internalisation of conscience, with its presumption of guilt and its simultaneous assumption of salvation, induces a psychical splitting which manifests itself in symptoms of doubling and of voices:

> I (*seemingly*) heard a Voice, saying with Great Anger, *Thou Wretch! Thou hast committed the Sin against the Holy Ghost*. This *Breath* I then believed to have been the *Holy Ghost* (. . .). And believing that I had been inspir'd and taught by *Him* in all these *ridiculous Acts* of *Humiliation*, (I am sure they were *so* as done by me.) I presently concluded, that I really had been guilty of the *Sin against the Holy Ghost*, and so could not possibly be *pardon'd*. (88)

As this passage proceeds, the narrator reasons energetically with the protagonist's madness:

> Thus by my careless and prophane Reading and Hearing of the *Word of God*, and not endeavouring to *understand* the *Meaning* of it, I gave the *Great Deceiver* an Advantage to make me believe, that the *Word*, perverted and understood in a wrong Sence was the *Word of God*: For, not *Receiving the Truth* in the *Notion*, much less in the *Love* of it, I was dispos'd to believe every *Falsehood* that the *Father of Lies* might impose upon me. But I am well assur'd that *this* was not the *Sin against the Holy Ghost*. (88)

The rationality of this discourse is impressive, but, in retrospectively reordering his previous disorder, Trosse discloses the underlying epistemological problem which characterises the 'dissenting, Protestant model of the mind.'[43] As the writer argues with himself, the urgency of the debate reproduces conflict at the very moment it denotes resolution.

In Puritanism there is no escape from the divided self. Self-division will usually take the form of an interiorisation of a repressive morality, with a consequent need for self-scrutiny. In Trosse this psychological pattern reveals its affinity with the experience of madness. His narrative does not merely report his madness, it actively seeks to reorder its deliriously misguided moral thrust. The hallucinatory voice which assails the protagonist is compensated by the retrospective voice of the narration: this reproduces the way in which a pathological split is therapeutically restored to balance. But the fact remains that the split voice of madness and the balanced, self-monitoring voice of sanity are, both, doubled voices. Just as an hallucinatory Devil mimics a morally rational God, so pathological self-division is, in Trosse, a bad form of rational self-scrutiny.

In a state of continuing delirium in the madhouse, Trosse sees a *doppelgänger* figure in a vision. This episode strikingly reveals how ambivalent the phenomenon of doubling is in the text:

> there was One who had liv'd a very wicked and lewd Life, & was born
> in the *same City* and *Street* where I was, who also had been in *France*, and
> learn'd the *Language* with me in the *same House*; and afterwards when I
> return'd from *Portugal*, He liv'd in this *City*; we were Associates in *Vice*
> and *Vanity*. This person I imagin'd to have been in *Chains*, *wrestling* and
> *striving* to get himself free; by which he underwent a great deal of
> exquisite Pain, and told me, That *He had gone thro' a great many Pains*
> *already, and was resolv'd to wade thro' this, and all others before him; that*
> *so at length he might be perfectly and everlastingly free from all Miseries.* (99)

The very narrative moment is ambivalent here. The vision seems
too good to be true, and Trosse may be rigging his account in the
interest of allegory. But whether the vision is invented or actual, the
portrayal of extremes of suffering and salvation through the figure
of the double is significant. If Trosse's experience is intrinsically
ambivalent then the vision of the *doppelgänger* shows a practical
awareness of that ambivalence. His narration of madness clearly
involves a project of meaning, so that the delirious phenomena
possess a paradoxical coherence. The insistently downwards movement of his self-abasement ('Yet more humble') is characteristic of a
thematic pattern, and the episode of self-abasement, situated at the
onset of the protagonist's madness, already anticipates the larger
narrative outcome, wherein the downward path of despair terminates not in destruction and damnation but in eventual salvation.

Trosse's individualism and psychological realism more usually play
down allegorical or emblematic tendencies. He possesses a practical
insight into the kinship between the psychological forms of unreason
and reason, and is able to turn this to a genuinely therapeutic end.
In the eighteenth century William Cowper's Evangelical autobiography will celebrate a 'miraculous' rebirth to sanity, whereas
Trosse presents a gruelling and prolonged re-education of the self.
Like Bunyan, he condemns Quakerism, but, writing in the early
1690s, he demonstrates, as Bunyan does not, the accommodation
English Protestantism reached with rationalist scepticism at the end
of the seventeenth century: 'I am perswaded, that *many* of the
Quakers formerly were deluded by *such Voices* and *Impulses* from the
Impure Spirit, which they mistook for the *Holy Spirit of God*' (87).
According to Trosse, enthusiastic Quakerism and 'Visions and
Voices among the Papists' all derive from 'the same Author, or
Cause, *viz.* A crack'd Brain, impos'd upon by a deceitful and lying
Devil' (87). His own careful discriminations, coming in the previous

paragraph, are eminently psychological in spirit: 'I either heard a *Voice*, which bid me, or *had a strong Impulse*, which excited me.' Christian truth requires a vigilant exercise of reason: it is not given but must be worked for.

In Trosse's prose a virtuous labour of reason seeks to penetrate beyond the deceit of surface appearances and arrive at an underlying truth: 'I was (. . .) haunted (. . .) with a great many terrifying and disquieting *Visions* and *Voices*; which tho' (I believe) they had *no Reality* in themselves, yet they *seem'd* to be such to me, and had the *same Effect* upon me, as if they had *been really* what they *appear'd* to be' (89). Reason involves hard work: the painstaking differentiations of this sentence define sanity in terms of the Puritan work-ethic. Inasmuch as effort is an index of moral value, Trosse's recovery is literally hard-won.

This becomes evident in his study of foreign languages. He possesses an initial facility: 'All my younger Years were spent at the *Grammar-School*, to learn the *Latine Tongue*. I had a *quick Apprehension*' (47). Following the interruption of his studies, his first trip abroad is undertaken with the aim of learning French: 'Within a Year, I arriv'd at a considerable Knowledge of *that Tongue* (. . .). And *this* was all the Good I got in *France*' (51). When, following his final recovery, he goes up to Oxford he sets himself to studying the ancient languages – not only Latin and Greek, but also Hebrew, in order to read the Bible in the original. In this way he seeks to remedy the deviation which took him from the virtues of Latin and grammar school to the vices of France and French (by inference, an ungodly language). His progress from the study of Latin to Greek and then Hebrew suggests a concern to arrive at a language of ultimate patriarchal authority. If French has been the language which Trosse learned with the least effort, Hebrew, at the opposite pole, is the one which costs him most pains. But the effort expended is proportionate to the virtue gained inasmuch as this is the original language of the Scriptures,

> which tho' I found very *difficult* and *tedious*, very *jejune* and *sapless*, (. . . now to beat my Brains about *Words* and *Terminations*, was for some time grievous to me.) yet apprehending it very *useful* for the attaining that End for which I design'd all my *other Studies*, which was the knowledge of *Divinity*, I waded thro' that Difficulty and got some considerable Insight into it; insomuch that now I have read the *Hebrew Bible* several Times thro'. (115)

God's 'original' language requires mastery of the technical

difficulties of meaning, an involvement with grammar and rules of syntax which is at the opposite pole from the Devil's spurious orality and hallucinatory conflations of signifier and signified. True meaning can only be established as a result of a learning of rules.

III

As Trosse recovers his faculties in the madhouse he correspondingly acquires a sense of Christian responsibility, but the improvement remains superficial: 'I now began now to favour somewhat the Matters of *Religion*, and *pray'd* with the Gentlewoman [Mrs Gollop] in her Family, and *constantly* attended Publick Worship (. . .). Time after this, as to all *external Actions*, I liv'd very commendably: But, in the mean Time, there was but little of *Heart-work*' (101). Out of Glastonbury, Trosse falls back into his bad old habits ('I *return'd to that Vomit*'), then relapses into torments of guilt and is returned to the madhouse in a state of frenzy. Once more his recovery coincides with a renunciation of licentiousness and a turn to Christian observance. But he has not yet truly opened his heart to God: '[I] contented my self with some *external Reformation*, and a *Pharisaical Religion*' (110). Again he relapses, and, for the third time, returns to Glastonbury. Yet again he recovers, but this time he at last commits himself decisively to God: there is no further question of moral or mental relapse. Assuming a new responsibility for his existence, he re-educates himself in the fullest sense by going up to Pembroke College to pursue a degree in Divinity (this is left incomplete owing to the circumstances of the Restoration). The interiorisation of the Puritan ethic of self-discipline is complete.

In a revealing phrase, Trosse states that he has (by God's grace) been 'brought out of a State of *Nature* into a State of *Adoption* (. . . .) that my strong and powerful *Lusts* might be subdu'd and renounc'd' (112). Stability has been attained at the cost of implementing the characteristically Puritan split between instinct and conscience. This split can be restated in Freudian terms, as the antithesis of id and ego/superego. This in turn suggests a psychoanalytical reading of Trosse's situation. His relapses constitute a regression to an infantile state, while the process of recovery involves a repetitious reworking of the conflicts of infancy and childhood: he can only break out of the cycle and achieve real growth by interiorising the father as superego, at which point the destructive bad father (Devil) is replaced by a benevolent good father (God), in whose name Trosse will henceforth act.

Such an interpretation encounters an obstacle in Trosse's uninformative narration of his actual childhood circumstances. It is entirely possible to speculate that his insanity derives from unresolved childhood traumas: indeed surviving extracts from another autobiographical manuscript written by Trosse indicate a deep and continuing resentment against his parents for having farmed him out as an infant to an uncaring nurse who almost starved him to death. The potential psychoanalytic significance of this detail has been explored by A. W. Brink. Following the precepts of the British school of object analysis, Brink hypothesises that

> Trosse's behaviour disorder, which led him to punish the adult world so severely, would answer to a fundamental failure of personal relationships in infancy. Lacking a good outcome of infantile dependence, subsequent moral independence did not develop normally. The wayward course Trosse entered ended only with Mrs. Gollop's ministrations in the madhouse at Glastonbury; his melancholy lifted after the regrowing of his personality with the help of a surrogate mother.[44]

This is a persuasive reading, one which offers an entirely convincing account of the crucial role of Mrs Gollop, the wife of the madhouse keeper. But Brink concludes that in the absence of available evidence (particularly of contemporary evidence which would lend weight to theories of childhood trauma), the psychoanalytic case remains unproven. This is all the more true of my speculative Freudian reading. However, even if we accept that hypothetical reconstructions of specific infantile and childhood trauma are disallowed, psychoanalytic interpretation remains potentially useful in relation to the broader socio-historical context.

In *The history of manners*, an examination of changes in social manners between the Middle Ages and the nineteenth century, Norbert Elias proposed that as succeeding social formations imposed increasingly formalised standards and codes of social behaviour on the educated classes, the expression of instinctual drives and impulses were correspondingly repressed. With the advance of an urban, bourgeois society, instinctual tendencies came to be viewed as 'infantile' residues: 'Much of what we call "morality" or "moral" reasons has the same function as "hygiene" or "hygienic" reasons: to condition children to a certain social standard. Molding by such means aims at making socially desirable behavior automatic, a matter of self-control, causing it to appear in the consciousness of the individual as the result of his own free-will, and in the interests of his own health or human dignity.'[45] This thesis offers a plausible

account of Trosse's process of recovery. Madness reduces Trosse to
a state of infantile helplessness, and in this condition he submits
himself to Mrs Gollop, who, as Brink suggests, becomes a surrogate
mother: 'She had great Compassion upon me; would many times sit
and discourse with me (. . .): if any one was more *eminently
Instrumental* in my *Conversion* than another, *She* was the Person' (96).
Trosse's tutelage under Mrs Gollop initiates a process of re-education
in the ways of faith, behaviour and reason, bringing him to God:
'at length (. . .) I began to be somewhat *quiet* and *compos'd* in my
Spirits; to be *orderly* and *civil* in my *Carriage* and *Converse*, and
gradually to regain the Use of my *Reason* and to be a *fit Companion*
for my *Fellow Creatures* (. . .) and hereupon I kept my self very *sober*
and *commendable* in my *outward Demeanour*' (100). As Trosse himself
goes on to acknowledge, this acquisition of outward restraint is not
sufficient to effect an inner change: 'there was but little of *Heart-
work.*' In other words, Trosse must interiorise his learning of
socialisation. Elias would interpret this as the socially determined
formation of a superego: in overcoming a madness which reduces
him to infantilism, Trosse necessarily initiates a process of repression: 'The pronounced division in the "ego" or consciousness
characteristic of man in our phase of civilisation, which finds expression in such terms as "superego" and "unconscious," corresponds to
the specific split in the behavior which civilized society demands of
its members. It matches the degree of regulation and restraint
imposed on the expression of drives and impulses.'[46]

Elias focused on the civilised standards imposed by the court
society of the absolutist monarchy as the key transitional stage
between medieval and bourgeois standards. This is a greatly over-
simplified schema: Roger Chartrier, in reviewing Elias's thesis, has
noted the need to take into account other large-scale developments,
notably the emergence of the 'public sphere,' also the Reformation
and the Counter-Reformation:[47] Elizabeth Eisenstein would, no
doubt, want to add the emergence of a print culture.[48] These are
factors which complicate but do not contradict the fundamental
proposition that social and ideological developments affect the
psychical life of individuals. In the English context, Lawrence Stone
argues that in the late sixteenth and early seventeenth centuries, 'a
new interest in children, coupled with the Calvinist premise of
Original Sin, gave fathers an added incentive to ensure the internalised submissiveness of children.'[49] Christopher Hill argues that
'despite the defeat of religious Puritanism in 1660, and the isolation
of nonconformity even after 1689, nevertheless much of the social

content of Puritan doctrine was ultimately accepted outside the ranks of nonconformity.'[50] This involved a tendency among the middle ranks of society to adopt the ethics of work, discipline and rationality which Trosse came so hard by in recovering from his crises.

Repression of instinctuality is already evident in Trosse's experience of madness, which involves obsessional guilt and self-punishment. This is consistent with Elias's broader proposal that Western European civilisation in the sixteenth and seventeenth centuries inaugurates a psychical divorce between 'adult' self-regulation and a 'childish' irresponsibility which will eventually be labelled 'infantile.' Trosse's recovery arguably permits a glimpse of the birth pangs of a socially determined superego, renouncing the pleasure-principle and paying its dues in full to the reality-principle.

Trosse's *Life* assumes that not only is there a period which precedes madness but also a period which succeeds it: this is confirmed by our knowledge that he led a virtuous and upright life from his eventual recovery in 1667 until his death in 1713. His autobiographical account of his converted life in the *Life* is brief and rational. If we compare Nerval's *Aurélia* in the nineteenth century, we find that it too asserts a therapeutic imperative, but, as is the case with many of the literary autobiographies of madness which followed in its wake in the twentieth century, the critical perspective implemented by the narrative voice is compromised by a reluctance to deny the 'truth' of the writer's experience. We are not surprised to learn that in Nerval's case the biographical record does not confirm the autobiographical claim to recovery: Trosse is the last of the writers discussed in this study to make a fully effective recovery from his experience of madness.

4 William Cowper (1): The Privatisation of Madness

I

William Cowper's autobiographical account of his madness, completed in 1767, and posthumously published as *Memoir of the early life of William Cowper*,[1] preceded his major literary writings.

By the time of Cowper's death in 1800, Romanticism had reestablished the ancient link between madness and poetry, broken during the Enlightenment. Cowper, a thoroughly unromantic figure, managed to acquire a measure of posthumous Romantic pathos on account of his mental problems. In the margin of a copy of J. G. Spurzheim's *Observations on insanity*, Blake wrote, 'Cowper came to me and said: "O that I were insane always. I will never rest. Can you not make me truly insane?"'[1] The *Memoir* hardly contributes to these developments: were it not for his poetry and letters Cowper, like Trosse, would have remained an isolated and unregarded figure. However, it is difficult to read the *Memoir* without an awareness of its author's subsequent eminence, along with his continuing history of breakdown and acute depression.

The *Memoir* is contemporaneous with Rousseau's *Confessions*. When Cowper started work on his autobiographical memoir in Huntingdon, Rousseau was finishing Part One of the *Confessions* not so very far away in Wootton. The proximity is tantalising. Even if we bear in mind the upsurge of personal writings in the seventeenth and eighteenth centuries, the *Confessions* remains a watershed in the history of autobiography. At a stroke it banished all previous autobiographies to the further side of a cultural divide. Cowper's *Memoir*, far from looking forward with Rousseau to Romantic individualism, looks back to the old model of the Puritan spiritual autobiography.

Trosse's *Life* exemplifies the assumptions of the older form. Rousseau's founding premise is that the continuity of a unique self can be retrospectively traced from childhood on. Trosse would have disagreed. Shattering his existence, madness enables a thoroughgoing renewal of identity. When Rousseau declares, 'I have displayed myself as I was, as vile and despicable when my behaviour was such, as good, generous, and noble when I was so,'[2] his metaphor of self-portraiture emphasises the overall unity of the various features: whether good or bad, the ensemble makes him what he is. Trosse's claim is altogether different: 'I am what I was not: I am quite contrary to what I was in the past years of my Life, both in my Judgement, my Heart, and my Conversation' (112). Cowper's *Memoir* similarly assumes that the meaning and pattern of the individual's existence can be shattered and remade, but his text also incorporates the complexities and tensions of a later cultural moment. His religious conviction sits uneasily with a measure of psychological self-awareness which he is reluctant to acknowledge, but which, at the same time, he doesn't entirely deny. The framework of the spiritual confession enables him to avoid directly confronting his particular psychological disposition, but, unlike Trosse, he never quite convinces us that he was truly remade as a new man.

In 1753 Cowper, then twenty-two years old and in pursuit of a legal career, took up residence at the Middle Temple of the Inns of Court. This move coincided with the first of the periods of severe depression he was to suffer throughout his life: 'I was struck not long after my settlement in the Temple with such a dejection of spirits as none but they who have felt the same can have the least conception of. Day and night I was upon the rack, lying down in horrors, and rising in despair' (I, 8). This crisis passed, but ten years later Cowper, now residing in the Inner Temple, suffered the calamitous breakdown which forms the main subject of the *Memoir*. As he tells the story, a relative (his uncle Ashley) held in his control two appointments to the House of Lords, the Clerkship of the Journals, and a more public but more lucrative position, the Clerkship of the Committees. By 1763 Cowper had almost exhausted his patrimony, and one day he remarked casually to a friend that if the current Clerk of the Journals should die he held some hope of being offered the post. As it happened, the holder did die shortly thereafter (causing Cowper considerable guilt), and both the clerkships fell vacant. The Clerkship of the Committees was offered to him by his relative:

he first accepted it, but, realising that he would be unsuited for this post, he then asked for his original preference, the Clerkship of the Journals. Unfortunately this appointment was contested by a rival claimant and Cowper was required to undergo an examination at the Bar of the House of Lords to prove his suitability for the post. The prospect of this ordeal appalled him so much that he suffered nervous debilitation and was unable to learn the required duties. As the date of the examination approached he began to wish madness on himself as a way out of his predicament, then decided on suicide. Various suicide attempts followed: he purchased some laudanum in order to poison himself, but could not bring himself to drink it, and eventually tried to hang himself with a garter. This incident put a stop to his candidature for the Clerkship, but his torment continued unabated, until, one morning, 'that distemper of mind which I had so ardently wished for actually seized me' (I, 32). He plunged into a state of religious despair which soon turned to mania. In this condition he was conveyed to Dr Nathaniel Cotton's private mad-house, the Collegium Insanorum at St Albans. Here his ordeals continued and he once more tried to kill himself. After this he became quieter, although his sense of total despair persisted.

After some months he began to feel a superficial degree of allevia-tion under Dr Cotton's kindly influence, and he also experienced some hopeful portents. Remission, when it came (in 1764), was dramatically sudden. Following a cheering visit from his brother, Cowper dreamed 'that the sweetest boy I ever saw came dancing up to my bedside' (I, 38). This dream immediately served to relieve his mind, and over breakfast the depression continued to lift. Then he opened a bible at 'the twenty fifth of the third chapter to the Romans where Jesus is set forth as the propitiation for our sins. Immediately I received the strength to believe it. Immediately the full beams of the sun of righteousness shone upon me' (I, 39).

There are significant parallels between Cowper's Memoir and Trosse's Life. Both feature narrators who led casually irreligious lives until the onset of their respective crises: both then became aware, in their despair, of a spiritual dimension of existence. Both felt that they had committed the sin against the Holy Ghost, and both were haunted by the prospect of the 'bottomless pit.' Both received beneficial Christian attention in private madhouses, where their recuperation coincided with the discovery of a living faith. Finally, both recounted their experiences in spiritual autobiographies of uncommon force.

However, differences between the two works are more important still. Cowper suffered a gradual, almost calculated descent into delirium, while his restitution was miraculously sudden, with visions, portents and messages playing a key part. This reverses the pattern found in the *Life*: Trosse's lapse into madness was inexplicably sudden, while his recovery was achieved only slowly and effortfully, with a total absence of inspirational shifts from darkness to light. His acquisition of religious conviction was as gradual as Cowper's was abrupt: 'I can tell neither the *Minister*, nor the *Sermon* whereby, nor the *very Time* wherein, I was *converted*' (111). Trosse did not write his autobiography until some forty years after his recovery, near the end of a long life, devoted entirely to his religion. Cowper, on the other hand, wrote his *Memoir* at a distance of only two or three years from the events it recounts: his fervent Evangelicalism was to cool somewhat following the subsequent crisis of 1773, and his God eventually became a torment to him, rather than a support.

The features of an historically determined private sphere emerge in Trosse's *Life* through his insistence on the need for 'secret Prayers.' Habermas explains the priority of religion here: 'The link to divine authority which the church represented became a private matter. So-called religious freedom came to insure what was historically the first area of private autonomy.'[3] At all points in the *Life*, references to family-related matters are subordinate to religious ones. Trosse's mother remains a shadowy figure in his account of his earlier years: she exercises little or no authority over her son, and although she is referred to at one point as 'My *tender Mother*,' the narrator's attitude to her is detached and unrevealing. Isaac Gilling's 1715 biography of Trosse provides intriguing additional information. As an infant Trosse was put out to nurse and almost died of consequent neglect. This circumstance left a deep mark on him: Gilling cites a now lost autobiographical manuscript: 'I may say with *David*, Tho' my *Father and my Mother forsook me*, nay tho' my *Nurse starv'd me*, yet *the Lord took me up*.'[4]

In the *Memoir*, Cowper is scarcely less reticent than Trosse concerning his family background: he refers only briefly to his early separation from his mother and makes no mention of her subsequent death (which, as we know, deeply affected him). Nevertheless the differences of detail are telling:

> At six years of age I was taken from the nursery and the immediate care of a most indulgent mother and sent to a considerable school in Bedfordshire. Here I had hardships of various kinds to conflict with, which I felt

the more sensibly in proportion to the tenderness with which I had been treated at home. (I, 5)

The contrast between the childhood experiences of Cowper and Trosse bears out the findings of social historians: 'between 1660 and 1800 there took place major changes in child-rearing practice among the "squirarchy" and upper bourgeoisie. Swaddling gave way to loose clothing, mercenary wet-nursing to maternal breast-feeding.'[5] The maternal sanctuary glimpsed in the opening of the *Memoir* is developed in Cowper's later poem, 'On the Receipt of my Mother's Picture out of Norfolk,' where the emotional implications of a mother-centred private sphere receive full expression. This is typical of what Lawrence Stone has described as a 'liberation of maternal love': 'Childhood came to be regarded as the best years of one's life, instead of the grim purgatory it had been in the seventeenth century.'[6]

Richard Sennett argues that in the later eighteenth century the public–private 'molecule' is split apart at the expense of the former, with the conventions of adult public life coming to be viewed in terms of 'inauthenticity.'[7] Cowper's reaction to the affair of the clerkships shows that he is in retreat from the increasing degree of psychical tension which accompanies the transformations of social and civic life that followed the constitutional settlement of 1688: 'They whose spirits are formed like mine, to whom a public exhibition of themselves on any occasion is mortal poison, may have some idea of the horror of my situation' (I, 15). His expulsion from the maternal realm of the nursery into the harsh environment of a school where he is a victim of bullying is already experienced as a fall into an alien social realm. It marks a specifically historical form of self-division, threatening the male adult in the urban society of eighteenth-century England with a potential condition of alienation.

Where Cowper's crisis occurs in relation to a public realm his recovery constitutes a retreat from this realm. Here, again, his experience is the opposite of Trosse's, whose recovery introduces him to 'adult' responsibilities. Trosse's *Life* makes no concessions to the notion that Glastonbury might be a scene of emotional as well as spiritual renewal. Mrs Gollop's role in the narrative is devoid of symbolic or affective content: she is portrayed as the moral steward of a community; there is no hint of the domestic intimacy which Cowper will discover in the Unwin household a century later. Trosse may well have received emotional support from Mrs Gollop, but he does not allude to this, paying exclusive tribute to her moral influence.

Rather than a learning of civilised behaviour and reason, Cowper will experience recovery as a return to a protected domain where he is not required to confront the outside world. Eighteenth-century bourgeois culture divided childhood and adulthood into separate spheres: 'the gradual concern with the special state of childhood marked off certain limits to public expression: (. . .) by 1750 a father would be embarrassed to dress up his son's dolls.'[8] If this is a development to which seventeenth-century Puritanism contributed (Bunyan was called away from adult play by the stirrings of conscience), then Cowper benefits on the distaff side. He finds his surrogate mother, Mary Unwin, only after he has recovered, and then clings closely to her for the following twenty years. The deeply ambiguous emotional intimacy of Cowper's relationship with his Mary is entirely absent from Trosse's relationship with Mrs Gollop. Far from clinging to Mrs Gollop (whose first name we never learn), Trosse returns to the outside world with a new sense of moral purpose.

According to Philippe Ariès, 'The modern family (. . .) cuts itself off from the world and opposes to society the isolated group of parents and children.'[9] In Cowper's case, a split between individual and 'society' may or may not have been fostered at home,[10] but it certainly relates to the home environment. This is where he returns, in search of a refuge from an intolerably stressful confrontation with the world of public affairs.

Public and private are strongly antithetical categories in the *Memoir*. An initial disjunction between public and private is instrumental in setting in motion the trauma of 1763. In the affair of the Parliamentary appointments, Cowper prefers the office of the Journals because 'the business of that place [is] transacted in private' (I, 13): by contrast the office of the Committees is unsuitable given his 'incapacity to execute a business of so public a nature' (I, 14). It is the prospect of a public examination before the Bar of the House of Lords which drives him towards suicide and madness. As the suicidal crisis gathers impetus, lack of privacy is an important factor: 'I was liable to continual interruption in my chambers, from my laundress and her husband' (I, 20). The servants are minor but intrusive characters in the drama of Cowper's attempts to do away with himself: 'I lay down in bed again [still holding a bowl of laudanum] (. . .) and while thus employed heard the key turn in the outer door and my laundress's husband come in'; 'In a few minutes I was left alone, and should certainly have done execution upon myself, having a whole afternoon before me, both the man and his

wife being gone to dinner' (I, 22). Subsequently the laundress is busy
in the dining room while he is trying to hang himself in the
bedroom, 'and must have passed by the bedchamber door (. . .)
while I was hanging upon it' (I, 24–5).

The contrast between Cowper's excruciating private drama and
the casual routine of the servants lends an element of black farce to
the proceedings. This is heightened by the narrator's avoidance of
nuance. The flat perspective of the narrative conveys a scene which
is devoid of hierarchical order. The protagonist is in no sense at
home in this milieu: the only relationship he can manage with the
servants is one of implied awkwardness and embarrassment, but this
is filtered out by the detachment of the narrative point of view, leaving only an incongruity of plot. This situation is absurd because the
received meanings which should order it have gone badly awry. In
the eighteenth century, domestic servants were gradually disappear-
ing from view in the houses of the well-to-do. The spaces of the
household were increasingly privatised, with corridors, closets,
dumb-waiters, bell-pulls and (in larger houses) service back stairs
coming into fashion. In the midst of these social developments,
however, the Inns of Court remained an island of pre-bourgeois
manners and mores. In the ensuing emotional catastrophe, it
becomes clear that neither in a literal nor a metaphorical sense is
Cowper at home in his quarters. The unhomely environment of the
Inns of Court houses an alienated self.

The gathering crisis is unleashed when he reads a letter in a
newspaper while breakfasting in a coffee house: 'it appeared
demonstrably true to me that it was a libel or satire upon me. The
author seemed to be acquainted with my purpose of self murder and
to have written that letter to secure and hasten the execution of it'
(I, 20). This recalls Trosse's hallucination of the voice which prompts
him to ever greater acts of self-abasement. In Cowper's case,
however, the mortification of the self is associated with a public
sphere wherein its inadequacy is made derisively manifest. The delusion that his most private concerns and motives are open to scrutiny
in a newspaper at length realises his fear of being publicly examined.
The letter becomes the literal text of self-alienation as the
apparatuses of the public sphere conspire against a painfully exposed
self. He rushes impulsively from the coffee house, intent on poison-
ing himself in a ditch with a newly purchased phial of laudanum.
Then he thinks to run away to France, 'But while I was looking over
my portmanteau my mind changed again' (I, 20): he goes to Tower
Wharf to drown himself, but the water is too low and a porter is

present. 'I returned to the coach and ordered the man back to the Temple.' The play of opportunity and deferral which has occurred outdoors is now introjected as an inner conflict, unfolding in the space of Cowper's private quarters:

I (. . .) once more had recourse to the laudanum, and determined to drink it off directly. But God had otherwise ordained. A conflict that shook me to pieces almost suddenly took place: not properly a trembling but a convulsive kind of agitation which deprived me in a manner of the use of my limbs. My mind was as much shaken as my body, distracted betwixt the desire of death and the dread of it. (I, 21)

The ensuing drama is a psychical one, but it involves both Cowper's physical self and his immediate environment. His hands are mysteriously paralysed when he forces the bowl of laudanum to his lips: 'I lay down in bed again to muse upon [this] and while thus employed heard the key turn in the outer door and my laundress's husband come in. By this time the use of my fingers was restored to me' (I, 21-2). There is an accelerated alternation between inner and outer impediments: 'In a few minutes I was left alone, and now unless God had evidently interposed again for my preservation, I should certainly have done execution upon myself (. . .). Outer obstructions were no sooner removed than new ones arose within. The man had just shut the door when a total alteration in my sentiments took place. . .' (I, 22). Cowper recognises the fluctuation of his alternating moods, but he does not recognise the symptoms of an inner split. His account of the conflict of initiative and counter-initiative highlights the psychological nature of the drama that is occurring, yet he is unable to acknowledge this, and the sudden and brief paralysis of his hands is misrecognised: 'It had the air of a divine interposition.'

Cowper is, nevertheless, acutely aware of the disparity between what is inside and what is outside. That evening a friend calls on him: 'We conversed a while with a real cheerfulness on his part and an affected one on mine (. . .). Behold to what sort of extremity a good man may fall. Such was I in the estimation of those who knew me best; a decent outside is all the good-natured world requires. Thus equipped, though all within be rank atheism, rottenness of heart, and rebellion against the blessed God, we are said to be good enough' (I, 22-3). The truth of the inner world clashes with the facade which conceals it.

The situation of his chambers in the Inner Temple provides a spatial counterpart of the inner–outer disjunction. Cowper's inner rooms – bedchamber and dining room – are bordered by communicating outer passages where the laundress and her husband come and go. The everyday activity of the outer sphere remains unaware of the crisis and agony of the inner, and the friend's visit underlines this disconnection, suggesting that it is indeed this alienating split from which Cowper is suffering: the laundress fails to notice the body hanging on the other side of the door.

When he attempts to hang himself, he believes that he has bolted the inner door of his bedchamber, but afterwards hears the laundress in his dining room: 'she had found the door unbolted notwithstanding my design to fasten it, and must have passed by the bedchamber door, for it opened into the passage' (I, 24–5). This 'slip' is easily interpreted as a silent plea: more specifically, we might suggest that the door is left open to the possibility of a lifesaving communication between the inner and the outer contexts. The world of inner–outer dissociations which Cowper inhabits constitutes a pathological inversion of the 'healthy' psychical duality of private man and public man in the bourgeois settlement. Like Carkesse, but in an altogether different way, Cowper is unbalanced to the extent that he is incapable of Pepys's judicious feat of balancing the books. Nevertheless he recognises that this feat is a norm in the social world he inhabits: 'a decent outside,' he comments bitterly, 'is all the good-natured world requires.'

If Cowper's descent into madness is marked by his inability to adapt to a social and public world, his recovery is marked by a rediscovery of the intimate emotional world in which he is required to take no responsibilities upon himself – the world of the child. In abandoning the obligations of public life he submits to the powers of a supernatural authority and assumes the role of an obedient child dependent on the benevolence of an all-powerful parent: 'God had ordered everything for me like an indulgent father.' The regressive direction of the *Memoir* is confirmed by the dream which signals his overnight conversion: 'The sweetest boy I ever saw came dancing up to my bedside. he seemed just out of leading strings, yet I took particular notice of the firmness and steadiness of his tread' (I, 38).

The Collegium Insanorum, where Cowper enjoys this dream, facilitates his withdrawal from active life. Dr Cotton's establishment provided a more supportive environment than that of the Inns of Court. Dr Cotton, himself a poet, was devout and benevolent: he restricted the number of patients in his care – 'the usual number was three or four' (in fact Cowper makes no reference to other patients).[11] Deprived of adult obligations, Cowper rapidly accepts a condition of passivity and dependence. Servants are again much in evidence, but his relationship with them is no longer one of awkwardness and distance. They watch over him (his final suicide attempt results in his 'being more closely watched than ever'), and in these circumstances, he becomes familiar with them as he evidently had not with the domestic help of the Inns of Court. This is accompanied by a renunciation on his part of an attitude of superior sophistication: 'The servants who attended me had been conversing together upon the subject of thunder and lightning. At length one of them asserted that he had seen several thunderbolts, supposing them to be round smooth stones which are found in brick walls.' The others servants are sceptical and ask Cowper's opinion. 'I answered: No; that it was a vulgar error' (I, 36). But shortly afterwards he revokes this reply. He is in the company of a servant during the course of a thunderstorm and witnesses a vision of a giant hand holding a thunderbolt. 'I asked the servant (one of the profanest wretches in the world) if he had seen it. He forced a kind of smile and answered "Yes, but I was afraid to look" (. . .). I gave him not the least intimation of what I understood it to be, but found presently after that as soon as he left me he declared to the servants below that he had seen a thunderbolt' (I, 36). The 'vulgar error' is now called on to lend credence to Cowper's vision.

The sight of the giant hand is one of two 'remarkable occurrences' which precede Cowper's spiritual revival: the other is a vision of a radiant cathedral:

> One evening as I was walking to and fro in my chamber, the day being now shut in, I saw myself suddenly enclosed in a temple as large as a cathedral. It had two cupolas, one at each end, and the roof supported by tall and straight columns in rows parallel to each other (. . .). The whole edifice was built with beams of the purest light, mild and soft indeed, but bright as those of an unclouded sun. I cannot conceive a more regular piece of architecture or imagine to myself a more delightful object. (I, 35)

If the design of Cowper's chambers at the Inns of Court represents his alienation in material form, then this architectural vision is a non-alienated counterpart. A place of light rather than darkness, it locates a promise of life rather than a quest for death. This too is an inner temple ('I saw myself suddenly enclosed in a temple') but its spiritual non-materiality, transforming the divided spaces and boundaries of the Inner Temple into a transparent whole, holds out

the promise that the damaged self of the previous residence will be
healed. For a brief moment, he is bathed in spiritual plenitude: 'Bless
me; I see a glory all around me.'

Again, he is accompanied by a servant at this moment. Throughout his convalescence and recovery he is attended by a servant with
whom he establishes a close rapport: 'He (. . .) maintained such an
affectionate watchfulness over me during during my whole illness
and waited on me with so much patience and gentleness that I could
not bear to leave him behind' (I, 42). This man, Sam Roberts, who
was to remain with Cowper for the next thirty years, becomes an
adjunct to an hospitable domestic space outside 'history' which the
self has come into possession of.

The madhouse itself initially embodies this space: Cowper stayed
on for 'near twelve months after my recovery'; 'it was with the
greatest reluctance that I thought of leaving the place of my second
nativity; (. . .) I had enjoyed so much happiness there that I dreaded
a change of place' (I, 42). The Memoir concludes with his search for
a congenial environment where he can be at home in perpetuity.
Whereas Trosse celebrates a political event at the end of the Life (the
Glorious Revolution), Cowper celebrates a found home and family
– the Unwins, to whom the final pages of the Memoir are dedicated:
'I took possession of my new abode on November 11 1765. I have
found it a place of rest prepared for me by God's own hand'. (I,
45–6).

Reversing the usual autobiographical pattern, Cowper's narrative
involves a traumatic break with adulthood and a return to a sanctuary associated with childhood.

II

Cowper's eventual return to a privileged private sphere ideally
abolishes the alienating split between interiority and exteriority.
However, the autobiographical narrative itself reproduces self-
division. Cowper takes no responsibility for the course of his
narrative: it is, quite literally, taken out of his hands: 'My life which
I had called my own and proudly claimed a right to dispose of as
my own was kept from me by Him whose property indeed it was and
who alone had a right to dispose [of] it' (I, 20–1).

An ambivalent project of passivity can be discerned in the Memoir.
Cowper's first crisis occurs when he comes of age and achieves
independence:

I became in a manner complete master of myself and took possession of a set of chambers in the Temple at the age of twenty one. This being a most critical season in my life and upon which much depended, it pleased my all-merciful Father in Christ Jesus to give a check to my rash and ruinous career in wickedness at the very outset. (I, 8)

For 'career in wickedness' we might well read 'career' (he is eventually restored to himself while on holiday in Southampton). In the *Memoir*, self-determination is usually an occasion of stress or inner turmoil. This can be clearly seen in a reading of Cowper's biography. The first depression (1753) occurred when he was called to the Bar, but also at a time when his youthful love affair with his cousin Theadora was running into problems. These, in part at least, stemmed from Cowper's reluctance to commit himself to the relationship. This conjunction of career and commitment recurred in 1763. The main cause of the second breakdown was the affair of the clerkships, but at this time he again rejected the possibility of an alliance with Theadora (there is in fact a connection between the two events – it was Theadora's father who held the Parliamentary posts within his gift). His third breakdown came in 1773, and was almost certainly initiated by an engagement to Mary Unwin, who he openly regarded as a mother-figure. In each of these episodes, the prospect of assuming responsibilities, whether those of earning a living or those of becoming a husband, is a common factor. However much he may have suffered in his life, Cowper always avoided responsibilities of a conjugal, economic or public kind. His conversion of 1764 provided him with a protective carapace which supported the self in its goal of withdrawal from institutional obligations: the *Memoir* concludes with a hymn, 'Far from the world, O Lord, I flee.'[12]

A pattern of effort, self-defeating indecision and distress also distinguishes the suicide attempts. Although these aim at terminating an intolerable situation, they nonetheless involve a degree of committed effort which Cowper finds understandably difficult, 'distracted betwixt the desire of death and the dread of it.' The effort to overcome his indecision in turn generates extraordinary psychical tensions. When he exerts himself to drink the laudanum, his initiative is checked by an influence which, as he persists, appears increasingly supernatural: 'Twenty times I had the phial [of laudanum] at my mouth and as often received an irresistible check, and even at the time it seemed to me that an invisible hand swayed the bottle downwards as often as I set it against my lips' (I, 21). Active determination is counteracted by an opposite tendency to passivity and inaction.

The termination of his candidature for the Clerkship following his suicide attempts is far from bringing his anguish to an end. Unable to project his torment onto an external cause, he focuses inwards to confront his acute state of inner alienation: 'A vein of self-loathing and abhorrence ran through all my insanity' (I, 33-4). When he is transferred to Dr Cotton's, he makes another attempt on his life, with the aid of a large needle he has secured: 'With my finger, as I lay on my left side, I explored the pulse of my heart, thrust in the needle nearly to the head. Failing in the first attempt I repeated it, and did so ten or a dozen times, till at length, having broken the point of it in a rib, I was obliged to give over' (I, 34). This is somewhat different from his suicide attempts in the Inns of Court: by stabbing himself in the heart, he now seeks to destroy his own alienated interiority. Following the failure of this initiative he sinks at last into an apathetic despair. But in the supportive environment of the Collegium, this inertia is converted into an inner hibernation: his rebirth follows not long after. But his recovered tranquillity of mind remains dependent on a continuing state of passivity, an avoidance of action and self-determination. Even his application to board with the Unwin family is a cause of unrest: 'such a tumult of anxious thoughts seized me that for two or three days I could not divert my mind to any other subject' (I, 46).

Cowper's disavowal of the meanings of his own story remains problematic. Whereas Trosse's Puritanism engages actively (and indeed psychologically) with the meanings of his breakdown, Cowper's Evangelicalism is a cover which enables him to draw back from the troubling symptoms of his breakdown in a way that short-circuits a potential narrative of self-recognition. The tension between, on the one hand, a psychological symptomology and, on the other, a refusal to confront the evidence of this, is apparent in the narrative:

> It would be strange to omit to observe here how I was continually hurried away from such places as were most favorable to my design to others where it was almost impossible to execute it – from the fields where it was improbable that anything should happen to prevent me, to the Custom House, where everything of that kind was to be expected; and this by a sudden impulse which lasted just long enough to call me back to my chambers, and then immediately withdrawn. Nothing ever appeared more feasible to me than the project of going to France till it had served its purpose, and then in an instant it appeared to me impracticable and absurd even to a degree of ridicule. (I, 20-1)

This assessment is cogent, but the 'official' point of view now intervenes, disavowing the psychological implications of the sequence: 'My life (. . .) was kept from me by Him whose property indeed it was.'

At other junctures, the narrator withdraws from the events he narrates. This occurs most notably in his remarkably detached depiction of his attempt to hang himself. There is no modulation or intensification in the meticulous account of the preparation for death: the scene is not so much described as anatomised, with each circumstantial detail impersonally recorded:

My garter was made of a broad scarlet binding with a sliding buckle being sewn together at the ends: by the help of this buckle I formed a noose and fixing it about my neck, strained it so tight that I hardly left a passage for breath or the blood to circulate. The tongue of the buckle held it fast. At each corner of the bed was placed a wreath of carved work fastened by an iron pin which passed up through the midst of it. The other part of the garter therefore which made a loop I slipped over one of these and hung by it some seconds, drawing my feet up under me that they might not touch the floor. But the iron bent, the carved work slipped off, and the garter with it. I then fastened the garter to the frame of the tester, winding it round and tying it in a strong knot. The frame broke short and let me down again. The third effort was more likely to succeed. I set the bed chamber door open, which reached within a foot of the ceiling. By the help of a chair I could command the top of it, which, being rough and ragged, the garter hitched upon it, and the loop being wide enough to admit a large angle of the door, was easily fixed so as not to slip off again. I pushed away the chair with my foot and hung at my whole length. While I hung I heard a voice say distinctly three times, ''Tis over, 'tis over, 'tis over.' (I, 23–4)

In the climate of Sensibility this passage is anomalous. The clinical neutrality of the narration voids the scene of moral or emotional meaning. The protagonist is objectified in terms of the surface detail on which the narrative focuses: the withholding of subjective meaning reduces his predicament to one of absurdity. Barthes observes that 'as soon as a fact is *narrated* no longer with a view to acting directly on reality but intransitively that is to say, finally outside of any function other than that of the very practice of the symbol itself, this disconnection occurs, the voice loses its origin, the author enters into his own death.'[13] The formula of 'the death of the author' acquires an ironic appropriateness with regard to Cowper's account of his preparations for his own death. He does not, it is true, die – the garter snaps after he has lost consciousness – nevertheless the discourse of the *Memoir* constitutes a post-mortem.

In retracing the descent into delirious madness which follows, the narrative engages in a *via negativa* which reflects the protagonist's inner collapse. A bare minimum of meaning remains available for the crisis of symbolisation which now unfolds:

> I arose from bed to look for my prayer book, and having found it endeavoured to pray, but immediately experienced the impossibility of drawing nigh to God unless He first draws nigh to us. I made many passionate attempts towards prayer, but failed in all. Having an obscure notion about the efficacy of faith, I resolved upon an experiment to prove whether I had faith or not. For this purpose I began to repeat the Creed. When I came to the second period of it, which professes a belief in Christ, all traces of the form were struck out of my memory, nor could I recollect one syllable of the matter. While I endeavoured to recover it, and just when I thought myself on the point of doing so, I perceived a sensation in my brain like a tremulous vibration in all the fibres of it. By this means I lost the words in the very instant when I thought to have laid hold on them. (I, 28)

Where the language of the Scriptures is, for Cowper, invested with a higher meaning which is at once transcendental and interiorised, the breakdown of this language results not merely in a conviction of death but in a species of anti-meaning which Cowper experiences as an interior sensation at the antipodes of significant language:

> The extraordinary sensation in my brain, just in the very article of recollection, I considered as supernatural interposition to inform me that, having sinned against the Holy Ghost, I had no longer any interest in Christ or in the gifts of the spirit. Being therefore assured of this with the most riveted conviction I delivered myself over to absolute despair. I felt besides a sense of burning in my heart like that of real fire, and concluded an earnest of those eternal flames which should soon receive me. I laid myself down in bed, howling with horror, while my knees smote against each other. (I, 28–29)

Cowper's discourse fully engages with the meaning of his experiences only when he is reborn in God. As narrator, he is eager to affirm the validity of his preliminary religious visions: they 'befell me indeed while in a state of insanity, but recollecting them now and weighing them in my cooler judgement, which I thank God was never more its own master, I am forced to admit the solidity and reality of the facts' (I, 35). The narrative of recovery affirms a higher, visionary reality, amounting to a renewal of the narrating voice itself.

The public norms of reason inherited from the Enlightenment would cast doubt on Cowper's visions, but these norms implement an adult and masculine standard of rationality now foreign to him. William Blake would have accepted Cowper's heavenly visions on their author's own evaluation, as a mark of rebirth to a domain whose holiness is guaranteed by the unmediated quality of its joy:

> My eyes filled with tears and my voice was choked with transport. I could only look up to Heaven in silence, overwhelmed with love and wonder! (. . .). Thus was my Heavenly father in Christ Jesus pleased to give me the full assurance of faith at once, and out of a stony heart to raise up a child unto Abraham. (I, 40)

Cowper's proximity to Blake in this instance points to the need to understand that these visions are not merely religious. The temple, the thunderstorm and the giant hand are all sublime according to Burke's *Philosophical enquiry into the origin of our ideas of the sublime and the beautiful* (1757). Burke states here, 'The mind of man possesses a sort of creative power of its own':[14] Cowper's visions manifest themselves in terms of such a 'creative' faculty: the renewed metaphorical capacity of his narrative coincides with a narrated renewal of symbolisation. Following his dream-vision of the child, Cowper opens his bible: scriptural meaning, previously withheld, instantaneously fulfils his inner emptiness: 'In a moment I believed and received the Gospel' (I, 39).

The *Memoir* is not, however, a 'creative' work. Responsibility for the narrative remains outside Cowper's control: meaning is not discovered but is given by God. Nevertheless, in the personal and emotional context of the *Memoir*'s conclusion, Evangelicalism opens the door to literature. The *Memoir* concludes with two of Cowper's hymns. The writing of hymns was his first notable literary activity following the composition of the *Memoir*, and these are an intermediate step between religious and literary enthusiasm.

III

If Cowper's acceptance of God in 1764 is understood to involve a renunciation of manhood, then, at the risk of indulging in 'wild analysis,'[15] we might understand the giant hand grasping the thunderbolt as an image of castration. The scene of Cowper's vision, it will be remembered, occurs in Dr Cotton's private madhouse where he begins to regain the (ideally) privileged condition of upper middle-class childhood.

The new private sphere fosters precisely the kinds of intimacy and tension between parents and children on which Freudian psychoanalysis is founded. The *Memoir* is a narrative of psychological homecoming, but one which is grounded in precise socio-historical circumstances. It is no coincidence that Cowper's next major personal and autobiographical writing, *The Task*, takes the sofa as the occasion of its composition, describing it in terms of its evolution as an item of domestic furniture. It is this item, or a close relation, which, in its bourgeois domestic context, will become the Freudian apparatus *par excellence*, the analyst's couch. As far as the *Memoir* is concerned, psychoanalysis helps to explain the work to the extent that the work itself helps to explain psychoanalysis. How we might choose to interpret a particular episode of the *Memoir* is perhaps of less significance than the perception that in considering the *Memoir* we seem to stand on the threshold of a psychoanalytic culture.

It is in this context that we might consider an interpretation of the vision of the thunderbolt as a symbolic image of castration. Alongside this hermeneutic conjecture I wish to place a biographical conjecture. Maurice Quinlan has suggested that a case history noted by William Heberden may possibly refer to Cowper. Heberden, a physician whom Cowper had consulted during his crisis (and to whom he refers by name in his poetry), tells of a 'Gentleman' (of Cowper's age and disposition) who 'fell into a great dejection of spirits (. . .) At length, by some perversion of the mind, he seized a razor, and amputated his penis and scrotum.'[16] Quinlan's tentative hypothesis is consistent with Cowper's self-punishing behaviour in 1763, and (though Quinlan only implies this) it makes some sense of the hints and rumours which surfaced in the nineteenth century concerning Cowper's alleged 'hermaphroditism.'[17] The possibility that Cowper actually castrated himself is admittedly a remote one,[18] nevertheless I may be permitted to entertain it for the sake of argument. If the *image* of castration derives not from symbolism but from biographical fact, then a Freudian interpretation of unresolved psychical conflicts deriving from infancy and childhood would become, strictly speaking, redundant. Following this line of argument, the meaning of the vision is not latent but manifest; Cowper must renounce manhood and return to the 'pre-Oedipal' condition of the child. Of course, there is nothing to prevent a psychoanalytical critic from going on to reconstruct Cowper's madness (including conjectural self-emasculation) in terms of the infantile processes which Freud posited as the necessary condition of all individual development. This would undoubtedly involve Cowper's failed or inadequate negotiation of the Oedipal scenario. But from a critical and historical viewpoint, psychoanalytic theory makes its most useful contribution by seeking its own reflection as reproduced by the specific traumas which both precede and succeed Cowper's return to the private domain between 1764 and 1766. In this respect, the problems involved in his recovery of an 'ideal' realm of childhood in 1766 are more significant than his representation of his actual childhood. His third breakdown of 1773 occurred not only in the private sphere, but through the medium of a dream, when he heard the voice of a personal God, cast in the image of an all-powerful father, excluding him from hope of salvation. Less immediately severe than the crisis of 1763, the 1773 breakdown was to prove more devastating in the long term.

5 William Cowper (2):
The Poet on the Couch

I

In October 1765 Cowper, delighting in his discovery of the Unwin household, wrote 'Go when I will I find a House full of Peace and Cordiality in all its parts (. . .). You remember Rousseau's Description of an English Morning; such are the Mornings I spend with these Good People and the Evenings differ from them in nothing, except that they are still more Snug and quieter' (I, 122). Cowper refers to *La Nouvelle Héloïse* (1760), where St Preux writes, 'today we have spent an English morning, gathered together and in silence, savouring at one and the same time the pleasure of being together and the sweetness of repose. How few people know the delights of this situation.'[1] The *matinée à l'anglaise* was an eighteenth-century phenomenon, an expression of a new domestic sensibility. Intimacy was consolidated in the absence of social converse: family and friends 'assemble with a new consciousness of their intimate solidarity, which can as well be expressed in silence, and which artificial and sterile words would risk spoiling.'[2] This version of a spiritual communion transplanted to a secular domain provides a memorable image of a 'feminised' domestic environment and its values. The emphasis on quiet distinguishes this society from the masculine and urban one of coffee house or club.

Two months later Cowper moved in with the Unwins as a boarder. He formed a close attachment with Mary Unwin, who quickly came to share his Evangelical enthusiasm. Mary's husband, the Reverend Morley Unwin, did not altogether approve and felt uneasy about the friendship between his wife and Cowper.[3] In 1767, however, Reverend Unwin died after a fall from his horse fractured his skull. A year later Cowper and Mary moved to Olney where their companionship was the subject of local gossip. This prompted plans for betrothal. Cowper's breakdown of January 1773 followed directly.

Cowper's fullest account of the ensuing episode of insanity is contained in a letter to his cousin, Lady Hesketh, written in 1786:

> in the year 73 the same scene that was acted at St Albans, opened upon me again at Olney, only covered with a still deeper shade of melancholy, and ordained to be of much longer duration. I was suddenly reduced from my wonted rate of understanding to an almost childish imbecility. I did not indeed lose my senses, but I lost the power to exercise them. I could return a rational answer even to a difficult question, but a question was necessary or I never spoke at all. This state of mind was accompanied, as I suppose it to be in most circumstances of the kind, with misapprehension of things and persons that made me a very untractable patient. I believed that everyone hated me, and that Mrs. Unwin hated me most of all; was convinced that my food was poisoned, together with ten thousand megrims of the same stamp (. . .). At the same time that I was convinced of Mrs Unwin's aversion to me, could endure no other companion. (II, 454-5)

Once more he was tempted by the thought of suicide (in his *Spiritual diary* of 1795 he regretted his failure to take his life at this time). We also know that near the onset of the crisis he experienced a terrible dream, 'before the recollection of which, all consolation vanishes' (II, 385). In it he heard a fatal 'Word': Thomas Wright, in his 1892 biography of Cowper, proposed that the 'Word' was, in effect, *Actum est de te, periisti* – 'It is all over with thee, thou has perished.'[4] Cowper now believed he was singled out for damnation by a God who, having first elected him, then condemned him:

> Hatred and vengeance, my eternal portion,
> Scarce can delay execution,
> Wait, with impatient readiness, to seize my
> Soul in a moment
> ('Lines Written During a Period of Insanity')

He slowly regained a tolerable mode of existence in the years following this breakdown, but remained convinced of his inevitable damnation and continued to suffer nights of insomnia and despair. Only after a prolonged period of silence was he able to resume writing. He later recounted the course of his convalescence to Lady Hesketh:

As soon as I became capable of action, I commenced carpenter (. . .). I
grew weary of this in about a twelvemonth, and addressed myself to the
making of birdcages. To this employment succeeded that of gardening,
which I intermingled with that of drawing, but finding that the latter
occupation injured my eyes, I renounced it, and commenced poet. (II,
454)

Cowper's recognition of the therapeutic dimension of his writing[5]
occurs at a decisive moment in the development of social responses
to insanity, namely the emergence at the end of the eighteenth
century of moral treatment as a therapeutic practice, concerned with
the socialisation of the madman. This development bears on *The
Task*. The poet's experiences of insanity are never openly broached
in the poem, but that threat is in some measure its precondition.
The Task is a therapeutic undertaking: it enlists the poetry itself in
the service of recuperation.

Cowper's depressive crises recurred at ten-year intervals: a minor
episode in 1753, major ones in 1763-4 and 1773-4 respectively. This
pattern was broken in 1783-4, at the time when he was working on
The Task. Cowper subsequently hinted that another crisis was
narrowly averted at this moment, and that it was the composition
of *The Task* which kept mental turmoil under control: '*In the year
when I wrote the Task,* (for it occupied me about a year,) *I was very
often supremely unhappy,* and am under God indebted in good part
to that work for not having been much worse' (II, 456).

In an introductory 'Advertisement', Cowper tells how the poem
came about:

A lady, fond of blank verse, demanded a poem of that kind from the
author, and gave him the Sofa for a subject. He obeyed; and having
much leisure, connected another subject with it; and pursuing the train
of thought to which his situation and turn of mind led him, brought
forth at length, instead of the trifle which he at first intended, a serious
affair - a Volume!

The Task is designed on explicitly psychological principles. The
'slight connections'[6] which constitute the poem's mode of procedure
are justified by Cowper's allusion to the doctrine of association of
ideas. The poem begins, 'I sing the SOFA,' and continues with one
hundred mock-epic lines on the development of domestic seating
from ancient to modern times:

> Thus first necessity invented stools,
> Convenience next suggested elbow-chairs,
> And luxury th'accomplish'd SOFA last.
>   (1, 86–8)[7]

Cowper here connects his other subject, to provide a famously abrupt connection:

> . . . The SOFA suits
> The gouty limb, 'tis true; but gouty limb,
> Though on a SOFA, may I never feel:
> For I have loved the rural walk through lanes
> of grassy swarth. . .
>   (1, 106–9)

No longer an objective historical referent, the sofa has become an idea in the poet's mind. This unostentatious change of status enables a provocative leap between topics that lack objective connection. The frequent shifts in argument which occur as the poem progresses through its six books are not determined by the logic of an overall design, but by the shifting focus of the poet's attention: his discourse is often forwarded by associative transitions.

The absence of an objective logic governing the poem did not hinder its success with contemporary readers. While responding to the direct address of a personal voice, they also detected the continuity of its moral concerns.[8] In 1783 Cowper had lost none of his commitment to Evangelicalism, but he had considerably moderated the intense enthusiasm of the years following his recovery and conversion of 1764. His therapeutic pursuits, including The Task, were designed to distract him from his self-punishing conviction that his God had abandoned him: 'the God that reveals himself in the world of nature in this poem is a God whose major mode is his gentler one.'[9] The poem's avoidance of extreme religious sentiments as well as its emphasis on social and moral themes are in tune with the broader development of Evangelicalism in the late eighteenth century:

> the moral revolution was the imposition on the whole of society, and particularly of its upper and lower levels, of the traditional puritanism of the English middle ranks. But it was traditional puritanism in a variety of mutated forms, some of them surprisingly secular (. . .). The most important mutation was the change from exhortation of the various ranks to support existing society (. . .) to a demand for a new and higher morality than that associated with the traditional ruling class.[10]

By this time, associationism, which had seemed such an upsetting doctrine in the hands of Locke and Hume,[11] had been tamed: both Scottish moral philosophy and Samuel Tuke's 'moral treatment' appropriated versions of associationism. In *The Task* too, a moral concern is evident in the associationistic transition which launches the poem proper. Having provided his potted history of domestic seating, the poet resumes a directly personal discourse in criticising the unhealthy lifestyle of the wealthy and fashionable classes:

> Oh may I live exempted (while I live
> Guiltless of pampered appetite obscene)
> From pangs arthritic, that infests the toe
> of libertine excess.
>   (1, 104–7)

The response to the gout as a moral infirmity is to be found not merely in the healthful rural walk, but in a parallel indoor situation which is depicted in Book 4, 'The Winter Evening'. Here, in some of the poem's most famous lines, it is the poet who reclines on the sofa in the company of his companion, enjoying a late afternoon cup of tea:

> And, while the bubbling and loud-hissing urn
> Throws up a steamy column, and the cups
> That cheer but not inebriate, wait on each,
> So let us welcome peaceful evening in
>   (4, 38–40)

Tea, in contrast with alcohol, is a source of healthful refreshment, thus a morally impeccable restorative. The sofa which furnishes the poet's retreat is not the luxury object of the poem's opening sequence but the seat of values which are feminine, middle-class and domestic, rather than masculine, aristocratic and à la mode.

Cowper's concern with moral renewal is simultaneously a concern with self-renewal. If the reference to inebriation is a critique of corrupt manners, the need for a beverage which nevertheless 'cheers' covertly acknowledges and addresses the poet's own ailment. Cowper tactfully avoided the topic of his mental troubles in his public poetry, but 'Retirement', the concluding poem of his *Moral satires* (1782), includes a description of a patient suffering from melancholia (which is identified as a nervous ailment).

In 1796, Samuel Tuke founded the Retreat (originally described as 'a retired habitation') for the care and treatment of insane and mentally ill Quaker Friends. Both 'Retirement' and *The Task* anticipate Tuke's landmark therapeutic initiative. The Retreat presented itself as a domestic dwelling situated in a rural environment: 'Beyond the low walls patients could see the open countryside which surrounded the establishment.'[12] In the urban culture of the later eighteenth century, nature was viewed as a therapeutic resource: 'The individual gets in touch with (. . .) the subjective truth about himself via the harmony and innocence of virgin, external nature, and the result corresponds to moral "naturalness" which tempers the behaviour towards the norm.'[13] This emphasis colours Cowper's handling of the *beatus ille* topic: for him, as for Tuke, the benefits of nature were founded in moral and spiritual values. 'Woe to the man,' he writes in 'Retirement',

> Who studies nature with a wanton eye,
> Admires the work, but slips the lesson by
> (ll. 213–14)

In the poem the physician William Heberden is introduced to recommend the virtues of nature:

> Virtuous and faithful HEBERDEN! whose skill
> Attempts no task it cannot well fulfill,
> Gives melancholy up to nature's care,
> And sends the patient into purer air
> (ll. 279–82)

Associationism provides a further link between Cowper and Tuke. Associationist theory was instrumental in determining both the situation and the therapeutic methods of the Retreat:

The findings of associationism were accepted on the importance of the emotions in the well-being of the patient: the grounds at the Retreat were made as varied and interesting as possible to manipulate the patient's emotions and so to cheer the melancholics. The need to balance the emotions and distract the patient from painful thoughts and assocations led to a central feature in the Retreat's moral therapy: the creation of varied employments and amusements.[14]

Following on from carpentry and gardening, the writing of poetry was, as we have seen, just such a therapy for Cowper. *The Task* was specifically commenced, at Lady Austen's suggestion, as both employment and (initially at least) amusement. The given task

leads, associationistically, to a rejection of unhealthy excess in favour
of the 'improving' theme of rural walks. Here again Cowper is at one
with Tuke: 'The significance that was attached to country walks in
the Retreat's moral treatment was as much because of the spiritual
as the physical benefits derived from them. Patients could regain
their serenity through contact with beautiful, unspoilt surroundings.'[15]

According to Michel Foucault, Tuke in England and, contem-
poraneously, Pinel in France removed the external constraints of
bars and chains, only to replace them with inner constraints.
Patients are 'free' providing they restrict themselves to a limited area
of movement.[16] This describes Cowper's situation. He was not
lodged in an institution at any time after 1765, but Olney itself often
seemed like one. In 1780 he wrote to Mrs Newton, who had just
moved with her husband to London, 'If I were in a Condition to
leave Olney too, I certainly would not stay in it; it is no Attachment
to the Place that binds me here, but an Unfitness for every other.
I lived in it once, but now I am buried in it, and have no Business
with the World on the Outside of my Sepulchre; my Appearance
would Startle them and theirs would be shocking to me' (I, 322). In
The Task, self-confinement is presented in more positive terms. In
Book 1, the poet likens himself to a weather-house figurine, alter-
nately retiring and sallying forth (1, 210-14): Martin Priestman
comments that the weather-house is 'a perfect symbol of the circumscribed and conditional freedom the poem needs at this point.'[17]
The poem's associationism maintains a balance, albeit a shifting one,
between indoor and outdoor environments: the limitations the poet
places on his freedom of movement are both designedly therapeutic
and consonant with the wayward and discontinuous but coherently
self-returning course of associationism itself. As a manner of movement, this may legitimately proceed in various digressive directions
without entailing either the responsibilities of an onwards-and-
upwards type of progress or the risks of regression and loss. Where
potentially stressful junctures arise in the poet's discourse, associationism enables him to negotiate or simply offset them.

The degree to which the associative procedure enables Cowper to
combine poetic exploration with prudent self-management can be
demonstrated in the sequence of linked passages which make up the
first 250 lines of Book 1.
  The movement from indoors to outdoors (1, 108-9) is one of

release: the constrained, prosy rhythm of the preceding lines disappears as the poet moves into nature: 'For I have loved the rural walk through lanes.' However his freedom is conditional: recollecting boyhood rambles, he remarks, 'No SOFA then awaited my return.' The adult must return to self-imposed domestic confines.

The rural walk commences with two set-pieces: first, a description of the River Ouse, then a contrasting passage in which nature is perceived empathetically through the ear. The first passage is an exercise in picturesque landscape description:

> How oft upon yon eminence our pace
> Has slackened to a pause, and we have borne
> The ruffling wind, scarce conscious that it blew,
> While admiration, feeding at the eye,
> And still unsated, dwelt upon the scene.
>
> (1, 154–8)

The poet identifies the familiar scene ('daily view'd') in terms which would have been recognised by cultured readers of the day, as a visual prospect of the type developed for English verse by James Thomson.[18] As such, it emulates a landscape painting of the classical genre more than it responds to an actual landscape:

> Thence with what pleasure have we just discerned
> The distant plough slow-moving, and beside
> His lab'ring team, that swerved not from the track,
> The sturdy swain diminished to a boy!
>
> (1, 159–62)

The terms of the description are perspectival ('The sturdy swain diminished to a boy') and decorative ('The stream that, as with molten glass, inlays the vale'). In this respect it provides an outdoor analogue to artificial indoor portrayals of pastoral scenes, such as the needlework designs which ornament upholstered seats in the poem's opening section: 'There might ye see the peony spread wide, / The full blown rose, the shepherd and his lass' (1, 35–6). In identifying the scene in terms of familiarity and continuity, the poet determines it as an objective correlative of self-identity:

> Scenes must be beautiful, which, daily viewed,
> Please daily, and whose novelty survives
> Long knowledge and the scrutiny of years.
> Here Ouse, slow-winding through a level plain
> Of spacious meads with cattle sprinkled o'er,
> Conducts the eye along its sinuous course
> Delighted.
>
> (1, 178–80)

In the succeeding paragraph, picturesque nature is abruptly juxtaposed with a sublimely disordered *natura naturans*:

> Not rural sights alone, but rural sounds,
> Exhilarate the spirit, and restore
> The tone of languid nature. Mighty winds
> That sweep the skirt of some far-spreading wood
> Of ancient growth, make music not unlike
> The dash of ocean on his winding shore,
> And lull the spirit while they fill the mind;
>
> (1, 181–7)

The previous landscape description freezes active processes: 'the distant plough slow-moving'; 'Ouse, slow-winding.' The gerunds function as adjectives, describing a static, two-dimensional scene. By contrast, nature heard is active and dynamic: winds make music; oceans dash. The two passages can be systematically contrasted: unity versus multiplicity ('Unnumber'd branches waving in the blast'); surface versus depths ('distant floods'; 'cleft rock'); pictorialism versus word-music ('rills that slip / through the cleft rock, and, chiming as they fall, / Upon loose pebbles, lose themselves at length. . .'). The overall contrast is between culture as determined by the educated eye, and wild nature, which is mediated by the untrained ear: the picturesque scene is a discourse of identity, while the sublime scene opposes it as a discourse of subjectivity.

The eye plays its part in the sublime scene too, but its function changes: it now actively interprets nature: streams of water 'lose themselves at length / in matted grass that, with a livelier green / Betrays the secret of their silent course' (1, 194–6). The eye which notices the patch of greener grass and apprehends its significance no longer belongs to an educated connoisseur viewing the scene in compositional terms. The position of the poet-subject has shifted; plunged into the midst of nature, he observes details that would have been not only invisible but incomprehensible from the previous vantage point. This shift affects the language of the poem. Whereas the picturesque passage is characterised by ease and urbanity of expression, sentences in the sublime passage are longer, their syntax more complex. In this section, language is energised by the effort the poet makes to convey perceptual meanings which are no longer disposed on an available surface.

The poet connects the two passages by means of an easy associative link between sight and sound: 'Not rural sights alone, but rural sounds. . .'. However, the degree of difference between the two passages is sufficiently pronounced to recall Hume's scepticism, in the *Treatise of human nature*, on the notion of a substantial self: 'I can never catch *myself* at any time without a perception and can never observe any thing but the perception. (. . .) I may venture to affirm of the rest of mankind, that they are nothing but a bundle or collection of different perceptions, which succeed each other with an inconceivable rapidity, and in a perpetual flux and movement.'[19] Conversely, identity is, for Hume, a psychological 'fiction':[20] 'Our notions of personal identity proceed entirely from the smooth and uninterrupted progress of thought along a train of connected ideas.'[21] *The Task*, with its 'slight connections,' would seem to illustrate Hume's psychological scepticism: the shift from a picturesque to a sublime mode involves a shift in subject position which displaces a composed identity. The educated man of leisure who views the River Ouse from his eminence is less easily identified when he gives ear to nature. We might, for example, compare the different uses of simile in the two sections. Picturesque simile – 'the stream / That as with molten glass, inlays the vale' – clearly differentiates between tenor (stream) and vehicle (molten glass). By contrast, sublime simile, operating negatively, blurs the tenor/vehicle distinction: 'Mighty winds (. . .) make music not unlike / The dash of ocean.' Negative capability ('unnumbered branches') involves a productive loss of certainties. Nature disseminates fixed points of identity: the poet's ear, far from imposing definition and order, is receptive to non-definable subjective meanings which 'exhilarate the spirit' and 'fill the mind.'

Yet there is no sense of psychological tension involved in the shift from eye to ear: the poet, making no attempt to 'catch' himself, briefly forgets himself. Outdoors scenes of nature do not constitute for him a primary context of self-definition. The culture–nature opposition must be situated in a context which is intrinsically invested with moral and psychological meanings if its personal significance is to become manifest.

The poem's opening sequence traces a progression from the

primitive to the cultured:

> Time was, when clothing sumptuous or for use,
> Save for their own painted skins, our sires had none.
> . . .
> The hardy chief upon the rugged rock
> Wash'd by the sea, or on the gravelly bank
> > . . . reposed his weary strength.
> > > (1, 8–15)

This primitive mode of existence is indirectly linked with the intui-tion of a past self which is freed from the constraints of civilised society: in his boyhood, the poet could 'pass his bounds,' happily ignorant of a waiting sofa. So too, *natura naturans* transcends the bounds of domestic identity. But as the passage proceeds, domestic confines are re-evoked with the reference to the weather-house (see above). Next on the itinerary is an isolated rural cottage which the poet has entitled 'the peasant's nest.' The primitive, non-bourgeois environment of the cottage evokes a tantalisingly ideal version of selfhood, one which, enabling inspiration and creativity, would free the poet from the obligation of the moral Task:

> hidden as it is, and far remote
> From such unpleasing sounds as haunt the ear
> In village or in town,. . .
> . . .
> Oft have I wished the peaceful covert mine.
> Here, I have said, at least I should possess
> The poet's treasure, silence, and indulge
> The dreams of fancy, tranquil and secure.
> > (1, 228–35)

These remarks on the cottage reintroduce the twists and turns of mental process to the unfolding discourse. Just as a sofa initiated the poet's associative discourse in the first place, so a self-aware process of thought is foregrounded as he encounters the cottage: the domestic context renews the train of self-reflection which the sublime landscape has dispersed. But there is no sofa in the 'peasant's nest': as the poet becomes self-consciously aware of a lack of modern conveniences, he abruptly dispels Rousseauesque notions of solitary communion with nature:

> Vain thought! The dweller in that retreat
> Dearly obtains the refuge it affords
> Its elevated site forbids the wretch
> To drink sweet waters of the crystal well
>   . . . nor seldom waits,
> Dependent on the baker's punctual call
> . . .
> So farewell envy of the *peasant's nest*:
> If solitude make scant the means of life,
> Society for me!
>
>   (1, 237–49)

Civilised man, refined in comparison with primitive man (the 'hardy chief'), can no longer inhabit an uncultured environment: Cowper is confronted with an image of sanctuary which is inappropriate to the conditions of his actual discourse. John Lukacs observes that the conditions of mental and material life in any given period are interrelated: 'as the self-consciousness of medieval people was spare, the interiors of their houses were bare (. . .). The interior furniture of houses appeared together with interior furniture of minds.'[22] If this statement appears oversimplistic, we might inflect it by saying that medieval people, even burghers, were not yet bourgeois subjects. For Cowper, certainly, living in the 'peasant's nest' would require the renunciation of a long, painstaking cultural-historical development: by the same token, a 'primitive' mode of poetic sublimity would involve renouncing the painstaking progress which has been attained through a self-administered psychological therapy. Just as there is no sofa in the 'peasant's nest,' so there would be no *Task* in a sublime poesis which renounced civilised restraint. The poet's subsequent encounter with 'crazy Kate,' driven mad by love, disappointment and despair (1, 534–56), suggests that this way lies madness.

It is the domestic context which provides the self with its point of psychological self-reference and its locus of moral self-recuperation. In this context, nature is a tonic, but one which must be taken in moderation.[23] As at the York Retreat the natural environment is a therapeutic accessory to the domestic institution and not a location of subjective transcendence:

>   . . . thou seeming sweet,
> Be still a pleasing object in my view;
> My visit still, but never mine abode.
>   (1, 249–51)

II

Cowper's avoidance of direct autobiographical reference to insanity and melancholia in *The Task* is more than a matter of poetic tact. The associationistic rationale for avoiding the topic is set out very clearly by Robert Southey's comments on the *Memoir* in his 1835 biography of Cowper: 'the train of thought to which he was led tended greatly to induce a return of the malady, over the remains of which those injudicious friends encouraged him to brood.'[24] This could well be close to Cowper's own view of the matter subsequent to 1773. When he eventually described the episode to Lady Hesketh, he did so at a distance from the event: 'It will be thirteen years in little more than a week since this malady seized me. Methinks I hear you ask, (. . .) Is it removed? I reply, in great measure, but not quite. Occasionally I am much distressed, but that distress becomes continually less frequent, and I think, less violent. I find writing, especially poetry, my best remedy' (II, 455). This account contrasts with the fundamentalist viewpoint of the *Memoir*. Insanity is a 'malady': recovery is not an inspirational rebirth accompanied by divine visions and messages but a moral struggle against unreason, with poetry in the therapeutic vanguard. The sequence which follows from the 1773 breakdown unfolds in secular and effectively psychiatric terms.

The emergence of a culture of sensibility in mid-eighteenth-century England disestablished the claims of reason to absolute authority: 'the insane ceased to be looked upon as completely irrational. On the contrary, the madman's visible irrationality and one's own hidden internal irrationality were seen to share certain qualities, such as intoxicating emotions, especially of a painful sort, passion, sensibility, irresistible desires, fancies and dreams and other aspects of the dark side of the soul.'[25] Tuke's initiative is the outcome of a larger response to what has now become a social and moral struggle against one's own asocial propensities. Fiona Godlee has suggested that the Retreat's therapeutic emphasis on self-restraint is implied by the historical development of Quakerism itself. The Retreat was specifically founded in order to care for insane Friends, and was opposed from within the movement by those who, at this juncture, feared further association between Quakerism and insanity.[26] In the seventeenth and early eighteenth centuries, Quakers were commonly accused of enthusiastic madness. The movement responded with an increased emphasis on reason and respectability. John Gough wrote a history of the movement in 1790 which sought retrospectively to rationalise early Quaker enthusiasm, 'testifying against vice and wickedness might produce warmth of expression and action also, which to an uninvidious eye might appear convulsive: But their convulsions did not bereave them of understanding.'[27] By 1790 such testifying was a thing of the past: so too it was for Cowper in the 1780s. The evolution of Cowper's attitudes between 1764 and 1786 resumes the larger evolution of the Protestant Dissenter groups from spiritual intensity and enthusiasm to a self-restrained, socially normative emphasis on conduct and behaviour.

The Retreat's patients, correctly dressed and properly behaved when taking tea with Quaker friends, suppressed the inner struggle which the maintenance of such appropriate behaviour required. Similarly, *The Task* carries no direct trace of the struggle against a resurgent crisis that marked its composition. If it implements a normative morality, this occurs less in its positive moral content than in the invisibility of the struggle with unreason which characterises the production of its discourse. Where Cowper is concerned, mental turmoil is constituted as the unseen, unspoken dimension of *The Task*.

While at work on the poem, Cowper read the *Dissertations moral and critical* by the Scots poet and commonsense philosopher, James Beattie. In the 'Dissertation on the Imagination', Beattie distinguishes between focused attention and the involuntary association of ideas which occurs in a state of reverie:

> That energy, which lays a restraint upon the fancy, by fixing the mind upon one particular object, or set of objects, is called Attention: and most people know, that the continued exercise of it is accompanied with difficulty, and something of intellectual weariness. Whereas, when, without attending to any one particular idea, we give full scope to our thoughts, and permit them to shift, as Imagination or accident shall determine, a state of mind which is called a Reverie; we are conscious of something like mental relaxation: while one idea brings in another, which gives way to a third, and that in its turn is succeeded by others; the mind seeming all along to be passive.[28]

Cowper probably had this passage in mind when he wrote Book 4 of *The Task*, 'The Winter Evening.'[29] In this section he evokes a state of reverie which, in effect, illustrates Beattie's abstract account:

                                              But me, perhaps,
The glowing hearth may satisfy awhile
With faint illumination that uplifts
The shadow to the ceiling, there by fits
Dancing uncouthly to the quiv'ring flame.
Not undelightful is an hour to me
So spent in parlour twilight: such a gloom
Suits well the thoughtful or unthinking mind,
The mind contemplative, with some new theme
Pregnant, or indispos'd alike to all.
Laugh ye, who boast your more mercurial pow'rs,
That never feel a stupor, know no pause,
Nor need one; I am conscious and confess,
Fearless, a soul that does not always think.
Me oft has fancy, ludicrous and wild,
Sooth'd with a waking dream of houses, tow'rs,
Trees, churches, and strange visages, express'd
In the red cinders, while with poring eye
I gaz'd, myself creating what I saw.
Nor less amus'd have I quiescent watch'd
The sooty films that play upon the bars
Pendulous, and foreboding, in the view
Of superstition, prophesying still,
Though still deceiv'd, some stranger's near approach.
                                        (4, 272-97)

One of the main planks of the commonsense school of philosophy
was that consciousness is not passive (as asserted by Locke and
Hume), but that the self possesses innate capacities of judgement and
intention. In the *Dissertations*, Beattie evokes the semi-conscious state
of reverie in terms of a seemingly passive association of ideas, but
makes clear that this is an activity of the liberated imagination. The
poet's reverie in *The Task* similarly relates what is, in effect, free-
association to the notion of an unthinking self. While conscious
identity is suspended, non-attentive and potentially creative
processes of awareness emerge. Beattie's discussion of reverie in the
Dissertations provides a distant anticipation of Freud's notion of
primary process. Attention and conscious thought are seen as
involving both authority and effort; conversely inattention is a mode
of relaxation whereby the imagination is allowed to play unsuper-
vised – the mind exerts 'little authority over its thoughts.' Fantasy
and daydreaming, 'harmlessly' bypassing the prohibitive authority of
the conscious ego, allow the instinctual desires of the unconscious a
mode of expression.[30] The anticipation of Freud is strikingly

underlined in *The Task*: in his reverie, the poet free-associates while relaxed on a sofa.

This emphasis on the freedom of reverie directly contradicts the pronouncements of Samuel Johnson. Confronted with the unsettling prospect of Hume's contingent self-in-consciousness, Johnson had expressed in *Rasselas* his fear of fancy: 'There is no man whose imagination does not sometimes predominate over his reason (. . .) No man will be found in whose mind airy notions do not sometimes tyrannise, and force him to hope or fear beyond the limits of sober probability. All power of fancy over reason is a degree of insanity.'[31] Beattie's discussion of reverie seems to be designed as a reply to Johnson. Where, for Johnson, fancy operates through a 'particular train of ideas [which] fixes the attention,'[32] for Beattie, fancy, operating below the level of attention, takes effect as an associative play. Against Johnson's concern to 'control and repress' fancy,[33] he proposes that intellectual relaxation and indulgence in fancy is valuable. For Cowper, Johnson himself personified an odiously censorious authority ('Oh! I could thresh his old Jacket 'till I made his Pension jingle in his Pocket'):[34] following Beattie, he too demurs from Johnson's verdict.[35] In the moral context of the companionable domestic retreat (different from the condition of solitude which Johnson so feared), fancy operates in terms of liberty rather than tyranny, while its associative play distinguishes it from the violence of insanity. Nevertheless it is the underlying kinship between relaxed control of fancy and the uncontrol of insanity which permits the substitution of the one for the other, enabling Cowper, in a post-Augustan culture, to introduce a therapeutically associative expression of 'fancy' in a poem which, in the very conditions of its composition, is psychologically embattled.

Given the poet's own self-administered moral treatment, the reverie, with its permitted upsurge of non-rational images, provides a psychological safety valve. The reverie seems to take the poet from his domestic point of reference towards an increasingly Gothic register of imagery: houses, then towers, trees, churches and strange visages. This is confirmed by the 'foreboding' superstition connected with the 'sooty film.' The passage provides an analogue to the topic so frequently encountered in subjective writings of madness, namely the *descensus Averno*. However, as Bruce Redmond has noted, the threatening underworld fires are contained within the reassuring limits of the modern domestic fireplace,[36] while the psychical descent is undertaken from the safety of the sofa, and the potentially delirious images return to the self-recuperative domestic context –

the poet is 'summoned home' to himself, and to a reassuring environment such as the 'peasant's nest' could not have provided:

> at length the freezing blast
> that sweeps the bolted shutter, summons home
> The recollected pow'rs; and, snapping short
> The glassy threads, with which the fancy weaves
> Her brittle toys, restores me to myself.
> How calm is my recess . . .
>
> (4, 302-8)

If mental turmoil constitutes the suppressed dimension of text, then the associative images of the reverie allow a safe and sanctioned defusing of repressed tensions:

> 'Tis thus the understanding takes repose
> In indolent vacuity of thought,
> And sleeps and is refresh'd
>
> (4, 296-8)

Some lines previous to the fire-gazing passage the poet and his companion (Mary) have closed the shutters against the weather and pulled the sofa round before the fire for tea:

> Now stir the fire, and close the shutters fast,
> Let fall the curtains, wheel the sofa round,
>
> (4, 36-7)

The opening section of *The Task* portrays the sofa as an historically produced item: the above detail too can be viewed in an historical perspective. In the eighteenth-century drawing room, 'Sofas were pulled away from the sides of rooms – a landmark moment in the evolution of domestic comfort.'[37] With reference to this moment, we may reconstruct the scene in specifically psychological terms. The fire is the focal point of interiority while the shutters and curtains indicate the limit-point which divides the interior from the exterior environment. The sofa, placed in the middle, determines the disposition of interior space. 'Interior space' should also be understood here in a psychological sense: domestic space emblematises inner space and so constitutes the material terrain of bourgeois subjectivity. This space is not fixed and rigid, it becomes mobile, with the sofa as particular instrument of that mobility. As it is wheeled round it predisposes and defines interior space, forming the supplementary boundary of an intimate interiority which radiates from the hearth, while at the same time it is the physical container of actual subjective interiority. That is to say, it is both a receptacle into which one sinks, and that receptacle whereby one can sink into oneself, to indulge, for example, in a reverie evoked by the play of the fire in the hearth.

Christopher Hill, writing of the mid-seventeenth-century domestic environment, indicates both the new features of that environment and their general significance: 'All roads in our period have led to individualism: more rooms in better off peasant houses, use of glass in windows; use of coal in grates, replacement of benches by chairs. All of this made possible the greater comfort and privacy for at least the upper half of the population.'[38] When, in 'The Winter Evening', the poet reclines before the fire, his fancy creating a play of imagery in the burning embers, we should note, following Hill, that the fire in his grate is indeed a coal and not a wood fire – the play of imagination devolves on the images perceived in the red cinders. A wood fire was more likely to be associated with a primitive and functional environment – that, for example, of the alluring but unsuitable 'peasant's nest.' Cowper's prefatory 'Advertisement' notes that leisure was a precondition of the poem: both coal fire and sofa abet an affluent extension of leisure, and so provide for specifically bourgeois modes of subjective interiority. A wood fire burns up and exhausts itself quickly, whereas a coal fire lingers on in its embers, encouraging just the kind of lethargic reverie in which the poet indulges here: not quite drowsing or dozing, but idly conscious; indulging in the play of imagination before the fire.

The parlour scene of 'The Winter Evening' induces a psychological self-communion which is quite different from the spiritual introspection of the *Memoir*. The fire-gazing passage, like the introductory 'Advertisement', assembles the essential elements of bourgeois subjectivity: the inhabiting of the private sphere, the possession of leisure and the notion of psychological process. But it goes considerably further and broaches a psychologically conceived notion of a pre-conscious mental process. The private sphere, of which Cowper's domestic interior constitutes a particular instance, is the crucial arena of this development: it both precedes and inaugurates the psychological style of his discourse in *The Task*.

His first breakdown occurred in the public domain, in response to external pressures, but the second breakdown occurred in the poet's domestic retreat. In the passage from public to private, Cowper's problems and their solutions come to seem psychologically rather than supernaturally motivated. These are the circumstances which set the *The Task* apart from the spiritual discourse of the *Memoir*. In the *Memoir* the alien and alienated self of madness is associated with an alien and alienating environment – London and the Inns of Court – and both are set decisively apart from the converted self who writes, and who has found a 'place of rest' outside history, prepared for him 'by God's own hand.' By contrast, the self of *The Task* starts from the assumption that its environment – the emergent private sphere, as delineated in the opening hundred lines of the poem – *is* historical. As such it inaugurates both secular psychology and psychological interiorisation.

In *The Family, sex and marriage in England 1500–1800* Lawrence Stone, commenting on the evidence of an increase in emotional affect among the upper bourgeoisie in eighteenth-century England, indulged in a hypothesis which has gained some degree of notoriety:

> The rise of affect (. . .) is only partly a product of individualism, and seems to have its roots also in a basic personality change. In the sixteenth and early seventeenth centuries there predominated a personality type with 'low gradient' affect, whose capacity for warm relationships was generally limited, and who diffused what there was of it widely among family, kin, and neighbours. In the eighteenth century there predominated among the upper bourgeoisie and squirarchy a personality type with 'steep gradient' affect, whose general capacity for intimate personal relationships was much greater, and whose emotional ties were now far more closely concentrated on spouse and children.[39]

A comparison of George Trosse and Cowper suggests that any 'rise of affect' is wholly rather than partly attributable to individualism, provided that we understand the psychological extent of that phenomenon. What is subject to variation between the sixteenth and eighteenth centuries is not a quantity but a quality of affect, and not its manifestation as such in family relationships but the ways in which it is manifested. In the case of Cowper, affect acquires a new intensity which is often psychologically self-conscious in character. Conversely it is this evidence of an interiorised, psychological quality of affect which remains undeveloped in Trosse. Affect, then, does not 'arise' in eighteenth-century culture, but its manner of expression undergoes a qualitative change: it becomes psychologically interiorised in a culture which is, to an increasing degree, psychologically self-conscious.

We may further conjecture that this interiorisation of affect corresponds to the increasingly enclosed and private character of domestic life in the period. Under these circumstances, the father and mother become potentially formative forces in the psychical life of the individual. The voice Cowper heard in the fateful dream of 1773 was a paternal one – the voice of his God personally excluding him from Election. In 1764, God was a stern but indulgent father-figure, but now this father-figure turned decisively against him at the very moment when he was preparing to marry Mary Unwin. Cowper's liaison with Mary in 1767 was hardly an amorous one, nevertheless it cast her husband, a priest, an older man and a pater-familias, in the role of jealous rival. The Oedipal complexion of this scenario is confirmed by Cowper's explicit identification of Mary as a mother-figure.[40] Thus the enmity of the interiorised father-God in 1773 coincided with the culmination of Cowper's project of reversing his childhood history and integrating himself 'incestuously' within the domestic sphere. Acting as interiorised agent of prohibition, the hallucinatory paternal voice denies the subject's project of union with the mother.

Stone notes that 'again and again it becomes apparent in the literature of the eighteenth century that this Golden Age of childhood under close maternal care had serious inhibiting conse-quences later on (. . .). Again and again the story is one of sexual love that goes unfulfilled, inhibited by Oedipal fixation on the mother.'[41] If a domestic maternal domain represents for Cowper a secure psychological refuge, then an introjected voice of paternal authority refuses the subject's possession of this space and fragments it from within – indeed from within the problematic dimension of the personal unconscious. Madness can no longer be laid at the door of an agent outside the self. It is, arguably, at this point that psychological crisis is inscribed as the limit experience of bourgeois subjectivity.

Yet Cowper was not wholly devastated by this outcome. The domestic and family context that located an inner trauma also provided psychological resources which enabled him to reach a limited accommodation with that problem. Tuke's Retreat implemented a familial structure and atmosphere, with mentally ill inmates cast in the role of children to be educated.[42] Cowper reported himself reduced in 1773 to a state of 'childish imbecility,' and helpless dependence on Mary Unwin (II, 454-5). If the psychologised domestic reverie of The Task shares points of reference with Freud, these are consequent on the epistemological link which Michel Foucault has traced between the therapeutic concerns, seem-ingly so far apart, of Tuke and Freud:

In the great reorganisation of relations between madness and reason, the
family, at the end of the eighteenth century, played a decisive part [. . .];
it is from the family that Tuke starts out, and toward it that he
progresses. Lending it the prestige of primitive values not yet
compromised in the social, Tuke makes the family play a role of disaliena-
tion; it was, in his myth, the antithesis of that 'milieu' which the eighteenth century saw as the origin of all madness. But he introduced it as
well, in a very real way, into the world of the asylum, where it appears
both as truth and as norm for all relations that may obtain between
madman and man of reason. [. . .] The entire existence of madness, in
the world now being prepared for it, was enveloped in what we may call,
in anticipation, a 'parental complex.' The prestige of patriarchy is revived
around madness in the bourgeois family. It is this historical sedimentation
which psychoanalysis would later bring to light, according it through a
new myth the meaning of a destiny that supposedly marked all of
Western culture and perhaps all of civilisation, whereas it had been slowly
deposited by it and only solidified quite recently at the turn of this
century.[43]

This suggests the paradoxical nature of Cowper's predicament: the
family can only 'surround' him as recuperative medium inasmuch as
it is already inscribed within his psyche as that matrix from which
his problems ultimately derive. When, in 1780, he described Olney
both as refuge and 'sepulchre,' he showed an indirect insight into
this paradox. The bourgeois interior, replete with familial affect, is
at once place of confinement, place of refuge, and place of burial.

III

Book 6 of *The Task* begins with a notable instance of associationism.
The sound of village bells on the poet's winter walk 'opens all the
cells / Where mem'ry slept.' He recalls the course of his life, his train
of thought centring on the figure of the father:

> Some friend is gone, perhaps his son's best friend!
> A father, whose authority in show
> When most severe, and must'ring all its force,
> Was but the graver countenance of love;
> Whose favour, like the clouds of spring, might low'r,
> And utter now and then an awful voice,
> But had a blessing in its darkest frown,
> Threatening at once and nourishing the plant.
>
> (6, 23–36)

The father is more severe and distant than the mother ('That softer friend') because, moving between the home and the outside world of work and public concerns, he is a more equivocal figure, his image more likely to be compounded of elements of both love and authority, intimacy and distance. These elements emerge in the poem's psychological discourse as a felt ambivalence: the father's authority, his 'awful voice', returns from the public sphere to the private domain where it does not lose its threatening quality, but is nevertheless converted into a blessing. The image however, is persistently equivocal: 'threatening at once and nourishing the plant.'

The significance of these lines consists less in their evocation of a given individual – Cowper's actual father[44] – than of a generalised 'father' who is felt to possess these attributes. The ambivalence is carried over from 'Retirement'. Both the onset as well as the remedy of nervous illness are here laid at the door of a God who is assimilated to the father:

> No wounds like those a wounded spirit feels,
> No cure for such, till God who makes them, heals.
> And thou, sad suff'rer under nameless ill,
> That yields not to the touch of human skill,
> Improve the kind occasion, understand
> A Father's frown, and kiss his chast'ning hand.
>
> (ll. 341–6)

Cowper's relationship with God is identified as a relationship with a father, as determined by the newly psychological and secular settlement of bourgeois culture. After 1773, Cowper experienced his own inner being in terms of a psychologically interiorised relationship with the Father and his negative–positive polarity. This was, inevitably, devastating. In 1787 he suffered another depressive crisis, one from which he never effectively recovered. The final, unrelievedly black period dates from 1794 until his death: 'In his last years,' Lilian Feder writes, 'Cowper experienced God as a "perpetual irresistible influence" that he felt controlled his "volitions" and "actions." The letters of these years are explicit in their bitterness toward the Being who, Cowper was convinced, regretted having "made" him and whom he increasingly held accountable for his frustration, rage and despair.'[45] The 'Word' which Cowper heard in his dream, 'thou hast perished,' is directly echoed in 'The Castaway', Cowper's final poem, where it gives force to what may be the first expression of existential (as distinct from spiritual) despair in modern literature:

> No voice divine the storm allayed,
>   No light propitious shone;
> When, snatch'd from all effectual aid,
>   We perish'd, each alone.
> But I beneath a rougher sea,
>   And whelm'd in deeper gulphs than he.

Written in 1799, 'The Castaway' can be read in the light of Foucault's pronouncement on Hölderlin:

> It seems to me that a change was produced in the relationship of language to its indefinite repetition at the end of the eighteenth century – nearly coinciding with the moment in which the works of language became what they are now for us, that is, literature. This is the time (or very nearly so) when Hölderlin became aware, to the point of blindness, that he could only speak in the space marked by the disappearance of the gods and that language could only depend on its own power to keep death at a distance.[46]

Cowper's final poem bears out the full consequences of his fateful dream of 1773. The dream-word of 1773 reverses traditional versions of inspiration: the message brings not exaltation but despair. The collapse of transcendental inspiration and the removal of a sense of the divine results in an existential consciousness: 'we perish'd, each alone.'

Discussing the poem, Vincent Newey recognises the significance of the *deus absconditus* theme.[47] Nevertheless, quoting Charlotte Brontë's *Shirley*, he comments, "Cowper found relief in writing 'The Castaway'." It must have alleviated the pressure of his melancholia'.[48] Against this conjecture must be balanced the distance between 'The Castaway' and Cowper's own assertion in 1780 that 'with a pen in my hand, if I am able to write at all, I find myself gradually relieved' (I, 366). By the late 1790s, there was no question of any such practice. 'The Castaway' announces Coleridge's 'Dejection: An Ode', written some three years later. Wordsworth, in his *Ode*: Intimations of Immortality, had written,

> To me alone there came a thought of grief:
> A timely utterance gave that thought relief
>   And I again am strong

Replying to this point in the 'Dejection Ode', Coleridge broke with the therapeutic assumptions of moral psychology:

> A grief without a pang, void, dark and drear
> A stifled, drowsy, unimpassioned grief,
> Which finds no natural outlet, no relief,
> In word or sigh or tear –

Dejection is perpetuated in a language which does nothing to undo it.

Whereas *The Task*, as therapeutic exercise, is a sustained act of discursive production, 'The Castaway', as poem of despair, reproduces the subject in a single, non-discursive image of utter abandonment: 'misery still delights to trace / its semblance in another's face.'

All the evidence indicates that Cowper's final years were unrelievedly black: we can only guess at whether the writing of the poem might have produced in him a reflex of relief, but the poem itself, in confronting his situation, reproduces his utter desolation. The fate of Anson, the castaway, is a mirror which, far from therapeutically relieving the poet, reveals to him his own negative condition of anomie.

'The Castaway' anticipates the introspective lyrics which John Clare wrote in Northampton asylum in the nineteenth century. Cowper's narrative of a sailor swept overboard in high seas is an extended metaphor for the poet, who is 'whelm'd in deeper gulfs than he.' Clare, in the most famous of the asylum lyrics, '"I Am"', inhabits the metaphor itself:

> Into the nothingness of scorn and noise,
> Into the living sea of waking dreams,
> Where there is neither sense of life or joys,
> But the vast shipwreck of my life's esteems;

In this development, an interiorised madness, precisely because it exceeds therapeutic resources, becomes fully available to literature.

6 John Clare: 'Literature has destroyed my head and brought me here'

Clare was the son of an impoverished and illiterate rural labourer, and was himself a labourer for a good part of his life. His first volume of verse, *Poems descriptive of rural life and scenery, by John Clare, a Northamptonshire peasant* (1820) was published in time to catch the tail-end of a vogue for 'peasant poetry,' following the success of Burns and Bloomfield. But Clare's subsequent volumes of verse, written in an increasingly distinctive voice, met with a diminishing response from his contemporaries. Such attention as he received after 1830 was largely on account of his pathetic biographical circumstances, culminating in his descent into madness.

Clare attempted at various times to tell his own story. A short autobiography, *Sketches in the life of John Clare*, was written in 1821 at the request of John Taylor, his publisher. He set out to write a full autobiography in the 1820s, but encountered difficulties connected with his refusal to construct an ideal narrative of the self:[1] 'Wrote 2 more pages of my life   find it not so easy as I at first imagind as I am anxious to give an undisguised narrative of facts good & bad   in the last sketch which I wrote for Taylor I had little vanitys about me to gloss over failings which I shall take care to lay bare for readers' (*Prose*, 115).[2] With the eventual onset of madness, the notion of a narrated life lost all meaning. Dr Nesbitt, the superintendent of Northampton asylum for much of Clare's time there, noted 'If there was one subject more than another that he had an aversion to it was biography – he designated it a parcel of lies.'[3] It is possible to trace, throughout his life, a gradual depletion of the very possibility of autobiography: his madness possesses the logic of an inexorable loss of self.

As a rural labourer in early nineteenth-century Northamptonshire, Clare witnessed the effects of agrarian capitalism at first hand, most notably through the enclosure of his native parish of Helpston. The elegies Clare wrote in 1832 lamenting the loss of his native environ-ment suggest that his historical experience of dispossession is implicated in his madness: 'Strange scenes mere shadows are to me / Vague unpersonifying things' (MC, 217). Testimony such as this is impressive, but it should be handled cautiously. Clare is not merely a victim of historical circumstances over which he has no control: his encounters with both literacy and literature (themselves historical in character) are determining factors in his experience of madness. One of his last recorded remarks in Northampton asylum, near the end of his life, was 'Literature has destroyed my head and brought me here.'[4]

The transformation of Clare's local map coincided with his appren-ticeship to poetry. The enclosure of Helpston was completed in 1820, the year that Clare published the *Poems descriptive*. *Sketches in the life*, recounting the writer's efforts to educate himself and become a published poet, was written a year later. The *Sketches* remained unpublished in Clare's lifetime, nevertheless he wrote with an eye to the effect his story would have on a better-off audience: as a narrative of self-improvement it is not above colluding with the socio-historical changes which overtook his environment. As literacy opens up the world of knowledge to the young Clare, the family's 'once unletterd hut' is

> wonderfully changd in its appearance to a schoolroom   the old table, which old as it was doubtless never was honourd with higher employ-ment all its days then the convenience of bearing at meal times the luxury of a barley loaf or dish of potatoes, was now covered with the rude begg[in]ings of scientifical requ[i]sitions, pens, ink, and paper one hour, jobbling the pen at sheep hooks and tarbottles, and another trying on a slate a knotty question in Numeration, or Pounds, Shillings, and Pence (JCAW, 4)

Clare's quest for self-education superimposes an alien and abstract perspective on his homely surroundings. At the same time, the calculation of entirely notional pounds, shillings and pence underlines the poverty of these surroundings: 'my mother woud often stop her wheel or look off from her work to urge with a smile

of the warmest rapture in my fathers face her prophesy of my
success, saying "shed be bound, I shoud one day be able to reward
them with my pen, for the trouble they had taken in giveing me
schooling"' (JCAW, 4). This occasions a celebratory prolepsis: 'I
have to return hearty thanks to a kind providence in bringing her
prophecy to pass and giving me the pleasure of being able to stay
the storm of poverty and smoothen their latter days.'

As the narrative of his boyhood continues, however, this happy
outcome seems increasingly unlikely. While he is still a child, Clare's
literacy becomes a factor which isolates him from the community at
large: 'About this time (. . .) I began to wean off from my companions and sholl about the woods and fields on Sundays alone'
(JCAW, 4). In a world where old ways and livings were in a state
of upheaval, the writer himself was encountering forms of literate
individualism which set him apart from the village community.
These new perceptual forms are embodied in the narrative of the
Sketches itself: as an instance of secular autobiography, and as an
edifying story of economic self-help, *Sketches in the life* is typical of
a number of early nineteenth-century working-class autobiographies.[5] In his survey of these, David Vincent comments, 'The
entry into the realm of literature was frequently accompanied by a
rejection of the reader's previous associates.' This tended to
precipitate 'a permanent crisis of relations between the readers and
those with whom they lived and worked.'[6] Clare's account of the
reactions provoked in the village community by his solitary pursuit
of literature places a question mark against Mrs Clare's hopes for the
future: 'conjectures filld the village about my future destinations on
the stage of life, some fanc[y]ing it symtoms of lunacy and that my
mothers prophecys would be verified to her sorrow' (JCAW, 4).
Notwithstanding Clare's self-congratulatory prolepsis, the community's alternative point of view lingers as a choric comment,
warning of the dangers inherent in the project of 'improvement,' and
contesting its likely outcome.

In 1831, frustrated by Taylor's lack of interest in his recent work,
Clare began to assemble a large collection of his unpublished and
new poems, vainly hoping to see them into print through his own
efforts. He entitled the manuscript collection *The midsummer cushion*,
and wrote a prefatory note explaining that the title derived from a
local tradition: 'It is a very old custom among villagers in summer
time to stick a piece of greensward full of field flowers & place it as
an ornament in their cottages which ornaments are called

Midsummer Cushions.' As the poems in the collection 'are field flowers of humble pretentions & of various hues I thought the above cottage custom gave me an oppertunity to select a title that was not inapplicable to the contents of the Volume' (MC, 1).

While Clare was at work on the manuscript, circumstances resulted in his moving, with his wife and children, to a cottage in nearby Northborough. The effect of this move was one of alienation: the group of poems which mark the event, 'Remembrances', 'The Flitting' and 'Decay', were included in *The midsummer cushion*. These poems express Clare's sense of personal devastation. In 'The Flitting' he experiences the move as a diminution of lived reality:

> Ive left my own old home of homes
> Green fields & every pleasant place
> The summer like a stranger comes
> I pause & hardly know her face
> . . .
> I sit me in my corner chair
> That seems to feel itself from home
> & hear bird music here and there
> From awthorn hedge & orchard come
> I hear but all is strange & new
> (MC, 216)

Far from resembling a living flower, or perpetuating a local custom in the form of a 'midsummer cushion,' poetry becomes a process of loss: 'O words are poor receipts for what time hath stole away.' Under these conditions, literature comes to seem part of an encroachment of urban fashion which is destroying both nature and tradition. In 'The Flitting', the unhappy poet seeks for consolation in books, but in vain,

> For books they follow fashions new
> & throw all old esteems away
> In crowded streets flowers never grew
> But many there hath died away
> (MC, 217)

Poetry itself is implicated in the loss of Clare's childhood world. 'Remembrances', one of the three elegies of 1832, is anticipated by an early poem, 'Helpston Green'. Here, the changes occurring in a landscape familiar to the poet from childhood initiate a self-consciously subjective departure:

The uplifted ax no mercy yields
But strikes a fatal blow

When ere I muse along the plain
And mark where once they grew
Rememberance wakes her busy train
And brings past scenes to view
(JC, 62)

These gently melancholic memories are no match for the urgently painful 'Remembrances' of 1832. Neither, however, are they altogether different in kind. In both poems, loss initiates a self-consciously subjective mode. When Clare focuses his attention on nature as that which is specifically given, then the 'I' of the poem is usually able to turn receptively outwards. But, as immediate objects of perception become remembered ones, a sense of the immediacy of outward reality is diminished, and the poet is confronted with the inward meanings of displacement and loss. In 'Helpston Green', the passage of time and the loss of scenes associated with childhood already hint at a loss of identity:

For all the cropping that does grow
Will so efface the scene
That after times will hardly know
It ever was a green
(JC, 63)

John Barrell has argued that, in this poem, Clare's response to the despoliation of his childhood environment is blurred by his dependence upon eighteenth-century models: Clare must unlearn these models before his own distinctive representation of environment can emerge.[7] This, however, is not simply a negative process of unlearning. Clare encountered the subjective themes of memory and regret in poems by Gray, Collins, Goldsmith and Wordsworth among others. In 1821 he wrote verse accounts of visionary dreams ('The Nightmare'; 'The Dream') under the direct influence of De Quincey's *Confessions of an English opium eater*.[8] 'Clare was a prodigious imitator from the earliest years and a great deal of his work bears very obvious intertextual traces of other authors':[9] Clare does not disappear behind the intertext, and what he learned from literary models included a poetical discourse of introspective subjectivity which he developed over the following two decades. Where in 'Helpston Green' we encounter borrowed literary mannerisms ('Ye injured fields'), in 'Remembrances' we encounter a subjective discourse of emotion and memory which determines the poem as a specifically personal and autobiographical utterance.

In 'Remembrances', the poet's unplaced discourse is thrown into contrast with local dialect terms. As he bids farewell to an oral lexicon which will largely disappear from his displaced verse of the 1830s, the division between orality and literacy is formalised by the quotation marks which set apart the dialect words:

> I thought them all eternal when by Langley bush I lay
> I thought them joys eternal when I used to shout & play
> On its bank at 'clink & bandy' 'chock' & 'taw' and ducking stone
> Where silence sitteth now on the wild heath as her own
> Like a ruin of the past all alone
>
> (MC, 369)

The silence of the penultimate line accords with the literacy of the poet's discourse. As a sign of this, we note the muting of the 'e' in 'Remembrances'. In the manuscript of 'Helpston Green' Clare had spelled the word as he no doubt pronounced it: 'rememberance' ('Rememberance wakes her busy train' – Taylor emended the spelling in the published version). In the silent discourse of subjective memory, the lexis is not in fact sounded, and so is deprived of its constitutive orality. The dialect words are displayed in this discourse as in an archive – the archive of personal remembrance, no less than that of the collector of local folklore which Clare had become.[10]

The child's oral lexis is characterised by an ostensive concreteness and immediacy: if the process of enclosure destroys the referential ground of that lexis, then the acquisition of a literate and subjective discourse provides an all too appropriate means of expressing silence and loss. While 'Remembrances' is a lament for the lost world of childhood, the very timbre of the lament institutes a rupture with that world. In boyhood, the poet is a pre-literate Adam, orally naming his new world and so creating it:

> While I held my little plough though twas but a willow twig
> & drove my team along made of nothing but a name
> 'Gee hep' & 'hoit' & 'woi' (. . .)

The child's verbal activity is reversed as the self-consciously literate adult names in writing what is being lost or destroyed. In this way, his poetry cannot but participate in the process of dissolution:[11] '– O I never call to mind / These pleasant names of places but I leave a sigh behind' (MC, 369). The process of dissolution culminates in the sublime lyrics written in Northampton Asylum.

Clare's earliest compositions imitated his father's oral repertoire, but in discovering 'literature' he encountered a mode of writing which was much more radically counterposed to the orality of the vernacular tradition:

> I think I was 13 years of age (. . .) this summer I met with a fragment of Thompsons Seasons   a young man, by trade a weaver, much older than myself, then in the village, show'd it me   I knew nothing of blank verse nor ryhme either otherwise than by the trash of Ballad Singers, but I still remember my sensations in reading the opening of Spring   I cant say the reason why, but the following lines made my heart twitter with joy   'Come gentle Spring ethereal mildness come' (JCAW, 9)

Clare remained faithful to a native and inherited folk tradition, but he also sought to take on board the sublime concerns of the literature of Sensibility. In 'The Fate of Genius', he creates a Rousseauesque fiction of himself as a poet-genius who, misunderstood by his community, communes with nature in solitude: 'Muttering to cattle – aye and even flowers / As one in visions claimd his talk for hours' (JC, 82). The poem gives the community's view of the 'rustic genius':

> We wonderd many times as well we might
> And doubted often if his mind was right
> Een childern startled from his oddness ran
> And shund his wanderings as 'the crazy man'
>   (JC, 81)

Clare's assumption of a non-traditional and literate voice complicates the issue of identity. The borrowings of 'Helpston Green', more than the debts of an apprentice poet, are a stage in Clare's encounter with concepts of self which, as mediated by eighteenth- and early nineteenth-century literary culture, are 'creative' and inwardly oriented. These concepts open up for Clare new practices of subjective writing, but, at the same time, they destabilise more familiar discourses of identity. Clare's 1821 visionary poems, 'The Dream' and 'The Nightmare', suggest how disruptive the acquisition of a Romantic discourse of subjectivity was for him. After writing 'The Dream', he stated, 'I mustn't do no more terrible things yet they stir me up to to such a pitch that leaves a disrelish for my old accustomd wanderings after nature' (*Letters*, 132).[12]

The kind of cultural simile which we find in 'Remembrances' -
'hollow trees like pulpits' - is much less in evidence in the poems
which Clare wrote in Northborough between 1832 and 1837. Such
metaphorical images familiarise nature in human or homelike terms,
yet the linked catastrophes of enclosure and displacement blight
Clare's sense of nature as a sphere of cohabitation. In 'The Mouse's
Nest', a representative poem of this period, the poet's encounter with
a female mouse feeding her brood is blundering and alienated:

> I found a ball of grass among the hay
> and proged it as I passed and went away
> And when I looked I fancy somthing stirred,
> And turned agen and hoped to catch the bird
> When out an old mouse bolted in the wheats
> With all her young ones hanging at her teats
> She looked so odd and so grotesque to me,
> I ran and wondered what the thing could be
> And pushed the knapweed bunches where I stood
> When the mouse hurried from the crawling brood
> The young ones squeaked and when I went away
> She found her nest again among the hay
> The water o'er the pebbles scarce could run
> And broad old cesspools glittered in the sun
>   (JC, 263)

The natural world becomes perverse to the displaced poet. Taken
unawares, his ironic bewilderment measures his distance from what
he observes. It is instructive to compare this with one of Wordsworth's most famous forays into nature, 'I wandered lonely as a
cloud.' This poem begins outdoors with the sight of the 'host of
golden daffodils,' but concludes indoors:

> For oft when on my couch I lie
> In vacant or in pensive mood,
> They flash upon that inward eye
> Which is the bliss of solitude;
> And then my heart with pleasure fills,
> And dances with the daffodils.

Wordsworth's and Clare's different experiences of nature are
qualified by different contexts. Wordsworth's explorations of nature
tend to culminate in an authentication of the subjective self. In
Clare's poem, any such possibility is confounded by the poet's error
- the casually confident assumption that the nest is a bird's nest.

What then ensues is both unexpected and out of the ordinary, hence
its grotesque character. But the specific circumstance also suggests
that the sight of the mouse running, 'with all her young ones hanging at her teats' is so insistently odd and disturbing in relation to
the self – 'so grotesque *to me*' – because it is *unheimlich* – uncanny,
but also unhomely, in the etymological sense which Freud drew on
in German: the maternal function becomes an unnatural sight as a
consequence of the human subject's violation of the nest.

The mouse returns to its nest, but there seems to be no possibility
that the poet can recover a disrupted home. In 'I wandered lonely
as a cloud', Wordsworth's interiorisation of nature corresponds to
the domestic interior wherein it occurs: it is the poet's couch which
enables the recreation of an exterior scene of nature in terms of the
poet's 'inward eye.' Here, Wordsworth performs his *accouchement*,
giving birth to the 'egotistical sublime' of his poetry. This outcome
possesses the confident self-reflexiveness which is the mark of a
psychologically self-aware subject. Just as the material conditions
which locate the private Wordsworthian interior are absent in
Clare's life, so there is no context in his poetry which might locate
a comparable measure of interiorised self-identity. The homeless self
of the Northborough poems is exposed and fragile.

'The Mouse's Nest' is typical of the poems of this period in the
vacancy of its subjective position. The first-person protagonist who
steps out so confidently goes nowhere: we are simply told that 'I
went away.' A projected narrative of discovery and self-definition
unfolds in terms of loss and puzzlement. The rift in nature caused
by an intrusive human presence corresponds to an insecurity and
vulnerability of identity. Only when the disrupted and disruptive
protagonist has absented himself can nature reformulate itself as
habitat: 'when I went away / She found her nest again among the
hay.' The paratactic final couplet, suspending discursive closure,
conveys an environment now free from human interference: 'The
water o'er the pebbles scarce could run / And broad old cesspools
glistened in the sun.' The poet absents himself as protagonist from
this environment because the relationship between nature and man
is one of mutual exteriority. 'The Mouse's Nest' is self-emptying, and
seems to renounce any designs which poetry itself might have on
nature.

II

In 1837 Clare's deteriorating mental condition caused him to be placed in High Beech asylum, a private madhouse in Essex, under the care of Matthew Allen, a practitioner of moral treatment. Clare was seemingly a model patient, but he came to detest High Beech. In 1841 he escaped and, without money, travelled back to Northborough on foot, a journey of some eighty miles. His aim was to find Mary Joyce, who had in fact died some three years previously. For a brief period Mary had been Clare's childhood sweetheart, and in his adult life she came increasingly to represent the Eden of his boyhood world: in High Beech he thought of her as his 'first wife.'

Clare recorded the journey from Epping to Northborough in a prose document written immediately on completion of his long tramp, the *Journey out of Essex*. It begins as a series of diary entries:

> July 18–1841 – Sunday Felt very melancholly – went a walk on the forest in the afternoon – fell in with some gipseys one of whom offered to assist in my escape (. . .)

> July 19 – Monday Did nothing

> July 20 – (. . .) having only honest courage and myself in my army I led the way and my troops soon followed (JCAW, 153)

Through a combative advance movement into enemy territory, Clare determines to deal with a hostile reality on its own terms: 'Reconnitered the rout the Gipsey pointed out and found it a legible one to make a movement.' But martial rhetoric is abandoned as the diary becomes a narrative proper. Thereafter the journey north is told in a sparse, neutral language which conveys a state of increasing dereliction (Clare wrote his account in a state of exhaustion immediately after his journey had reached its conclusion). Half-way to Northborough, the soles of his shoes were flapping open and one of his feet was hurt by gravel: at this point, 'the odd houses on the road began to light up and show the inside tennants lot very comfortable and my outside lot very uncomfortable and wretched' (JCAW, 157). The cosy domestic interior represents everything from which he is excluded, but he does not dwell on his sorry state: movement is the overriding concern: 'I was forced to brush on pennyless and be thankfull I had a leg to move on.' The intervening terrain is unrelated to self-identity. The route the gipsies had proposed to him at High Beech may well have been 'legible' in terms of the network of national routes which were now in place. For the most part Clare travels along the Great North Road (the future A1), part of the turnpike road system which had been developed in the eighteenth century, enabling the rapid expansion of a national market economy: at the same time, it diluted local and regional characteristics.[13] The new roads, however, suit Clare's purpose: at one point he falls briefly into company with a gipsy woman who advises him to take a short cut, but he rejects her vernacular knowledge: 'I thanked her and told her I should keep to the road.' The landscape through which his journey takes him is an historicised and linearised one, but like this landscape, the narrative of the journey is an empty space to be traversed; self-presence and self-identity depend on the destination in view – home and Mary. The minimalism of a narrative which is now devoid of metaphors expresses the condition of the subject, reduced to a bare will to movement in an alien, inhospitable territory:

> on the third day I satisfied my hunger by eating the grass by the road side which seemd to taste something like bread   I was hungry and eat heartily till I was satisfied and in fact the meal seemed to do me good   the next and last day (. . .) I took to chewing tobacco and eat the quids when I had done and I was never hungry afterwards (JCAW, 159)

Clare's uncomplaining satisfaction with this sustenance is typical of his unintrospective mode of narration. One of the biblical paraphrases which he wrote later that year directly relates a sense of self-loss to a lack of interest in food and eating. Depersonalisation is expressed as a hollowed-out self: so empty is it that physical nourishment becomes superfluous:

> My heart is smitten like the grass
> That withered lies and dead
> And I so lost to what I was
> Forget to eat my bread.
>   (LPJC, 137)

The distance the journey seeks to overcome is, in the event, irreducible: Clare's story of exhaustion and loss becomes a loss and exhaustion of story: 'I was (. . .) soon at Northborough but Mary was not there neither could I get any information about her further than the old story of her being dead six years ago which might be taken from a bran new old Newspaper printed a dozen years ago but I took no notice of the blarney having seen her myself a twelvemonth ago

alive and well and as young as ever' (JCAW, 160). Clare's narrative,
far from recovering a meaningful reality, terminates in failure and
disillusion. This is his last exercise in autobiographical prose: his
attempt to determine himself as an historical identity, first projected
in the *Sketches*, is finally played out.

Clare's flight from High Beech and his recording of that event,
occurred when he was working on his Byronic poems, *Don Juan* and
Child Harold. The *Child Harold* song 'I've wandered many a weary
mile' recapitulates the journey home:

> I've wandered many a weary mile
> Love in my heart was burning
> To seek a home in Mary's smile
> But cold is love's returning
> . . .
> No ray of hope my life beguiles
> I've lost love home and Mary
>   (LPJC, 43–4)

In the notebook which Clare started using after his return to
Northborough (Northampton MS 6 – it includes fair copies of the
two Byronic poems and the narrative of the journey)[14] he
comments that this song was written 'directly after my return to
Northborough last Friday evening.' With the failure of his expedition, Clare had no alternative but to confront an irreparable frac-
ture in his world. The song is a lyrical conversion of the narrative's
bleak conclusion: 'July 24th 1841 Returned home out of Essex and
found no Mary – her and her family are as nothing to me now
though she herself was once the dearest of all – "and how can I
forget"' (JCAW, 160). On July 27, Clare wrote a letter to Mary
which forms an epilogue to the narrative: 'Though my home is no
home to me my hopes are not entirely hopeless while even the
memory of Mary lives so near me' (JCAW, 160–1). This epitomises
in prose the subjective mode of *Child Harold* – a circular, self-
consuming dialectic, revolving round the ever-tantalising figure of
Mary.

On the final page of the *Journey*, Clare quotes a couplet from
Byron's 'Sonnet on Chillon': 'May none those marks of my sad fate
efface / For they appeal from tyranny to God.' During this period
he identified with various individuals, most notably with Lord
Byron. Clare's editors have traced only a few minor poems dating
from the first three years of his residence in High Beech. If there was

a hiatus in Clare's production after the removal to High Beech in 1837, then it seems likely that Byron and his poetry were instrumental in his renewed activity in 1841. Cyrus Redding, the editor of a literary periodical, visited him early that year: 'he wanted books. On being asked what books, he said BYRON.'[15] Redding sent the requested volumes, and Clare commenced work on his two Byronic poems, *Don Juan* and *Child Harold*. These poems continue Clare's assimilation of a subjective discourse through intertextual engagement with other writers.

By 1841 he had reached a particularly painful threshold in his dealings with reality: his writings of this year reveal an individual who, for reasons of class and culture, lacks a psychological sense of identity and experiences self in terms of frustration and perplexity. Both *Don Juan* and *Child Harold* directly refer to the traumatic conditions in which he found himself, and it is probable that his work on them contributed to an increasing restlessness: the escape from High Beech coincided with his composition of the poems. For Cowper in 1783–4, *The Task* was a therapeutic exercise, but Clare's non-psychological discourse aggravated his sense of personal crisis.

Lynn Pearce has argued that the 1841 poems must be considered in terms of a dialogical multiplicity.[16] Certainly, Clare's Byronism cannot be reduced to a single formula. *Don Juan* and *Child Harold* provide a striking set of contrasts: in *Child Harold*, the poet exposes his inner, subjective concerns, but in *Don Juan*, written in a public rather than a private voice, he pushes aggressively outwards, reacting to his situation as inmate of a lunatic asylum. In an accompanying satire, he wrote,

> Nigh Leopards Hill stand All-ns hells
> The public know the same
> Where lady sods & buggers dwell
> To play the dirty game
>
> A man there is a prisoner there
> Locked up from week to week
>   (LPJC, 37)

Clare's squib disagrees bitterly with the general nineteenth-century view of moral treatment: 'The rule is gentleness – not force and galling chains.'[17] Allen's regime was in fact a liberal one, and Clare had little difficulty in escaping. He clarified his objections in a letter he wrote to Allen from Northborough (August 1841), 'the greatest annoyance in such places as yours are those servants styled keepers who often assumed as much authority over me as if I had been their prisoner & not likeing to quarrel I put up with it till I was weary of the place altogether' (*Letters*, 203). Clare's experience of moral treatment is consistent with his career as poet generally: Allen's treatment is the latest in a series of well-meant but authoritative interventions which Clare had suffered at the hands of social superiors, notably John Taylor and Lord Radstock. In the angry satire of *Don Juan*, the poet attacks the imposition of moral constraints: in particular he exposes the hypocrisy on which an imprisoning moral regime is founded. The 1841 poems assert that Allen's madhouse is a place of 'dirty sights' and low sexual misconduct – 'Earth hells or b-gg-r sh-ps or what you please.' *Don Juan* portrays Dr Allen collecting urine samples – 'for analysis, especially for signs of VD.'[18] In labelling the madhouse 'whoreshop' and 'buggershop,' Clare inverts the scene of medical and moral surveillance, revealing the obscene content hidden within the moral 'prison':

> Theres Doctor Bottle Imp who deals in urine
> A keeper of state prisons for the queen
> As great a man as is the Doge of Turin
> Yclept old A-ll-n – mad brained ladies curing
> Some p-x-d like Flora & but seldom clean
>
> (LPJC, 98)

Discussing the socio-historical context of nineteenth-century moral treatment, Andrew Scull argues that a therapy which implements an 'internalization of norms' is continuous with the organisation of social and ethical disciplines imposed by capitalist market relations:

> Just as the peasantry who formed the new industrial workforce were to be taught the 'rational' self-interest essential for the market system to work, the lunatics too were to be made over in the image of bourgeois rationality: defective human mechanisms were to be repaired so that they could once more compete in the marketplace. And finally, just as hard work and self-discipline were the keys to the success of the urban bourgeoisie from whose ranks Tuke came, so his moral treatment propounded these same qualities as a means of reclaiming the insane.[19]

Clare is caught at point where the ideological pressures which bear down on labour and lunacy intersect, but, written precisely from this point, *Don Juan* refuses the process of coercive internalisation. It does so not as 'literature,' but, on the contrary, as what must be described as 'anti-literature.'

In the nineteenth century, the writing of poetry was encouraged as a therapeutic activity in a number of lunatic asylums. In 1860, a French observer, Octave Delepierre, noted that 'In several of the great institutions for the insane which exist in the kingdom of Great Britain, the encouragement regularly given to literary composition has had the happiest results.'[20] Delepierre does not discuss the regimes which promoted these activities, but it is clear that the various asylum journals which were being produced at the time (one of them edited and published by the inmates themselves) were products of the asylum reform movement, inspired by the therapeutic ideal of moral treatment. The comment on moral treatment quoted above comes from a poem written in Hanwell asylum in 1843:

> No gloomy cells where sullen madness pines
> In squalid woe, where no glad sunlight shines,
> But here kind sympathy for fall'n reason reigns;
> The rule is gentleness – not force and galling chains.[21]

John Conolly, the leading Victorian proponent of reformed treatment of the insane, managed Hanwell from 1839 to 1843, and instituted radical changes in its running:[22] the stanza evidently celebrates his achievement. Another of the verses from Hanwell cited by Delepierre ('by John P____ whose moments of lucidity are rare, and who has been confined for some time') offers a more whimsical celebration of moral treatment:

> Sing, sing to the harp, to the year that is past;
> To the year now a coming, fill, fill to the brim;
> To the mistletoe bough, and the Christmas, the last –
> May the Christmas forthcoming, fly away half as fast!
> And, to him who promulged *Non-Coercion* to him
> Sing, sing to the harp, and fill up to the brim.[23]

Delepierre found evidence of derangement in the penultimate line, but it is undoubtedly a direct tribute to Conolly. Nevertheless the line throws into relief the conventional form and content of the rest of the stanza. Delepierre, in citing with approval samples of verse which are typically conventional, confirms the agenda that underlies the progressive character of moral treatment: 'the madman (. . .) must feel morally responsible for everything within him that may disturb morality and society.'[24] In the verse by 'John P.' the coercion imposed by a conventionally correct poetic form is abruptly highlighted by the poignant intervention of a heterogeneous personal message: 'to him who promulged *Non-coercion.*' The irony is superb, if unintentional.

In 1840 Dr Allen reported on Clare's condition in a letter to *The Times*: 'the moment he gets pen or pencil in hand he begins to write most beautiful poetic effusions.'[25] Clare seems to have produced very few of these 'beautiful effusions,' and, a year later, *Don Juan* might have been written expressly to repudiate Allen's complacent claim. Certainly there is a stark contrast between *Don Juan* and the sanctioned verses produced at Hanwell and other 'reformed' asylums. Clare's repudiation of the pressures of moral treatment is whole-hearted, and extends to the forms and procedures of literary decorum itself (an antagonism which should be read in the light of John Taylor's earlier efforts to 'normalise' Clare's idiosyncratic style for the benefit of a well-to-do readership). By virtue of Byron's satirical precedent, Clare's *Don Juan* is able to constitute itself as a grotesque inversion of 'literature.'

However confused he may have been at this time, Clare remained sharply aware of his situation. Byron directly provides him with a surrogate identity in *Don Juan*, but this is as much a gambit as a delusion. Tim Chilcott, in a cogent reading of *Don Juan*, asks 'to what extent is the poem a conscious address to another poem, and to what extent a manifestation of Clare's insanity?'[26] *Don Juan* in fact plays these alternatives off against each other: madness and lucidity are not mutually exclusive:

> Lord Byron poh – the man wot rite the werses
> . . .
> And still in Allens madhouse caged and living
> . . .
> Though laurel wreaths my brow did ne'er environ
> I think myself as great a bard as Byron.
>   (LPJC, 99–100)

The poem (which includes various theatrical references) acts out a self-image – sexual and social iconoclast, bestselling poet – as reflected in the mirror-poem provided by Byron. The poet, assuming his Byronesque identity as a role which is performed for an audience, directly addresses the poem to a prospective readership. At points, it becomes a series of one-liners as the poet improvises his performance of the ironic self-consciousness of Byron's *Don Juan*:

I love good fellowship and wit and punning
I love 'true love' and God my taste defend
I hate most damnably all sorts of cunning
I love the Moor and Marsh and Ponders end –
I do not like the song of 'cease your funning'
I love a modest wife and trusty friend
– Bricklayers want lime as I want rhyme for fillups
– So here's a health to sweet Eliza Phillips
                                                    (LPJC, 95)

Chilcott acknowledges that *Don Juan* marks a 'radical develop-ment,'[27] but concludes nevertheless that it attests to an 'erosion of understanding [which] destroys all sense of nucleus.'[28] Given the search for a nucleus, such a conclusion is unavoidable, yet the *Don Juan* poet does not lapse from 'nuclear' norms of expression so much as he contests them. The poem which results, far from attesting to a disintegration of identity, stages a parodic improvisation of iden-tity. At Northampton in 1844, Clare was recorded as saying, 'I'm John Clare now. I was Byron and Shakespeare formerly. At different times you know I'm different people – that is the same person with different names.'[29] This reflects back on *Don Juan*, tending to confirm it as the performance of an identity which is always aware of its own provisional and fictional status.[30]

This play of identity specifically involves issues of value. Situated in an urban milieu, *Don Juan* seeks, with transparent cynicism, to sell itself. It begins by matching poets with whores:

'Poets are born' – & so are whores – the trade is
Grown universal – in these canting days
Women of fashion must of course be ladies
& whoreing is the business that still pays
Playhouses Ball rooms – there the masquerade is
                                                    (LPJC, 89)

The contemptuous reference to female venality reflects directly back on the status of the poem itself. Clare's notebooks include advertisements for the Byron poems: 'Speedily will be published / The Sale of Old Wigs and sundries.' The poem, which foregrounds the monetary theme of buying and selling (Carlyle's 'cash nexus'), markets itself as a commodity:

Now i'n't this canto worth a single pound
From anybodys pocket who will buy . . .
. . .
So reader now the money till unlock it
& buy the book & help to fill my pocket.
(LPJC, 100–1)

Self-advertisement merges with exhibitionism. The filled pocket of
the final line may not be intended as a sexual pun, but the poet
puns elsewhere by cross-referring consumer goods, money ('blunt')
and sexual wares:

Childern are fond of sucking sugar candy
& maids of sausages – larger the better
Shopmen are fond of good sigars & brandy
And I of blunt – & if you change the letter
To C or K it would be quite as handy
(LPJC, 92)

Don Juan is aggressively anti-Romantic: in a period much
concerned with versions of sublimity, its obscenity is desublimatory.
It presents a non-interiorised, self-aggrandising mode which is
opposed to the interiorised and fluctuating self of Child Harold. The
concern with market value presents a strategy of physical sexuality
and gain which is counterpointed with Child Harold's oscillation
between sublime idealisation and loss.

Don Juan holds up a mocking glass to the hopeful poet who,
twenty years previously, had written the story of how he overcame
the disadvantages of class and education to achieve his vocation.
The economic concerns of the poem recycle Clare's portrait of his
education in Sketches in the life, working at 'a knotty question in
(. . .) Pounds, Shillings, and Pence.' In resuming the financial theme,
Don Juan provides an ironic comment on Mrs Clare's prophecy of
success in the Sketches: '"shed be bound, I shoud one day be able
to reward them with my pen."' Don Juan's injunction to buy merely
serves to underline the fact that Clare's pen had not brought any
significant financial rewards. As though acknowledging that the
pursuit of poetry is indeed a pursuit of loss, Clare here brutalises
literature, writing a poem of extreme and provocative crudity. Only
through a desecration of 'literature' and its values can the poet-
whore service the market.

In the era of copyright and 'possessive individualism,'[31] poetry
enters into new relationships with the self of the poet. From his

boyhood, Clare knew well that the 'higher' value of poetry could not be divorced from its value as private property: the *Sketches* includes a memorable account of the obstacles he had to overcome in order to obtain a copy of Thomson's *Seasons*.[32] This episode, along with others recounted in the *Sketches*, should remind us that Clare's class position tended to exclude him from literature in the most literal sense – as property. In High Beech he once more found himself chronically underprivileged with regard to this form of private property, having to beg the works of Byron. Correspondingly, it is only as Byron that he is able to address the poetry-reading public with an injunction to buy: his own name, John Clare, is utterly lacking in value. In a capitalist marketplace where identity is correlated with value, then the use value of an identity gives way to its exchange value – hence the poet's changes of identity in a poem which commodifies itself (there is no comparable system of exchange in *Child Harold*, a poem which eschews the world of the marketplace).

As the prospect of financial independence vanished in the 1820s, Clare reflected bitterly on the poverty of his class: 'for the poor have many oppressors and no voice to be heard above them' (JC, 446). This statement acquires a suggestive resonance in the light of his situation in 1841, when he considered himself a direct victim of oppression in High Beech and wrote out much of his anger in the adopted voice of Byron. It is as though Clare's lack of marketable value as poet directly impinges on his loss of inner self-value. It is only through an act of theft that some measure of self-value can be had, by adopting Byron's identity and 'plagiarising' his poetry. The advertisements he wrote for *Don Juan* and *Child Harold* ('Speedily will be published . . .'; 'In a short time will be published . . .') echo the advertisement which, as the *Sketches* tell us, he wrote with such difficulty in an attempt to get his early poems into print. He had, in the long term, failed to sell himself as a poet, but he might sell himself as Byron.

Clare's identification with Byron and his writing of *Don Juan* and *Child Harold* provide a negative proof of the extent to which the value of poetry increases proportionally with the value of the individual name whose property it is. In their very literality, these identifications demystify the empathetic identification of middle-class poetry readers with the 'romantic' image of the poet. In a materialist age, Byron and Burns (while they both wrote subversive satirical poems) represented 'spiritual' values in which the reader could participate by consuming their poetry. But, in the name of Byron the satirist, the poet-whore of *Don Juan* systematically denies the higher, spiritual values of poetry through emphasising the material values of the literary marketplace.

It would be a mistake to see Clare's literary – and literal – identifications with Byron and Burns as a wholly individual aberration. In his *Home memories and recollections of a life* (1886), Benjamin Brierley, looking back on his life as a self-educated labourer, remembered his early literary affectations: they are strikingly close to Clare:

> I had begun to take solitary walks on summer evenings in company with Burns and Lord Byron. I could recite all the choice passages in 'Childe Harold', and repeat all the more popular songs of the gifted ploughman. I was aspiring to be a poet myself, and went so far as to adopt the 'Byron tie' and try to look melancholy.[33]

David Vincent, who cites this passage, comments, 'all the [working class] readers were fired by the possibility of making contact not just with the writings but the personalities of the great literary figures.'[34] In taking this 'contact' a stage or so further than most, Clare's identifications bring to the surface the contradiction that underlies the self-conscious posing of Brierley and others. The society that emerged in the nineteenth century was a club which valorised individualistic ideologies while simultaneously barring membership to the labouring classes. Clare's Byronic poems, *Don Juan* and *Child Harold*, explore this contradiction as an antithesis between, respectively, an ideologically radical assertion of identity and an existentially radical loss of identity.

The negative pole of the antithesis is set out in the opening stanzas of *Child Harold*. Whereas the poet of *Don Juan* casts himself in the high-status role of a recognised poet, *Child Harold* begins by dissolving this identification and returning poetry to the anonymity of the oral tradition. Rural labour is opposed to the sexual, political and financial dealings of the city: 'real' poetry is opposed to the literary marketplace:

> Many are poets – though they use no pen
> To show their labours to the shuffling age
> Real poets must be truly honest men
> Tied to no mongrel laws on flatterys page
> No zeal have they for wrong or party rage
> – The life of labour is a rural song
>   (LPJC, 40)

An affirmation of pastoral song frees the poem from the relentless commodification of *Don Juan*, and reconciles the poet with language itself. Where this has been reduced to the status of graffito in the urban context of *Don Juan*, *Child Harold* returns language to its 'origin' as transcendental logos:

> & he who studies natures volume through
> & reads it with a pure unselfish mind
> Will find Gods power all round in every view
> As one bright vision of the almighty mind
> (LPJC, 42)

However this 'return to source' entails passivity. In *Don Juan* the poet's discourse, for all its apparent randomness, is self-consciously assertive, enabling him to protest his lack of freedom: 'I wish all honest men were out of prison' (LPJC, 91). By comparison the *Child Harold* poet, rejecting the polemical mode of *Don Juan*, comes to terms with his situation by claiming inner freedom:

> Summer morning is risen
> & to even it wends
> & still Im in prison
> Without any friends
> . . .
> Still the forest is round me
> Where the trees bloom in green
> As if chains ne'er had bound me
> Or cares ne'er had been
> (LPJC, 40–1)

But this is the 'freedom' of powerlessness.[35] Turning to nature, the poet assumes an inert and contemplative posture: 'I love to stretch my length 'tween earth and sky / And see the inky foliage oer me wave.' Such passivity leaves the self defenceless in the threatening environment of the madhouse. The hyperbolically masculine egotism of *Don Juan* is a mode of defence, one way in which a painfully exposed and vulnerable self can sustain itself in the alienating conditions of 'Allens hell.' Two stanzas in *Child Harold* resemble *Don Juan* in their language and concerns:

> My life hath been one love – no blot it out
> My life hath been one chain of contradictions
> Madhouses Prisons wh-re shops (. . .)
> (LPJC, 45)

However, the *Child Harold* poet looks inward to confront a shattered life. In *Don Juan*, bigamy is a matter of self-assertion (LPJC,
100): in *Child Harold*, by contrast, the absence of the two wives coincides with the poet's unfreedom and powerlessness:

> abscence claims them both and keeps them too
> & locks me in a shop in spite of law
> Among a low lived set & dirty crew

While reaffirming lyrical utterance, the poet must also admit the
extent of his vulnerability to the conditions in which he finds
himself. The 'dirt' which is encountered on its own terms in *Don
Juan* is here repudiated: the 'refined' poet seeks to direct attention
away from a situation which is too appalling to contemplate:

> Here let the Muse oblivions curtain draw
> & let man think – for God hath often saw
> Things here too dirty for the light of day
> For in a madhouse there exists no law –
> Now stagnant grows my too refined clay
> I envy birds their wings to flye away
>   (LPJC, 46)

In the succeeding stanzas the poet indeed turns away from the
madhouse and towards its grounds, with their adjacent scenes of
nature: 'How beautifull this hill of fern swells on' (this, as further
details confirm, is the rural setting of High Beech). Thus he returns
to nature as poetic source and consolation: 'I love thee nature in my
inmost heart.'

Again, *Don Juan*'s practice of literary defacement provides a
counter-image. The only flower to feature in the poem, if we except
the heterogeneous pastoral song which is inserted into it, is an
allegorically diseased city flower: 'Flora was p-x-d – and womans quite
as nasty.' The ideal poetic values of love and pastoralism are jointly
expelled in the urban context, so that the failure of nature or of
woman's love present no threat. But where, in *Child Harold*, the ideal
presence of the beloved founders in hope or memory, pastoral meaning founders too, leaving the self locked into contradiction:

> My hopes are all hopeless
> My skyes have no sun
> Winter fell in youths mayday
> And still lingers on
>   (LPJC, 41)

When the meanings of Mary and nature are called into question, poetry itself is unsettled by an inner crisis. In *Child Harold*, instability affects poetic discourse itself. With its intermingling of song-lyrics and Spenserian stanzas, as well as the self-subverting circularity of its themes, *Child Harold* presents itself to the reader as a labyrinth. Mary might provide a means of orientation for the poet, but the underlying unreliability of her image corrodes a seemingly positive indication: 'Mary thou ace of hearts thou muse of song / The pole star of my being *and decay*' (italics added). If the anti-poetry of *Don Juan* enables a provisional (improvisational) securing of identity, the poetry of *Child Harold* unfolds through the dispersal of identity. The fluctuations of the poem are not distinguishable from the fluctuations of the lyrical subject. In *Don Juan*, the poet is concerned with locating himself spatially: 'Muse tell me where I was / O – talk of turning.' This playful self-referentiality serves to reorient the poem while allowing its waywardness:

> But to our text again – and pray where is it
> Begin as parsons do at the beginning
> Take the first line friend and you cannot miss it
> 'Poets are born' and so are whores for sinning
>   (LPJC, 97)

This is a discourse which invents its continuity as it proceeds: discursive identity is projected as a surface which denies any hint of existential or affective depths. In *Child Harold* there is no comparable concern with a surface continuity: 'My life hath been one love – no blot it out / My life hath been one chain of contradictions.' Formal self-interruption doubles the thematic assertion of contradiction over unity. Chilcott has pointed out that *Child Harold* is a poem of continual oscillations which defeat any expectation of a progressive unfolding of meaning.[36] Indeed, its procedure not infrequently involves outright contradiction: statements made at one point – '& I shall find rest on her bosom agen' (LPJC, 42) – are cancelled by statements made elsewhere: 'Man meets no home within a womans breast' (LPJC, 55).

Eric Robinson, in his edition of the *Autobiographical writings* [JCAW], provides an intriguing variant reading of the Byronic lines quoted in other editions of the *Journey out of Essex*:

> Mary none those marks of my sad fate efface
> For they appeal from tyranny to God

The play between 'May' ('May none of those marks. . .') and 'Mary' converts the Byronic quotation into a personal reference to Mary Joyce. This transformation exemplifies the Byronism of *Child Harold*. Where *Don Juan* mimics an identity based on the charismatic image of Lord Byron, *Child Harold* opens out the self through the literary dimension of subjective lyrical verse. As the melancholy of Byron's *Child Harold* is assimilated to Clare's subjective concerns, it is 'literature' itself, in the privileged sense Romanticism gives to this term, which expresses the instability of subjective meaning through the dispersal of a given identity.[37] The Romantic literature of subjective affect emphasises inner values which are apparently countervalent to possessive individualism and its material affirmation of identity. The poet of *Child Harold* accordingly allies himself with the spiritual axis of interiority, in opposition to the *Don Juan* poet's self-consciously economic and acquisitive motives. However, for Clare in 1841, inner value is a problem without a solution; thus where, in *Don Juan*, modes of identity are conditional on modes of possession, *Child Harold* inscribes poetry as self-dispossession.

Child Harold, in short, resumes Clare's learning, through literature, of a writing which is appropriate to a subjective experience of absence and loss. But where, in 1832, the poetic discourse of 'Remembrances' was not itself destabilised by a crisis that could be attributed to external forces ('Inclosure like a Buonaparte. . .'), in *Child Harold*, the poet takes as poetic subject the ebb and flow of inner emotions which are continually re-enfolded and dispersed by the unstable meanings of literature itself.

For the *Child Harold* poet, these meanings are primarily manifested through the figure not of Byron but of Mary. The gathering intensity of Clare's emotional investment in Mary Joyce while in High Beech is inversely proportional to the brevity of his boyhood acquaintance with her. Before 1841, her most significant appearances in his writings are in his renderings of dream visions. In 'The Nightmare' (1821) the dreamer meets with an 'angel guide' who is eventually identified as Mary (*PJC*, 407). In 1832, shortly after the move to Northborough, Clare left a prose record of an encounter in dream with a female 'Guardian spirit' whom he recognises from previous dreams (*Prose*, 231–3). She remains unidentified, but it seems clear that Mary is implicated. The 1832 fragment insists on the actuality of this female vision: 'I cannot doubt her existence'; 'I believe in her ideally almost as fresh as reality'; 'the lady divinity left such a vivid picture of her visits in my sleep dreaming of dreams that I could no longer doubt her existence'. While the memory of

Mary Joyce was of crucial importance to Clare, his remembered experience of her individual reality was of little account, as he himself had acknowledged in 1824:

> I was a lover very early in life my first attachment being a school boy affection but Mary _____ who cost me more ballads then sighs was belovd with a romantic or platonic sort of feeling   if I could but gaze on her face or fancy a smile on her co[u]ntenance it was sufficient   we played with each other but named nothing of love (. . .) she was a beautiful girl and as the dream never awoke into reality her beauty was already fresh in my memory   she is still unmarried (JCAW, 72–3)

The ideal of Mary was a poetic one, and, as Edward Strickland suggests, the reality she came to possess for him derived from this very ideality: 'The essence of his delusion about Mary is the confluence of woman and archetype, the subsumption of human memory by a literary convention become a pathological reality.'[38]

This scenario underlies the tormenting circularity of meaning in which the poet of *Child Harold* is caught up: Mary is an ideal which remains unavailable, but which for this very reason assumes the proportions of a mental reality. It is a mental reality in the sense that it is fantasmatic, but it can never be incorporated as an element of subjective experience.[39] In Cowper's *The Task*, a self-aware mental process operates out of a private space which, functioning as an extension of the private self, mediates between outer and inner reality. The discourse of this mediation is specifically psychological: we re-encounter it in Coleridge and Wordsworth. Coleridge adapted Cowper's fire-gazing passage for his 'Frost at Midnight,' while Wordsworth seems to have drawn on the same passage in the final stanza of 'I wandered lonely as a cloud,' where the poet reclines on his couch in a vacancy of thought which in fact confirms his inner identity. The mental reality of Clare's Mary is different from that of Wordsworth's daffodils inasmuch as the self-identity which would incorporate her external being as an internal, psychologically meaningful form of knowledge is absent.

In *Child Harold* poetry itself, as it revolves round Mary, always carries the simultaneous meanings of a fantasmatic presence and an inner absence:

> Say What Is Love - To Live In Vain
> To Live And Die And Live Again
>
> Say What Is Love - Is It To Be
> In Prison Still And Still Be Free
>
> Or Seem As Free - Alone And Prove
> The Hopeless Hopes Of Real Love
>   . . .
> Say What Is Love - What E'er It be
> It Centers Mary Still With Thee
>   (LPJC, 78).

Mary provides the song's attempts to define the meaning of love with its point of reference, but this is already hollowed out by the repetitive circularity of the preceding definitions.[40] Precisely as a central reference, Mary cannot constitute a mode of knowledge. Instead the possibility of knowledge returns to the repetitive circularity of a poetic meaning which is subjective, but which can never be realised as a discourse of personal identity. Mary, then, marks the site of an interior fault line, destabilising those inner meanings which, whether positive or negative (positive in the manner of Wordsworth, negative in the manner of Coleridge's 'Dejection Ode'), would found a psychological sense of the self:

> On that sweet bosom I've had hours of rest
> Though now through years of abscence doomed to dwell
> Day seems my night & night seems blackest hell
>   . . .
> - But hell is heaven could I cease to mourn
>
> For her for one whose very name is yet
> Hell or heaven - & will ever be
>
>   (LPJC, 50)

In *Child Harold* introspection never takes the form of self-knowledge. Clare does not transform psychological experience into literature as, for example, Coleridge does by way of the 'Dejection' poems (the *Letter* and the *Ode*). Indeed Clare may be glimpsed proceeding in an inverse direction when he incorporates two lines of Coleridge's 'Pains of Sleep' into *Child Harold*, assimilating literature to his own inner situation ('"To be beloved is all I need / And them I love are loved indeed"' (LPJC, 51). In her unresolvable oscillation between plenitude of meaning and deficiency of meaning (heaven or hell), Mary is a poetical mode of reference in a poem wherein the precedence of literature confirms the absence of psychological self-identity.

The *mise en abîme* of literature in *Child Harold* must be understood in a literal rather than a theoretical sense. When, in the course of the poem, the poet descends into the abyss of his own crisis, it is Milton who provides the point of departure:

> Like Satans Warcry First In Paradise
> When Love Lay Sleeping On The Flowery Slope
> Like Virtue Wakeing In The Arms Of Vice
> Or Deaths Sea Bursting In The Midst Of Hope
> Sorrows Will Stay – & Pleasures Will Elope
> In The Uncertain Cartnty of Care
> . . .
> My Mind Is Dark & Fathomless & Wears
> The Hues Of Hopeless Agony & Hell
> No Plummet Ever Sounds The Souls Affairs
> There Death Eternal Never Sounds The Knell
> And Love Imprisoned Sighs The Long Farewell
> & Still May Sigh In Thoughts No Heart Hath Penned
> Alone in Loneliness Where Sorrows Dwell
> And Hopeless Hope Hopes On & Meets No End
> Wastes Without Springs & Homes Without a Friend
>
> (LPJC, 77)

The poem does not draw near to any kind of conclusion with these lines. The precipitous downwards plunge bottoms out in the exhausting circularity of the motif which the reader has come to recognise as being peculiarly Mary's: 'Hopeless Hope Hopes On & Meets No End.' Nevertheless these stanzas anticipate a subsequent stage in Clare's improbable poetic career. In pointing the way downwards into the abyss of a non-psychological subjectivity, they foreshadow the visionary lyrics of Northampton asylum.

III

At some point in 1841 Clare wrote a fragment entitled 'Self-identity':

A very good commonplace counsel is *Self-Identity* to bid our own hearts not to forget our own selves & always to keep self in the first place lest all the world who always keeps us behind it should forget us altogether – forget not thyself & the world will not forget thee – forget thyself & the world will willingly forget thee till thou art nothing but a living-dead man dwelling among shadows and falsehood (*Prose*, 239)

This is a final flickering of autobiographical concern: remembering guarantees self-presence, whereas the disintegration of experience through forgetting entails self-loss. Nevertheless 'Self-identity' acknowledges that memory has become a problem. The opening generalisations rapidly give way to more personal concerns: 'I am often troubled at times to know that should the world have the impudence not to know me but willingly forgetting me wether any single individual would be honest enough to know me – such people would be useful as the knocker to a door or the Bell to a cryer to own the dead alive.' Clare seeks to conjure up a *memento vita* at a moment when the death of the self has become a pervasive psychical possibility. He back-handedly acknowledges the prospect of madness: 'a person who denies himself must either be a madman or a coward.' Given the instability of the phenomenological self, he turns for reassurance to the material identity of the body: 'I shall never be in three places at once nor ever change into a woman & that ought to be some comfort amid this moral or immoral "changing" in life.' Corporeal identity is the only material support that reality has to offer in a mutable world. A few years later, even that touchstone will count for little: 'And yet I am, and live – like vapours tost / Into the nothingness of scorn and noise' (LPJC, 396).

In setting out continuity of memory as the guarantor of 'self-identity,' Clare implies a corollary relationship between forgetting and non-identity. It is this counter-condition which is realised in 'An Invite to eternity,' written some four years later in Northampton asylum: the poet enters a realm 'Where Parents live and are forgot / And sisters live and know us not' (LPJC, 349).

Where Clare seeks, in some measure, to assert continuity of identity, he tends to do so in his subjective prose writings – the autobiographical prose, the *Journey* and 'Self-identity'. Verse seems to be less suited to such assertions, and Clare's subjective poetry often expresses the sense of an identity which is either tenuous or under threat. It is appropriate, then, that in 'Self-identity' the prospect of forgetfulness is reserved for a stanza inserted into the prose argument:

> The mother may forget her child
> That dandled on her knee has been
> The bridegroom may forget the bride
> That he was wedded to yestreen
> (*Prose*, 239)

The *Journey out of Essex* and 'Self-identity' are, aside from Clare's letters, his last subjective prose writings, and also the last writings which attempt to sustain, however minimally, coherent versions of the self. In the introspective lyrics written in Northampton in 1844–5, discourse turns obsessively in on itself as identity enters into crisis:

> I am – yet what I am, none cares or knows;
> My friends forsake me like a memory lost
> I am the self-consumer of my woes
> (LPJC, 396)

In the light of the Northampton asylum lyrics, the warning sounded by 'Self-identity' looks like a self-fulfilling prophecy: 'forget thyself & the world will willingly forget thee till thou art nothing but a living-dead man dwelling among shadows.' In 'An Invite to eternity' (1844–5), the enabling conditions of autobiography have dissolved, as indeed have all recognisable landmarks. The 'Invite' proposes a journey which transforms the (literally) prosaic reality of the *Journey out of Essex* into a metaphorical, inward odyssey through a nebulous realm of non-being, a 'strange death of life to be,' where 'Things pass like shadows.' This is the *terra incognita* of the non-identified self.

Clare was admitted to Northampton asylum early in 1842, and remained there until his death in 1865, largely (but not entirely) forgotten by the outside world. History, in effect, came to a halt for him. Nevertheless he maintained a prolific output of poetry, and it was here that he underwent his final development, emerging as a lyric poet. A very large quantity of song-lyrics date from this final period – numerous nature poems, and lyrics on various subjects. They include the well-known group of introspective and sublime lyrics, most of which date from 1844 and 1845, although some were written later. Until recent years, these have been some of the best known of Clare's poems. Under the most unpromising conditions, Clare was at last writing poems which were in tune with the taste of 'cultivated' readers. This only gradually became apparent in the years following his death, but the trend was anticipated in Clare's lifetime: those few people who concerned themselves with Clare at this time recognised the quality of the visionary lyrics. Thomas Inskip, who succeeded in getting '"I Am"' published by a local newspaper in 1848 (the *Bedford Times*, which also published 'An Invite to Eternity' in the same year), said of the 'Invite,' 'there is

nothing in all his writings has lifted his genius so high in my estimation.'[41] 'Cultivated' readers, from Inskip onwards, have had few
problems in responding to poems such as 'An Invite to eternity'
because there is no trace left in them of that awkward materiality
of discourse which makes Clare's poetry of the 1820s and early 1830s
so unlike anything else in nineteenth-century English poetry. Pre-
Romantic and Romantic literary models had always involved for
him, along with an inward displacement of voice, a corresponding
tendency to elide or generalise the specificity of his perception of
places and people.[42] In Northampton asylum Clare was, in reality,
cut off from the world he knew: his painful loss of a foundation in
lived reality provided an appropriate condition for a genuinely
sublime lyrical practice.[43] After 1841, 'literature,' as this term is
newly understood at the beginning of the nineteenth century,
became his of right.

The major introspective lyrics, most notably 'An Invite to eternity,' are not without literary debts. In his excellent discussion of the
poem, Edward Strickland has listed a number of generic antecedents
involving invitations to the beloved:[44] the most plausible of these
are the folk-song 'Wild Mountain Thyme' ('Will ye go lassie, go'),
and Christopher Marlowe's 'The Passionate Sheepheard to his Love'.
Clare would have known both, and it is probable that a conscious
or subliminal echo of these sources provided a point of departure for
his poem:

> (a) Come live with mee, and be my love
>   And we will all the pleasures prove,
>   That Vallies, groves, hills and fieldes
>   Woods, or steepie mountaine yeeles.

> (b) Wilt thou go with me sweet maid
>   Say maiden wilt though go with me
>   Through the valley depths of shade
>   Of night and dark obscurity

'An Invite' retains the directness of the ballad form, but the
reader, in the position of the addressee, is invited not into a seductive pastoral scene, but into a dark night of the soul. The poem
derives much of its effect from the employment of the four-stress
ballad metre (with ballad repetitions) while conveying such a dark
spiritual content.

Strickland notes that 'when the itinerary of [Clare's] voyage is
revealed, the convention [of the invitation lyric] is transformed.'[45]

'An Invite' is in fact a poem of transformations. It presents a land-scape where

> stones will turn to flooding streams
> Where plains will rise like ocean waves
> Where life will fade like visioned dreams
> And mountains darken into caves
> (LPJC, 349)

The old commonplace of the world turned upside down[46] is remotivated here by a simultaneous inversion of the discourse of poetry itself. Marlowe's poem is a rhetorical fiction of seduction, but we might ask (and indeed critics have asked) how is Clare's 'sweet maid' to accompany him into the non-place which the poem evokes?[47] The formal occasion of the poem is thoroughly under-mined by the self-referentiality of the interiorised landscape to which the invitation beckons. As the status of the invitee is problematised,[48] Clare sets discourse into self-contradiction: the resulting tension resonates throughout the poem.

Poetic self-subversion is accompanied by an erosion of referential contexts. In the first stanza, the landscape is already lost in 'night and dark obscurity.' In the second it dissolves into an unstable flux: 'stones will turn to flooding streams'; 'plains will rise like ocean waves.' The process of dissolution corresponds to an absolute dispossession: as exteriority is transformed into a vacant interiority ('mountains darken into caves'), the psychical dimension of the scene is revealed:

> Say maiden wilt thou go with me
> Through this sad non-identity

Set out vertically on the page, the poem enacts a literal descent: the invite cannot be distinguished from the 'downwards' process of reading the poem itself as it mines an abyss of self-problematisation. This recessive interiorisation explores the limits of self-loss:

> The land of shadows wilt thou trace
> And look – nor know each others face
> The present mixed with reasons gone
> And past, and present all as one

Beyond any recognisable horizon of recovery, the poet inhabits his madness as a condition which deconverts all given forms of identity.

The mad poet's non-location is the unidentified and interiorised movement of subjective literature itself.

In examining the lines which conclude the poem, Edward Strickland fastens attention on the theme of the wedding:

> Say maiden can thy life be led
> To join the living with the dead
> Then trace thy footsteps on with me
> We're wed to one eternity

Strickland's initial comment on this is perceptive: 'Just as the marriage ceremony traditionally symbolizes social cohesion and elemental fecundity, so this insane marriage becomes the crowning symbol of a confounding rather than a communion of identities.'[49] In the conclusion of his paper however, Strickland resolves the 'insane marriage' into a positive meaning:

> Clare is searching his soul, questioning his own imagination: Muse, wilt thou go with me? Even here - to the disoriented world of madness which he proceeds to delineate, and in depicting which he answers the questions finally in the affirmative (. . .). The concluding affirmation is nothing less than a hierogamy of poet and Muse, complete with a grimly courageous procession to a visionary altar.[50]

The resulting consummation of poetry and madness amounts to the poet's rape of his muse: 'She is invited to a landscape that is without substance or stability, which the poet succeeds in traversing and infusing with form by forcing his Muse, the emblem of the transformative imagination, to accompany him.'[51] Strickland goes on to counterbalance this 'complex triumph' against the ultimate desolation of Clare's historical situation, quoting his final letter (March 1860) from Northampton asylum: 'I have nothing to communicate or tell of & why I am shut up I don't know I have nothing to say so I conclude' (*Letters*, 223). It would seem to me, however, that poem and letter are complementary rather than contrasting documents. The metaphorical 'wedding' which concludes 'An Invite to eternity' conjoins the painful contradictions expressed in 1841 through the simultaneous and opposite discourses of *Don Juan* and *Child Harold*. The visionary ambience of the 'Invite' may marry such antitheses, but this is not the type of dialectical Marriage envisaged by Blake ('Without Contraries is no progression'). In proposing the 'intercourse' of the conflicting extremes which the third stanza has brought into juxtaposition ('In this strange death of life to be / To live in death . . .'), the wedding is a knot that ties together the chiasmuses which constitute the centre as well as the circumference of the poem. Such a consummation entails not an act of possession, but an enactment of dispossession. The contradictions of Clare's situation are, I would suggest, unresolvable. The wedding does appear to present a concluding resolution, but it is one which acquires the inverted form of a paradox: if we follow Strickland in converting the maiden into the muse, then what is metaphorically consummated here is the very poetry of self-loss. For all the considerable body of poems he had yet to write – a few of which can hold their place with the finest lyrics in the language – Clare had, in the long term, nowhere to go from the 'Invite' save towards his final utterance: 'I have nothing to say so I conclude.'

7 Gérard de Nerval (1): Romanticism, Medicine and Madness

I

In the period of the European Romanticism, the old kinship between madness and inspiration returned with a vengeance. In a number of instances, figures who stand as embodiments of creativity endured real experience of madness:

> The Romantic mentality attains a new experience of illness in the perspective of a conversion to interiority. The illness is characteristic of its sufferer, an internal debate which involves his identity; a dialogue of self with self from which he must emerge renewed. In struggling with his shadow (. . .), the sufferer undergoes an initiation, a proof of truth. Novalis and Gérard de Nerval, Hölderlin, Schumann, Nietzsche are witnesses of this combat, won even as it is lost.[1]

Of the major literary madmen of the Romantic era, Hölderlin, Clare and Nerval, it is Nerval who best exemplifies the ironies and ambiguities of the encounter between Romanticism and madness. Théophile Gautier provides eyewitness testimony: 'In those days of literary eccentricity, it was quite hard to give the impression of really extravagant behaviour (. . .). Every kind of lunacy seemed somehow justifiable, and the most balanced among us would have seemed a suitable case for treatment in the *Petites-Maisons* (. . .). It was probable, therefore, that Gérard was mentally unbalanced long before any of us consciously noted it.'[2]

Born in 1808, Nerval was a founding member of the French Romantic movement. While still in his teens, he translated an acclaimed version of Part One of Goethe's *Faust*: a few years later,

in 1830, he was one of Victor Hugo's lieutenants in the 'battle of
Hernani.' In 1837 he declared his love for the actress and singer
Jenny Colon, the Aurélie/Aurélia of his writings. He was an ineffectual suitor, and Jenny had already formed an attachment with
another man, whom she married. She was to die in 1842, but her
image haunted Nerval for the rest of his life. In 1841, in the midst
of financial difficulties, he suffered his first mental crisis. His
problems seriously recommenced in 1851 when he suffered a fall
which left him in a feverish state. He recovered, but from then until
his death in January 1855, his stability was extremely fragile, with
a renewed bout of fever in 1852, and serious relapses into delirium
in 1853 and 1854. This, though, was also an intensely productive
period, and Nerval's most celebrated literary achievements date from
these years: the story Sylvie, the sonnet sequence, Les chimères, and
Aurélia, which explores his dreams, visions and hallucinations during
the crises of 1841 and 1851–3. During the final years he was treated
by Emile Blanche at his maison de santé at Passy: the final episodes
of Aurélia are set in this clinic.

Against the advice of Dr Blanche, Nerval managed to secure his
release from the Passy clinic in October of 1854. The winter of 1854–
5 found him in a state of vagabondage. On a freezing night in
January he was unable to secure lodgings, and in the morning was
found hanged in an alleyway.

The Romantics considered dreams, visions and inspired or exalted
states of mind to be inherently poetic conditions. Nerval's own
interest in dreams extended to somnambulism, drugs and mystical
transports: he claimed to have composed Les chimères in a state of
trancelike reverie. Such considerations coloured his encounters with
madness, which rapidly acquired the makings of a legend. In 1853
Alexandre Dumas announced his friend's condition in the journal
which he edited:

This is a charming and distinguished spirit (. . .) in whom, from time to
time, a certain phenomenon takes place, which, happily, we hope is
seriously disturbing neither for him nor his friends; from time to time,
when some piece of work or other has strongly preoccupied him, the
imagination, that lunatic of the house, evicts for a brief time reason, who
is only the housekeeper; then the former remains in sole possession, in a
brain neither more or less nourished with dreams and hallucinations than
an Egyptian opium smoker (. . .); – then, for the men of science, our poor
Gérard is ill and in need of treatment, whereas for us, he is quite simply
more storyteller, more dreamer, more spiritual and more sad than ever.[3]

Dumas's unfriendly reference to 'the men of science' illustrates a quarrel over views of madness which has become familiar to us. The Romantic revaluation of poetic madness coincided with far-reaching changes in the medical management of insanity, carried through in France by Pinel and Esquirol. This is the period of professional specialisation in mental disorders – the period of the 'mad-doctors,' to use Roy Porter's term.[4] A letter which Nerval wrote to Dumas's wife in the wake of the 1841 crisis depicts the poet embattled with the doctors:

> He [Dumas] will tell you that I have recovered what is commonly called reason, but don't you believe it. I am still and I always have been the same person, and I am only surprised that I was found to have *changed* for the space of some days last summer. Illusion, paradox and presumption are all enemies of good sense, which I have never lacked. Basically, I have had a very amusing dream, and I miss it; I even ask myself if it wasn't more *true* than that which seems to me alone natural and explicable today; but inasmuch as we have here doctors and commissars who watch out that the field of poetry isn't enlarged at the expense of the public highway, I was only allowed to leave and finally mingle with reasonable people when I had formally agreed to having been *ill*, something which cost my *amour propre*, and even my truthfulness, a good deal. Confess! Confess! they cried, as they used to do with witches and heretics, to finish with I agreed to let myself be classed according to an *affliction* defined by the doctors and indifferently called Theomania or Demonomania in the medical Dictionary. With the help of the definitions included in these two articles, science has the right to conjure away or reduce to silence all the prophets and seers predicted by the apocalypse, one of whom I flattered myself with being! (*Pléiade*, 904–5)[5]

The *Dictionnaire médical* to which Nerval refers is probably the *Dictionaire des sciences médicales* (1812–22), to which Esquirol, the pioneer of scientific psychiatry, contributed various articles on mental illness.[6] Nerval was diagnosed as suffering from either theomania or demonomania, the latter a variety of melancholia: Klaus Doerner takes Esquirol's discussion of demonomania as an instance 'of the "clinification" of the irrationality of the insane. Esquirol demonstrated Comte's law via the example of suicide, which was subject first to religious law, then civil law, but now as an illness, had become a medical concern. The same holds true for demonomania, the religious form of melancholia.'[7] It is this development, replacing religious perception with 'positive' definition, which Nerval contests. In a rhetorical inversion, he likens the doctors who have medicalised spiritual experience to medieval inquisitors.

In recent studies, Kari Lokke and Frank Paul Bowman have pointed out that Nerval's resistance to the definition of theomania was ideologically subversive. Bowman, who has explored theomania as a utopian tradition in French Romantic culture,[8] summarises the argument:

> Religious fanaticism was, for Pinel and Esquirol, the central and, so to speak, essential form of madness, no doubt because, as Lokke suggests, it seemed to them the one which most put in question the *statu quo* of society; here, in any case, medical discourse seeks to reduce not only the religious content but also the political aspect of extreme manifestations of religious enthusiasm.[9]

This is persuasive, but we must also note that medical discourse could not be only an ideological opponent for Nerval. His reactions to his condition were complicated by the fact that his own father, Dr Etienne Labrunie, was a doctor (a gynaecologist). Nerval had, in his youth, briefly followed in his father's footsteps, but had then abandoned his medical studies (along with his father's name), becoming an unrespectable bohemian. This occasioned bad feelings between father and son, and it can hardly be a coincidence that tensions resurfaced on the occasion of Nerval's first crisis in 1841. Hospitalised at a clinic in the Rue Picpus in May (he was shortly to be transferred to the *maison* of Esprit Blanche, father of Emile) Nerval sought permission to come and go during the day, but his father was proving unhelpful: 'Unfortunately, among so many people who are well-disposed towards me, you seem to be the only one (I say this to you alone) who has maintained a prejudice against my conduct and my future.' This is one of the few occasions on record when Nerval directly reproaches his father. 'I don't know,' he continues, 'to what extent my lack of taste for the profession of doctor has placed me in a bad light in your mind' (*Pléiade*, 884). When, some months later, Nerval wrote to Mme Dumas about doctors who placed limiting conditions on his cherished freedom of movement, Dr Labrunie must have been in the back of his mind: in quarrelling with medical authority he also quarrelled with paternal authority.

Nerval never abandoned the idealism of the 1841 letter, but, in the accelerating crisis of his final years, he did modify it in important ways. Writing to Dr Labrunie from Emile Blanche's clinic in late 1853 his words and tone of voice are in marked contrast with the unrepentant letters of May and November 1841. He now sought to realign himself with both his father and the medical profession: 'I can't persuade anybody here that I'm a little bit of a doctor, having followed two years of courses at the *Ecole* and the Hôtel-Dieu clinic' (*Pléiade*, 1067). Recovering from his latest breakdown, he was eager to place his new work-in-progress, *Le Rêve et la vie*, at the service of science. He not only sought Emile Blanche's approval for this project, he passed draft passages on to the doctor. At the same time (December 1853), he wrote to Dr Labrunie, 'I'm undertaking to write and record all the impressions which my illness has left me. This will not be without use for observation or science. I have never known in myself more facility for analysis and description. I hope you will judge so yourself' (*Pléiade*, 1088).

Dr Labrunie remained unpersuaded. However, a few years later, another doctor, Moreau de Tours, a pupil of Esquirol, read Nerval's account of his madness with considerable interest.[10] In 1855, the year in which *Aurélia* was published, Moreau had published a treatise entitled *De l'identité de l'état de rêve et de la folie*. In a subsequent treatise, *La Psychologie morbide* (1859), Moreau cited Nerval's description of the onset of delirium in capital letters 'L'EPANCHE-MENT DU SONGE DANS LA VIE REELLE' – 'the overflowing of dream into real life': *Aurélia* provided direct confirmation of his own postulate that the state of dream and the state of madness were congruent, and that madness was a form of waking dream.[11]

Moreau shared Nerval's interests in dreams, visions and hallucinations, but from the viewpoint of medical pathology. He experimented with hashish in order to scientifically investigate hallucinated states of mind: in so doing he introduced Balzac, Gautier and other writers to the drug. Such investigations were not always undertaken in a collaborative spirit, and in the course of one hashish session, recorded by Alphonse Karr, Nerval found himself under the observation of Esquirol. Karr, Gautier, Nerval and a few other writers and artists had been invited to experiment with the drug at the home of a writer of popular scientific textbooks, Ajasson de Grandsagne. The hashish was ingested in the form of tea, and the company then retired to a salon: 'In the salon,' Karr reported, 'we found a dozen individuals, including Esquirol, the celebrated doctor of madmen. I understood that we were being exhibited.'[12]

In *Aurélia*, the given relationship between Romanticism and medicine remains complicated and unresolved. In employing the word 'illness,' rejected in 1841, Nerval gestures in the direction of medical discourse: 'I am going to try to describe the impressions of a long illness which took place entirely within the mysteries of my own soul.' But the word prompts an immediate qualification: 'I do not know why I use the word illness, for as far as my own being was concerned, I never felt better. My imagination gave me infinite delight. In recovering what men call reason, do I have to regret the loss of these joys?' (115).

In a work which is subtitled *Le Rêve et la vie*, it is the complexity of 'dream' which brings into sharpest focus the alternation between a pathological madness on the one hand, and a Romantic madness on the other. As Lawrence Porter has pointed out, Nerval was influenced by the dream literature of the German Romantics, also by Charles Nodier, a writer who was in many respects his mentor. For all these writers, dreams possess a symbolic efficacy:[13] Nerval, unlike Moreau, did not simply assimilate dream to the pathology of insanity.[14] Nevertheless the domain of dream was for him a problematic one. Nerval's view of the relationship between dream and madness was derived from Nodier, who displayed a concern with the pathological as well as the symbolical dimensions of dream: 'most mental obsessions (. . .) are probably only the continuing perception of an impression acquired from that fantastic existence which makes up half our lives, the existence of the sleeper.'[15]

Jacques Bousquet, in a study which seeks to place the literature of dreams in an historical perspective, has argued that, before Romanticism, dream experience is narrowly circumscribed: 'dream, such as we know it – gratuitous supplement to daily life, strange scenes, bizarre games lacking in meaning – dates from the end of the eighteenth century.'[16] Before then, 'dreams are spoken of and referred to; but their content, their form, their function are altogether different.'[17] Bousquet further notes that there is a convergence of dream and madness in the nineteenth century. He traces the themes of the Romantic dream back to the two major forms of the medieval dream, namely heaven and hell. Dreams of heaven evolve through a genealogical sequence: paradise as the heavens (theological images) then as the sky (astronomical images); paradise as garden, then as nature. The genealogy of dreams of hell descends through images of the underground, then the interior and the city.[18] The derivation of dreams of hell is complicated by a further factor. Bad dreams draw on a more primitive repertoire of images – demons, monsters etc. These 'belated' dreams constitute the Romantic nightmare and underlie the modern dream of the bizarre and the absurd. In this category Bousquet places dreams of fear and anguish – fear, above all, of damnation: 'The themes of the most acute modern nightmares are of inhibition, the involuntary or unconscious act; these are linked not to merited damnation, but to a fatal damnation –

Calvinist or existential – which is less the punishment of a fault than
the negative destiny of man.'[19] The evolution of this kind of dream
(in accordance with the link between Calvinist and existential
notions of fatality), comes to express a pure anguish which dispenses
with the images of the medieval inferno. In the modern period these
are replaced with the topics of psychiatry: 'The rise of madness
parallels the rise of philosophical anguish and the two no doubt have
common causes (. . .). Metaphysics furnishes the general categories of
explanation of anguish and psychiatry provides metaphysical
anguish with its expressions and its examples (. . .). The role of
psychiatry in the nightmare increases as the nineteenth century
advances.'[20] Referring to the writings of Hoffmann, Poe, De
Quincey and Baudelaire, Bousquet proposes that 'from 1820 the
nightmare refers more and more to pathologically *classified*
phenomena.'[21]

Bousquet's 'history' of transformations in dream imagery relies in
good measure on Comte's and Weber's sociological accounts of the
secularisation and 'disenchantment' (*Entzauberung*) of the modern
world. This is relevant to the way in which the positivistic
('Comtean') medical definitions which Nerval rejected in 1841 rein-
sinuated themselves in the later narrative of *Aurélia*. Here, Nerval,
albeit strategically and ambiguously, admits the pathological
character of his exorbitant experiences: 'Only my actions were
apparently insensate, subject to what is called illusion, according to
human reason' (120);[22] '(. . .) a series of visions which were perhaps
insane [*insensées*], or vulgarly diseased' (120). As Michel Jeanneret
affirms, 'analysis of delirium in *Aurélia* maintains a close relationship
with the psychiatric discourse of the period':[23] in 1853–4, Nerval's
visionary Romanticism, while it did not submit to the pressure of
normalising medical definitions, was at least inflected by this
pressure.[24] Correlatively his report on madness is located in
specifically contemporary contexts, notably those of the city and the
asylum.

Nerval defines his madness as the overflow of dream into reality.
The clue to this breaching of the border between the two states can
be found in the introspective account of the process of going to sleep
with which *Aurélia* commences:

> Our dreams are a second life. I have never been able to penetrate without
> a shudder those ivory or horned gates which separate us from the invisi-
> ble world. The first moments of sleep are an image of death; a hazy

torpor grips our thoughts and it becomes impossible for us to determine
the exact instant when the 'I' [*le moi*], under another form, continues the
task of existence. (115)

The 'ivory or horned gates' refer us to Book VI of the *Aeneid*,
which recounts Aeneas's journey to the underworld to speak with
his dead father. Géza Róheim suggests that the Virgilian gates of
sleep, entrance to the underworld, take the form of a labyrinth:[25]
correlatively, labyrinths, in the view of W. F. Jackson Knight, 'serve
the purpose of gates, giving entrance of certain terms.'[26] Hallucination occurs where the gateway, as site of transition, and the
labyrinth, as site of self-loss, converge on each other to reproduce in
space the indeterminate time of going to sleep. The disruption of the
integral self is enacted on a stage provided by these spaces: Gérard's
first transport occurs at a 'junction of three streets' (119); in the
asylum near the end of the narrative, he sees a fellow inmate as a
sphinx stationed 'at the last gates of existence' (171).

The form of Gérard's breakdown is prefigured in the ominous first
dream of the narrative, where the dreamer loses himself in a
labyrinth and then encounters the image of Dürer's *Melencolia*.[27]
As the dream begins, Gérard is 'wandering about a vast building':

> [I] went to look for my own room in a sort of inn with gigantic staircases
> crowded with hurrying travellers, I got lost several times in the long
> corridors and then, as I was going through one of the central galleries,
> I was struck by a strange sight. A creature of enormous proportions –
> man or woman I do not know – was fluttering painfully through the air
> and seemed to be struggling with heavy clouds. At last, out of breath and
> at the end of its strength, it collapsed into the middle of the dark court-
> yard, catching and rumpling its wings on the roofs and balustrades. For
> a moment I was able to observe it closely. It was colored with ruddy hues
> and its wings glittered with a myriad changing reflections. Clad in a long
> gown of antique folds, it looked like Dürer's *Angel of Melancholy*. I could
> not keep myself from crying out in terror and this woke me with a start.
> (119)

In *Les Nuits d'Octobre*, a first-person journalistic writing of 1853,
the writer undertakes to explore the nocturnal city, which is both
underworld and labyrinth: 'And now, let us plunge still more deeply
into the inextricable circles of the Parisian inferno' (*Pléiade*, 88). He
initially intended an expedition to Meaux, but has missed the coach
in a moment of inattention: in this way he descends into the night-
time city. This seemingly banal sequence anticipates the psychical
drama of *Aurélia*. In *Les Nuits*, an attitude of *désinvolture* maintains

control and distance in dealing with potentially distressing material, turning it to self-mockery. Following his night-time adventure, Gérard, when he reaches Meaux, dreams of a vast labyrinthine dungeon composed of corridors and stairways which the dreamer fears he must endlessly traverse (*Pléiade*, 104): the dream proceeds with a parodic chorus of gnomes demolishing the partitions of his brain lobes while chanting 'The *self* and the *non-self* of Fichte engage in a terrible combat in this being so full of objectivity' (*Pléiade*, 106). In Part Two of *Aurélia*, such stylisations disappear: the underworld of nightmare is manifested in openly pathological terms as Gérard is drawn ever deeper into an hallucinatory traversal of Paris by an ongoing process of indecision, uncertainty, inachievement and failure.

> I went and saw my father whose maid-servant was ill; he seemed in a bad-temper (. . .). I left in dismay. In the street I met with a friend who wanted to take me along to dine with him in order to distract me a little. I refused his offer and, without having eaten anything, I made towards Montmartre. The cemetery was closed, which I considered an ill-omen. (158)

Book VI of the *Aeneid*, also the myth of Orpheus, may provide underlying parallels for these events, but they are skewed. In a reversal of Aeneas's journey, the sequence commences with a visit to a living father, who is bad-temperedly uncommunicative. Gérard then seeks to visit the grave of the beloved, but is unsuccessful. He passes through a gate [*barrière*], and enters into the labyrinth: 'As I went through the Clichy gate, I saw a fight. I tried to separate the combatants, but without success (. . .). From that moment I wandered about in despair through the vague territories [*terrains vagues*] that separate the suburbs from the city' (158). His movements through Paris form a chain of broken trajectories: each movement, frustrated in its goal, initiates a further fruitless initiative: 'It was too late to go on with my projected visit. So I went back through the street towards the centre of Paris.' He meets a priest, but is denied religious comfort: 'in my distressed condition I wanted to confess to him. He told me that this was not his parish' (158–9). Gérard's alienation and displacement eventually reach cosmic proportions:

> When I reached the Place de la Concorde, I thought of killing myself. Several times I started towards the Seine, but something stopped me from completing my plan. The stars shone in the sky. Suddenly it seemed to

me that they were all extinguished (. . .). I thought that the hour had
arrived and that we had come to the end of the world predicted in the
Apocalypse of Saint John. I thought I saw a black sun in an empty sky
and a red ball of blood above the Tuileries. I said to myself: 'The eternal
night is beginning, and it will be terrible. What will happen when men
find that there is no more sun?' (159)[28]

Stranded in a transitional space which blurs the boundary
between *vie* and *rêve*, Gérard experiences reality as nightmare. His
hallucination of the black sun again alludes to Dürer. The image
occurs, famously, in the sonnet *El Desdichado* ('le *Soleil noir* de la
Mélancolie'), also in the *Journey to the Orient*: 'The black sun of
melancholy (. . .) sheds its gloomy rays over the countenance of
Albrecht Dürer's dreaming angel.'[29] In *Aurélia*, the iconic image,
projected as an hallucination, contaminates Gérard's experience with
a literal representation of melancholia.

At the beginning of Part Two, Gérard notes that his soul is hover-
ing 'uncertainly between the life and the dream' (147). Throughout
the subsequent crises he experiences difficulty in going to sleep, and
when he does sleep, dream, no longer a vehicle of transcendental
meaning, is disrupted and disordered: 'Sleep brought me dreadful
dreams' (152); 'The next night I slept only a few moments' (154);
'The successive visions of my sleep had reduced me to such despair
that I could barely speak' (157). Unable to complete the passage to
the higher state of dream, he moves in the uncertainty and impreci-
sion of the given moment, his attention unfocused, assailed by
chimerical images which signify death or annihilation. In *Les Nuits
d'Octobre*, Nerval (with reference to Dickens) had associated explorations of the city with literary realism (*Pléiade*, 79): in *Aurélia*, the
city is experienced as the inverted realism of hallucination. Gérard's
urban delirium takes the form of pathological literalisations of
symbolic meanings. With the boundaries between *rêve* and *vie* in
flux, the ego experiences an oneiric reality, one which corresponds
to Bousquet's notion of the nightmare as a psychiatrisation of hell,
relayed through the context of the city, and manifested in
pathologically irrational images.

The negative character of Paris as milieu contrasts with the asylums
to which Gérard is committed. In Part Two, he is taken first to a
hospice, then transferred to 'an asylum outside Paris' (164). This latter
relocation constitutes a narrative fulcrum. In the asylum, Gérard's
beneficial treatment of a fellow inmate results in a dream ('my first for
a long time') which signals the positive outcome of the narrative:

I was in a tower, so deep in the earth and so high in the heavens, that all my life seemed to be passed in going up and down it. Already my strength was spent, and my courage failing, when a door in the side opened, a spirit appeared and said: 'Come, brother! . . .' I do not know why but I had the idea that he was called Saturninus. He possessed the features of the poor sick man, only transformed and intelligent. (. . .) Immediately one of the stars I could see in the sky began to grow larger, and the divinity of my dreams appeared, smiling (. . .). She said to me: 'The ordeal you have undergone is coming to an end. The countless stairways which wore you out so going up and down were the bonds of old illusions that impeded your thoughts.' (172)

This dream reverses the negative meanings of the dream that initiates Gérard's *descensus*. Rather than losing himself in a labyrinth of stairways and corridors, the dreamer is released from a labyrinth of 'countless stairways.' The Düreresque angel who plummets into the courtyard in the first dream is a counterpart of Saturninus, the spirit-creature who releases Gérard from the tower (Saturn is the sign of melancholy, and governs the imagery of Dürer's *Melencolia 1*).[30] But whereas the angel is trapped, Saturninus is an agent of release. Finally, whereas the first dream is interrupted by Gérard's cry of dread, this one results in 'a wonderful awakening.'

The two dreams outline, respectively, an initial movement of descent and entrapment, and a concluding one of ascent and release. In the Saturninus dream, a symbolic pattern of trial by ordeal becomes intelligible at the point of exit ('"The ordeal you have undergone is coming to an end"'). This corresponds to the conclusion of the narrative: 'I compare this series of trials I went through to that ordeal which, for the ancients, represented the idea of a descent into hell' (198). If descent into an oneiric underworld is marked by a disordering of self, then successful ascent signals a resolution as the self rejoins the upper world of reality. The two dreams represent the patterns of Gérard's breakdown and recovery: they are located respectively in terms of the city as labyrinthine underworld and the asylum as place of spiritual release and regeneration.

The real sanatoriums in which Nerval was treated – that of Esprit Blanche (corresponding to the asylum of Part One, 'the house which had been a paradise for me') and that of his son Emile (corresponding to the asylum of Part Two) – implemented the notions of moral treatment set out by Pinel and further elaborated by Esquirol. Following these notions, Gérard's delirium would have been described as a condition of *aliénation mentale*. The term was not a

new one (Tasso employed it in the sixteenth century), but for Pinel
and his followers the notion acquired a specifically modern
character. Pinel's employment of moral treatment was influenced by
his reading of Jean-Jacques Rousseau (a writer of central importance
for Nerval): 'Even the Rousseauan motif of alienation from and
restoration to one's own nature is completely applicable to Pinel's
therapy. For not only was insanity by its very name "mental alienation" (. . .) but Pinel's rhetoric typically depicted cure as an overcoming of alienation, a return to one's true self, a *retour sur lui-même*, and
an act of being *ramené à lui-même*.'[31] Consistently with the
Rousseauesque strand of his views, Pinel proposed that 'cities more
than countryside (. . .) were nurseries of insanity.'[32] The asylum,
then, was an ideal site in which to combat mental alienation: 'Both
Rousseauan schooling and Pinellian healing require a controlled
environment withdrawn from the larger society: "The most powerful
remedy . . . can only be found in a well-ordered hospice."'[33] If
Gérard is eventually able to regain a non-alienated and symbolic
perception, it is thanks to his relocation in the asylum. In Paris, his
sleep is disordered, but he now identifies the asylum as the mythical
underworld of sleep – a perception which betokens his imminent
reawakening: 'My companions around me seemed to be asleep and
to resemble the spectres of Tartarus, until the hour at which the sun
arose for me' (166). This prefaces his recovery of spiritual meaning
in the climactic dream of his release from the tower.

In Gérard's perception, the asylum is closely associated with
ancient mysteries and initiations – he refers to Isis, the pyramids and
Tartarus. Located through the symbolism of the ancient world, the
asylum counteracts the baleful effect of the modern city. Crucial to
this outcome is Gérard's encounter with a young inmate, who
embodies an ultimate withdrawal into melancholia: 'a young man
(. . .) who had refused to take food for six weeks' (171). Pinel would
have recognised Gérard's treatment of his fellow patient as an
instance of moral treatment. 'Men who [are] strangers to the principle of medicine, guided only by sound judgment or some obscure
tradition, have devoted themselves to the treatment of the insane,
and they have effected a great many cures.'[34] These men were the
untrained caretakers and superintendents of the insane, 'who had
"the habit of living constantly in the midst of lunatics" (. . .) They
were specialists in the old sense: lay healers.'[35] Gérard, encouraged
by his doctor, becomes such a caretaker: 'I spent hours examining
him mentally, my head bowed over his, and holding his hands. It
seemed that a certain magnetism united our two spirits, and I was

delighted the first time a word came from his mouth' (172). Gérard attempts to magnetise the madman (a practice with which Pinel had been prepared to experiment),[36] and also sings to him. All this is consistent with Pinel's doctrine of *douceur* (gentleness): 'the lunatic was not to be considered "absolutely deprived of reason," (. . .) He was, rather, feelingful and responsive; and hence *douceur* (. . .) produced therapeutic success.'[37] In the very element of its unorthodoxy, Gérard's practice of healing reconciles his visionary perception with nineteenth-century French therapeutic practice.

Gérard's recovery from this illness is simultaneously a recovery of a symbolic dimension of meaning which has been threatened by the disorder of pathological experience. In Part One, Gérard, in a state of delirium, is taken into custody by a patrol (an event which corresponds to the breakdown of 1841). He overhears the soldiers talking with an unknown individual:

> By a strange effect of vibration it felt as though his voice was echoing in my own chest, and that my soul was, so to speak, divided between vision and reality. For a second I thought of making an effort to turn towards the person in question; then I shivered as I remembered a well-known German superstition which says that everyone has a *double* and when you see him death is close at hand. (121)

Ambivalence of voice here effects a literal confusion between self and other: Gérard's voice, displaced, is dispossessed of its identity. At the narrative's conclusion, however, hallucinatory doubling and inner scission are reworked at the regenerative level of symbol through Gérard's encounter with the young madman in the asylum. The logic of the text makes it clear that the madman is a symbolic counterpart of Gérard, but the specificity of their relationship is best established on the basis of textual evidence. A passage in which Gérard sings to the madman transposes a cognate passage from an early draft fragment of *Aurélia*, which deals in fact with the events of Gérard's own first bout of delirium and fever:

> [draft]: On my awakening I was enchanted to hear a rendering of old airs of the village where I had been born. The young boy who watched over me sung them with a moving voice.[38]

> [*Aurélia*]: The poor boy from whom intelligent life had been so strangely withdrawn was so well cared for that gradually his torpor was overcome. I learnt that he had been born in the country, and so spent whole hours singing to him old village songs, which I tried to make as moving as possible. (177)

Through the doubling of successive versions of the text, Nerval
reverses Gérard's position and reclaims a voice which has been dispossessed. Returned to self-mastery at the conclusion, the voice of
the autobiographical protagonist is now fit to become that of the
autobiographical narrator, imposing coherent form on a pathological
content. In *Aurélia*, the narrator not only tells the story of a triumph
over illness and hallucination, his narrative also overcomes a split
which wounds the symbolic coherence of the self's discourse.

This resolution is thematically as well as formally effective. The
early appearance of the hallucinatory double, coinciding with the
onset of Gérard's delirium, confuses the boundaries of the ego.
These boundaries are redefined in the concluding encounter with
the symbolic double, who functions as a kind of scapegoat, a bearer
of Gérard's own unreason. As Gérard assumes the role of healer, his
madness is transferred to a representative of the self: in relation to
the young madman, Gérard is able to objectify his experience in the
very element of its inner irrationality: he is in control of his madness
rather than controlled by it.

Nerval's celebrated sonnet *El Desdichado* is closely related to *Aurélia*:

> Je suis le Ténébreux, - le Veuf, - L'inconsolé,
> Le Prince d'Aquitaine à la Tour abolie:
> Ma seule *Etoile* est morte, - et mon luth constellé
> Porte le *Soleil noir* de la *Mélancolie*

(I am the dark man, the widower, the unconsoled one, The Prince of Aqui-
taine of the destroyed Tower, My sole *Star* is dead, - and my constellated
lute Bears the *black Sun* of *Melancholia*.)

Alexandre Dumas who published this poem in his journal,
suggested that it confirmed Nerval's mental condition. In the preface
to *Les Filles du feu*, Nerval contested Dumas's account and outlined
his own version of events:

I was moved by this love for a fugitive *star*, which abandoned me alone
in the night of my destiny, I cried, I trembled at the vain apparitions of
my sleep. Then a divine ray of light shone in my hell; surrounded by
monsters against which I obscurely struggled, I seized this thread of
Ariadne, and since then all my visions have become celestial. Some day
I shall write the story of that 'descent into hell.' (*Pléiade*, 158)

This summarises the narrative pattern which is common to both
the poem and the autobiographical discourse: the loss of the beloved

precipitates a melancholic plunge into a dark, infernal underworld.
The protagonist, however, re-emerges from his ordeal in the likeness
of an epic hero: 'I imagined myself a hero living under the gaze of
the gods' (*Aurélia*, 166):

> Et j'ai deux fois vainqueur traversé l'Achéron
> Modulant tour à tour sur la lyre d'Orphée . . .

('And twice I have victoriously traversed the Acheron, Modulating turn and
turn about on Orpheus's lyre . . .')

In replying to Dumas, Nerval was at pains to make clear that *El
Desdichado* was not a document of madness but a dream-poem: 'you
have been imprudent enough to cite one of those sonnets composed
in that state of *super-naturalist* reverie, as the Germans would say.'
A form of dream-writing is at once the medium of a pathological
(melancholic) collapse of meaning, and the reconquest of meaning as
Orphic revelation – Orpheus's lyre, we remember, possesses the
power of vanquishing melancholy.

In the concluding pages of *Aurélia*, the climactic dream of Saturninus is succeeded by a section of visionary prose, entitled
'Mémorables' after Swedenborg's visionary reveries. This section is
close to *Les chimères* in its inspiration (Nerval also invoked the name
of Swedenborg in connection with the sonnet-sequence): it enacts
Gérard's dream-visions in the inspired language of prophecy:

> 'Oh death, where is thy victory,' now that the all-conquering Messiah has
> ridden between us? His garment was of the colour of hyacinth, and his
> wrists and ankles sparkled with diamonds and rubies. When his light
> switch touched the pearly gates of the new Jerusalem, we were all three
> bathed in light. It was then that I came down among men to give them
> the glad tidings. (174)

As the alienating milieu of the city is succeeded by the therapeutic
one of the asylum, delirious derangement is transformed into a
visionary reverie. As in the address to Dumas, a bizarre spiritual
disorder is transformed into spiritual illumination, communicated
through an inspired practice of literature: 'I seized this thread of
Ariadne and since then all my visions have become celestial.'[39]

Moreau de Tours may have appropriated *Aurélia* for a
physiological theory of insanity,[40] but Nerval pre-empts him. As a
Romantic writer, he assimilates the moral and therapeutic character
of contemporary medical treatment of the insane in order to assert
his own higher understanding of spiritual health. In an historical

perspective this is by no means an eccentric project. Gérard's spiritual therapeutics, while it may exceed the concerns of Pinel, is consistent with the theories of German Romantic medicine,[41] of which Nerval, steeped as he was in German Romantic thought, probably had some notion.

II

Gérard's sojourn in the asylum in the final section of *Aurélia* corresponds to Nerval's stay in Emile Blanche's *maison de santé* from August 1853 to May 1854. When he left in late May, it was in order to undertake a journey to Germany. The journey was a troubled one, and climaxed in a fresh crisis in Leipzig. Most of the letters Nerval wrote from Germany are addressed either to his father or to his doctor. As he penetrated deeper into Germany, these letters acquired the momentum of a double address. In a valuable discussion of Nerval's trajectory during 1853–4, Ross Chambers goes to the heart of the matter:

> Not content with having made the doctor an intercessor with the father, Nerval confounded in a single movement the rapprochement which he sought with Dr Labrunie and the parallel impulse which propelled his wish to repair the wrongs he had done to Blanche, a figure who is at one and the same time fraternal (for he is young) and paternal.[42]

Nerval's problematic relationship with medical authority, as represented by Dr Blanche, is inextricably bound up with his relationship with his father.

In Bousquet's history of the imagination, the themes of heaven and hell evolve in response to empirical socio-historical developments, notably the progressive secularisation of Western life, and the correlative need for literature and the arts to compensate for the decay of authorised versions of the supernatural: this culminates in Romantic literature, with its enriched repertoire of imaginative and poetic evocations of 'otherness.' Bousquet's thesis, however, ignores corresponding changes in conceptions of selfhood, and so disregards the implications such changes might have for individual experiences of both dreams and madness. From Trosse to Nerval, the theme of the *descensus Averno* becomes the image and experience of a descent into the problematic depths of the subjective self. As madness acquires a new subjective complexity at the end of the eighteenth century, so too does dream itself. In the literature of the period, dreams are not only poetically and imaginatively enriched, they are also, as Alain Corbin has noted, understood in terms of a new sense of the complex latency of the subjective self: 'Dreams now frequently related to the personal history of the dreamer. The romantics led the way with their insistence that dreams represented a return to the very roots of being, preserved in memories of early childhood.'[43] Bousquet discounts Freud's psychodynamic theory of dreams, but a more nuanced historical perspective would require us to reintroduce at least the autobiographical data on which the theory is based – particularly where Nerval is concerned.

Aurélia is not an autobiography in the accepted sense: in narrating his psychical ordeals, Nerval gave himself licence to imaginatively recast and reshape his experiences. Nevertheless his autobiographical intention is important. Two of the figures referred to in the narrative, Georges and Gérard's doctor, are historically real individuals:

> One of my friends, called Georges, undertook to overcome this despondency of mine. (157)

> The kind and compassionate face of my excellent doctor brought me back to the living world. (171)

Georges is Nerval's friend George Bell; Gérard's doctor is, of course, Emile Blanche. The therapeutic role they play is not limited to the content of Gérard's narrative. Their concern with restoring Gérard to norms of reality coincides with the formal fact of their identification in the narrative. Named or designated, they take their place as historical individuals: by virtue of identifying them, the writer engages with a non-subjective reality. Conversely, experiences of illness or unreason suspend formal identification along with referential reality. Near the beginning of Part Two, Gérard visits an unwell friend. This is probably Antony Deschamps;[44] however, the possible identification of the friend is less revealing than the formal fact of his non-identification in the text. As Gérard perceives him, he is 'a somewhat different person from the man I had known' (149–50). Transformed by illness, he is 'no longer the happy companion of my work and play' (150). The friend remains unidentified because his identity in the real world no longer matters as such. The descent into illness, with its blurring of identity, is a perilous one for the very form of the discourse which recounts it. In this context, the persistence of references to identifiable people and events possesses a therapeutic force which is objective rather than subjective. In contrast with the unidentified *ami malade*, the figures associated with health and healing are identified: Georges and Gérard's doctor. The identity of Gérard's unwell friend is withheld to the extent that his illness enters into dialogue with Gérard's own illness, withdrawing him from *le monde des vivants*. Conversely, Georges and Gérard's doctor undertake to combat Gérard's lapse from norms of reality. In being identified, they in turn identify an autobiographical discourse which aspires to a healthful reality.

In addition to the information contained in *Aurélia* itself, Nerval's contemporaries provided testimony which bears on the events of the narrative. Maxime Du Camp, in his *Souvenirs littéraires*, retells, rather amusingly, the episode of Gérard's treatment of the young madman:

> On another occasion, and during another crisis, Gérard, in the lodge where he lived, had come across a lunatic who presented a very curious case of mental pathology. This was a self-absorbed individual with an impulsion to pyromania. He never said a word, never opened his mouth and refused to take any nourishment; for six months Dr Blanche fed him by means of an oesophageal tube. Gérard imagined that his companion was frozen and said to me: 'He has been that way since the crossing of the Bérésina. Blanche has given me the job of thawing him out.' Then he rubbed his nose against that of the poor wretch and blew his breath in his face. The lunatic drew back a little, made a 'Pfooh,' but didn't resist. This continued until the day when the self-absorbed individual wanted to strangle Gérard, who gave up trying to defrost him.[45]

In *Aurélia*, the young man, far from having been frozen in the Napoleonic retreat from Moscow, is a soldier who has served in Africa. It was, in fact, Nerval's father, Dr Labrunie, who, as a military doctor in the Grand Army, was lucky to survive the Bérésina crossing. The transposition from cold to heat is a strategic one: in *Aurélia*, Nerval both conceals and acknowledges that the 'young soldier' is a symbolic image of the father as well as of the self.

To read *Aurélia* as an autobiography is to read it as a psychobiography.[46] Nerval solicits such a reading. His most directly autobiographical writing is to be found in *Promenades et souvenirs* (1854), where, in a psychologically resonant outline of his parentage and childhood, he states that the affective meaning of his madness derives from his own life history. He directly links the occurrences of his 'fever' with his mother's death:

She died at the age of 25, in the fatigues of war, of a fever which she caught crossing a bridge littered with corpses, where her carriage almost overturned. My father, compelled to rejoin the army at Moscow, later lost her letters and jewelry in the currents of the Bérésina. I never saw my mother, her portraits were either lost or stolen; I only know that she resembles an old engraving, entitled *Modesty*, in the style of Prud'hon or Fragonard. The fever of which she died has seized hold of me three times, at intervals which form regular, periodic divisions in my life. At these intervals I always feel my spirit stricken by the images of grief and desolation which surrounded my cradle. (*Pléiade*, 134–5)

Male and female are differently constituted in *Aurélia*. The female is rarely a specific figure, and never an identified individual. But she is often a spiritual essence which contains all the female forms that haunt Gérard's visionary imagination. A dream-vision of Part One of *Aurélia* takes him back to his maternal grandfather's house:

Three women were working in the room and, without exactly resembling them, they stood for relatives and friends of my youth. Each seemed to have the features of several of them. Their facial contours changed like the flames of a lamp, and all the time something of one was passing to the other. Their smiles, the colour of their eyes and hair, their figures and familiar gestures, all these were exchanged as if they had lived the same life, and each was made up of all three, like those figures painters take from a number of models in order to achieve a perfect beauty. The eldest spoke to me in a voice I recognized as having heard in my childhood. (130)

The absent mother is implicated in this dream through the analogy with the aesthetic image of an ideal, composite female: 'she resembles an old engraving (. . .) in the style of Prud'hon or Fragonard.' The absence of a specific mother in reality is translated into the presence of an ideal but non-specific mother in the realms of both dream and memory, a mother who gathers together all females in the dimension of their ideality. In Part Two of *Aurélia*, during Gérard's delirious perambulations in Paris, he enjoys one privileged revelation: 'I had a marvellous vision. It seemed to me that the goddess appeared to me, saying, "I am the same as Mary, the same as your mother, the being also whom you have always loved under every form"' (162).

Jean-Paul Sartre, in *The Problem of Method*, remarked, 'psychoanalytic monographs would (. . .) by themselves, throw light upon the evolution of the French family between the eighteenth and twentieth century.'[47] In the French context, Rousseau marks a dividing line. Post-Rousseau, personal and autobiographical writings (at the levels of both documentation and 'bourgeois literature') are distinguished by the wealth of material they make available for the kind of monograph Sartre has in mind (his remark occurs in the context of a brief discussion of Flaubert – a foretaste of the monumental psychobiographical study he was soon to embark on). When Nerval traces his problems back to the circumstances and events of a childhood in which his mother and father were largely absent, he merely underlines the point: the fact of their absence in no way diminishes either the emotional affect or symbolic significance which invest their figures in his writings. In the era of Romantic individualism, the hero of subjectivity (usually male) comprehends his identity as a process of inner development commencing with infancy ('The Child is Father of the Man'). The actual circumstances involving the mother and the father are psychologically consequential, but only to the extent that they relate to the essential roles allotted to them by the process of subjectivity (i.e. the production and reproduction of subjectivity as the dramatic narrative of individual interiority). In Nerval, the absent mother is converted, by way of a personal mythology, into a spiritual ideal which can never be tarnished by reality: Mme Labrunie will never 'betray' her son in the ways that Baudelaire's mother does.

By contrast, the father, Dr Labrunie, who returns from the Napoleonic campaigns to claim the child, embodies the realities of history. The weight of his presence is exerted as a determinate psychological pressure against which his son reacts by turning to mythic and visionary images of the mother. Nerval's resonant account, in *Promenades et souvenirs*, of his first encounter with his father reveals the tensions of their relationship:

> I was seven years old, and I was playing without a care by my uncle's door when three officers appeared in front of the house; the blackened gold of their uniforms barely gleamed underneath their greatcoats. The first one embraced me with such an effusion that I cried out: 'Father! . . . you're hurting me.'
> From that day, my destiny changed.
> All three came back from the siege of Strasbourg. The oldest, saved from the currents of the Bérésina, took me with him to teach me what was called my duties. (*Pléiade*, 135)

The father-stranger, having traversed a river of death, clearly possesses an heroic stature.[48] At the same time, however, his uncannily abrupt apparition is fateful for the son: Nerval captures the compound of love and antagonism which characterises much of their relationship in a memorable recognition scene.

Ambivalence in the autobiographical discourse is more radically relayed in the subjective text as a split which fissures the image of the father. Jean Richer has noted that Nerval 'attentively discerned all the figures of the mother, but did not see that symbols such as Pluto, Adoniram, the dragon, the Revenger, related to his father.'[49] Among the negative but unrecognised versions of the bad father must be included the *doppelgänger* Gérard encounters in Part One of *Aurélia*. L.-H. Sebillotte's psychobiographical interpretation focuses on the climactic dream which brings Part One of *Aurélia* to a conclusion.[50] On discovering that the double is to marry his beloved in the spirit-world, Gérard is involved in a violent confrontation:

> He was holding a long bar at the tip of which was a red-hot ball. I wanted to fling myself upon him, but the ball which he held out before him seemed to be continually threatening my head. Everyone around me seemed to be jeering at my impotence [*impuissance*] . . . I stepped back to the throne then, my soul filled with unutterable pride, and raised my arm to make a sign which to me appeared to have magical power [*puissance*]. A woman's cry, vibrant and clear, and filled with excruciating agony, woke me with a start. (142)

If Sebillote and subsequent critics are correct in discerning Oedipal meanings in this dream, then the implications are carried over to Gérard's awakening to the world of reality, where the father can be openly referred to. The narrative shifts into the present tense as the writer states his belief in the impossible reality of the cry which awoke him: 'I am still sure that the cry was real and that the air of the real world had rung with it.' The premise of Nerval's autobiographical discourse is that the narrated ordeals lie in the past: the writer himself has recovered. But, at this juncture, the present tense of narration fails to distinguish between a reliable narrator and an unreliable protagonist. Part One comes to an ominous close, and Part Two opens with a crisis which affects the form as well as the content of the writing: 'Lost once more! All is finished, all is over. Now I must die and die without hope' (147). The subsequent reflections on God, religion and science confirm that it is the writer and not the protagonist who utters these words:

> We must not hold human reason so cheap as to believe that it gains by complete self-humiliation, for that would be to impeach its divine origin. . . God will no doubt appreciate purity of intention: *and what*

father would like to see his son give up all reason and pride in front of him?
The apostle who had to touch to believe was not cursed for his doubt.
What have I been writing? These are blasphemies. (148; italics added)

As discourse itself is disrupted by the pressures of self-contradiction, the specific relationship with the father, is foregrounded. Whereas the mother belongs to the realm of vision and revelation, a realm which transcends the ego's construction of reality, the father, along with his counterparts and equivalents, belongs to the world of ego and identity. It is this world, however, which is transformed into an hallucinatory and nonsymbolic underworld, exposing how fragile is the ego's construction of reality, and how vulnerable it is to dissociation and fragmentation. The problem of self-identity in the realm of reality is related to a father who has abruptly intruded on the non-paternal paradise of childhood in order to remove Gérard to the city.

In *Aurélia*, Nerval associated Revolutionary unorthodoxy with his maternal uncle, Antoine Boucher, with whom he spent his childhood, and who rejected Christian belief. Elsewhere, Nerval described himself as a 'Child of a century which was more sceptical than unbelieving, floating between two contrary educations, that of the Revolution which denied everything, and that of social reaction, which pretends to re-establish the ensemble of Christian beliefs' (*Pléiade*, 299–300). The post-Revolutionary return to order coincided, for him, with the appearance of the father and relocation in the city. In his association of social norms with an imposition of paternal authority, he reveals the subversive implications of both his rebellion and his restlessness: 'My early years were too impregnated with revolutionary ideas, my education had been too free, my life too full of rambling, for me to be able to accept easily a yoke which still, on many points, would offend my reason' (156). This rejection of orthodoxy, however, distances father from son: 'Dr Labrunie often did not even read Gérard's letters, often anguished pleas for help or attempts at reassurance. The doctor refused to visit his son in the mental clinics during his stays.'[51] It is this negative father-son relationship, with its divisive and damaging consequences for the son, which Part Two of *Aurélia* seeks to remedy.

Aurélia has been described as a two-part sequence: revolt followed by submission, expiation or reconciliation.[52] In Part One, Gérard stages a rebellion against structures of authority: in Part Two, however, he attempts to reach an accommodation with norms of reality as the delirious crisis worsens. This is, simultaneously, an accommodation with the figure of the father and with the medical authority he represents. Just as the father is an identified figure in the autobiographical dimension of the writer's discourse, so other figures who are designated as historical individuals, notably Georges and Gérard's doctor, are relevant to the father–son relationship. On the threshold of a devastating crisis of delirium, Gérard acknowledges the need to effect some kind of stabilisation through heeding the post-Revolutionary voice of paternal and medical authority, as manifested in Georges:

> One day his expressive and quasi-monastic countenance seemed to me to give import to the eloquence he was calling forth against the years of scepticism and political and social depression that had followed the July Revolution. I had been one of the young men of that period and I had tasted its ardours and bitternesses. An emotion took hold of me; I told myself that such lessons could not be given without the intention of Providence. (157)

Nerval and Emile Blanche were both doctors' sons – Emile was the son of Esprit Blanche, who had treated Nerval during the 1841 crisis. But where Nerval had rejected his father's name and profession, Emile, by contrast, retained both of these, and so perpetuated the father's mode of identity. In terms of their respective relationships with the paternal mode of identity, Gérard and Emile are formally antithetical. In Part Two of *Aurélia*, Georges intervenes to mediate this antithesis. George Bell was born Joachim Hounau and was, like Gérard and Emile, the son of a doctor. He had, like Nerval, rejected his father's name and profession, yet, by virtue of caring for Gérard, he was, at the same time, aligned with Emile Blanche (in a letter of December 1853, Nerval wrote to Bell, 'You have been one of my doctors, and I remember with gratitude those far-flung walks we undertook last summer when you managed me with so much patience and solid friendship' (*Pléiade*, 1091)). Georges, then, is able to mediate the father–son opposition: like Gérard, he has renounced the paternal mode of identity, and yet he now assumes the ideal paternal role of healer *vis-à-vis* his troubled friend. Apropos of Georges's discourse, the narrator remarks, 'no doubt a spirit was speaking through him' – 'sans doute un esprit parlait en lui.' If we remember that Nerval had been treated by Emile's father, Esprit Blanche, we might further hypothesise that Georges's discourse manifests the therapeutic return in the son of a paternal-medical signifier: *un esprit parlait*. This would compensate for the pathological trigger-event of Part One, when Gérard is invaded by the hallucinatory voice of the double: 'By a strange effect of vibration it felt as though his voice was echoing in my own chest' (121). Gérard's subsequent conviction that Georges is 'possessed,' while unorthodox, is not hallucinatory: this perception in fact predicates eventual cure. Georges functions as the vehicle of a paternal utterance which is no longer experienced as a hostile and aggressive signified: *Esprit*, the voice, breath or spirit which, in the guardhouse, had penetrated Gérard as an alien thing, becomes a benevolent discourse on moral order and authority.

Georges prepares the way for Gérard's eventual symbolic identification with the 'good son,' Emile Blanche, who has successfully taken the father-doctor's place.[53] This, finally, enables Gérard's return to *le monde des vivants* by way of his treatment of the young madman, with whom he is able to construct a reciprocal, mutually beneficial father–son relationship. Inasmuch as a crisis of identity is resolved in *Aurélia*, it is in terms of the relationship with the father.

In *Aurélia*, a properly Romantic project of spiritual reintegration involves a mother who is absent in reality but omnipresent in *le monde des Esprits* – the transcendental realm of dream. At the same time, a therapeutic initiative which would restore the ego's damaged relationship with accepted norms of social reality involves an interiorised identification with a father-doctor who possesses a positive rather than a negative value. The 'good' father embodies a reality-principle and a mode of identity which can be embraced as therapeutic, rather than rejected as pathologically alienating.

There remains, however, the cautionary proviso that such a reconciliation occurs only under special circumstances, in the privileged realm of the asylum. This is a proviso which we will examine in the next chapter.

8 Gérard de Nerval (2): 'Madness tells her story'

I

Gérard's sojourn in the asylum in the final episodes of *Aurélia* parallels George Trosse's experience in Glastonbury and Cowper's in St Albans. Each protagonist undergoes a spiritual resurrection in a place of healing. In *Aurélia*, however, the asylum, for all its historical specificity, remains a fictional construction. The tension between autobiographical history and autobiographical fiction reflects the tension which characterises the work as a whole: as an autobiographical discourse, it is bound up with the relevant historical and biographical contexts, but as a writing of subjectivity it is independent of them. The two levels of discourse subvert each other. Meanwhile, the relationship between the life and the work itself remains problematic: the narrative of Gérard's recovery is coherent, but in biographical terms that very coherence is fictional.

The ambivalence of Nerval's actual relationship with Dr Blanche and his establishment is not apparent in *Aurélia*, yet traces can be detected in a description of Gérard's private room at the asylum: 'On the whole I found nearly everything that I had possessed there' (169). The asylum, seemingly, provides Gérard with a space in which to realise a sense of identity. For Nerval, however, home was not a private interior: it was located by memories of his maternal uncle's house in Loisy, and comprised an entire locality. As *Sylvie* shows, this is not a space which Gérard can reinhabit, for it no longer exists in reality: the sites of childhood still exist, but their meaning derives from the lost plenitude of the childhood world.

A domestic retreat might conceivably have compensated Nerval for that alienating objectivisation of social reality which he saw occurring in contemporary life. In *Sylvie* both Gérard's 'old-fashioned apartment,' full of 'bric-a-brac splendours,' and his celebrated proposal that 'the only refuge left to us was the poet's ivory tower' imply a domestic aesthetic of the type which assumed increasing importance as the century progressed – the private 'palace of art' into which sensitive souls such as Huysmans's des Esseintes could withdraw from the insufferable vulgarities of the era. For Nerval, however, the private interior was usually a point of departure, and he was rarely *chez lui.*

Dr Blanche attempted to persuade Nerval not merely to take up residence in his clinic, but to treat it as a home. In a period when a settled domicile acquires a psychological character, Blanche was evidently concerned about his patient's chronic vagabondage. In October 1853, he took delivery of Nerval's possessions and installed them in a private room at Passy, seeking, in effect, to anchor him to a stable environment. As reported in *Aurélia*, however, the personal possessions that surround Gérard obstinately refuse to coalesce into the domestic circumference of a centred self:

> I found there the debris of my various fortunes, the confused remains of several sets of furniture scattered or resold over the past twenty years. It is a junk heap as bad as Doctor Faust's. A tripod table with eagles' heads, a console supported on a winged sphinx, a Seventeenth-Century commode, and Eighteenth-Century bookcase, a bed of the same period, with an oval-ceilinged baldequin covered with scarlet damask (. . .), a rustic dresser laden with faïence and Sèvres porcelain, most of it somewhat damaged; a hookah brought back from Constantinople, a large alabaster cup, a crystal vase; some wood panelling from the destruction of an old house I had once lived in on the site of the Louvre. (169)

The list of antiques, exotic curios and bric-à-brac, all of it lacking in use value, continues for half a page further. The disparate and heterogeneous nature of this collection, so far from placing Gérard, bears witness to his endemic displacement: 'For some days I amused myself by rearranging all these things, creating in this narrow attic a bizarre ensemble composed of palace and hovel, that aptly summarises my wandering existence.'

The age of the commodity had dawned with the Paris of the Second Empire and Gérard's room in the asylum is a fantastic version of the commodified private interior of the mid-nineteenth century.[1] Like that interior, it perpetuates the connection which is traced between person, property and desire in the bourgeois era, but in the inverted forms of heterogeneity, eccentricity and lack of permanence. Under these conditions bourgeois reality becomes extravagant, fantastic and unstable. Later in the century, Maupassant's naturalist fiction took an increasingly fantastic turn as his mental condition deteriorated (he was to be another patient of Dr Blanche's at Passy). One of his later stories, 'Qui sait?' (1890) would have delighted Marx: it concerns a roomful of furniture which comes to life one night and makes its way out of the house.[2] Some time later, the narrator inspects an antique shop full of bric-à-brac, where he discovers his furniture. By the end of the story he has taken refuge in a private mental clinic. Nerval's possessions, although not so fantastically animated, were scarcely more restful in their effect: 'Dr Blanche thought he had done well in re-establishing him in his past; that would help him, he hoped, to cope better with his solitude. On the contrary, the reappearance of his fondest memories provoked an acute crisis of exaltation; he wept day and night (. . .). After several days, the doctor decided to suspend the experiment and moved him to another room.'[3]

In a psychoanalytic study of *Sylvie*, Sarah Kofman has itemised 'narcissistic' female motifs in Nerval's *oeuvre*:

> rhythmically repetitive rounds, accompanied by songs with set refrains, garlands, bowers [*berceaux de fleurs*] – these have a maternal, protective value; they are linked to the cycle of natural fecundity, to the cycle of the seasons, to that of woman; they are linked to the moon, to the cult of Artemis-Isis, to that of the Great Mother and her avatars. They refer to the need to be regenerated and reborn through maternal exhalation, to the desire to be enclosed in an enveloping uterine form.[4]

In Nerval, such female-maternal circles are rarely if ever 'enveloping' in the claustrophobic sense of the reference to the uterus. None of the womb motifs noted by Kofman involve an interior space; all, on the contrary, are situated in the open, and associated with nature. From an historical point of view, this alfresco emphasis is untypical. In his paper, 'The uncanny' [*'Das Unheimliche'*], Freud assimilates the female womb to a home: 'It often happens that neurotic men declare there is something uncanny about the female genital organs. This *unheimlich* place, however, is the former *Heim* [home] of all human beings, to the place where each one of us has lived once upon a time and in the beginning.'[5] According to Freud, this (repressed) association is primeval, but the literature he cites tells a rather different story. His final example, immediately prior to this identification of womb and home, is a story encountered in the *Strand* magazine which exemplifies the Victorian-Edwardian genre of the haunted house story, 'about a young married couple who move into a furnished house (. . .).'[6] In Nerval, the non-interiority of the womb corresponds to the non-materiality (and non-sexuality) of the ideal female, which in turn derives from the absence of the mother. Conversely, if the domestic interior rarely constitutes for him a womblike space of retreat from the reality of the world at large this is because he does not associate it with the image of the mother presiding over hearth and home. His lack of interest in the forms of bourgeois reality extends to the private sphere.

As well as seeking to surround Nerval with a homelike space, Blanche further sought to integrate him into a surrogate family. 'Dr Blanche held it to be important that his establishment was above all a family dwelling: the boarders' meals were shared and presided over by the doctor's family (his mother and sister) and his assistants.'[7] Blanche married in the summer of 1854 while Nerval was absent from the clinic on the ill-fated journey to Germany. When he returned to Blanche's care in August, the doctor sought to assert a paternal authority over his patient. Nerval resisted this: in a letter written on October 17, and left behind at Passy for Blanche to discover, he insisted on his seniority in years: 'You are young! in fact I forget what age separates us, because I still act as a young man, which stops me from perceiving that I am several years older than you.' As the letter continues, Nerval transfers his own sense of rivalry to his doctor:

> I saw you at your father's so young that I took advantage of my presumed state of madness to inspire the friendship of a young lady (. . .). Do you want me to think and let it be thought that, from that period, a dark jealousy has made you unjust towards me. . . Perhaps even this cruel sentiment will be newly manifested here. I fear to go too far, and in order to reassure you, I need to appeal to my entire life. Never having aspired to the wives or mistresses of my friends, I wish to always rank you among these (. . .) (*Pléiade*, 1155)

The letter continues with a bizarre paragraph which seems to provide evidence of derangement. It is not, however, incoherent: full of masonic references, it resumes the themes of seniority and rivalry in a pseudo-occult language:

> I don't know whether you are *three years* old or *five*, but I am more than *seven* and I have *metals* hidden in Paris. If you have for yourself the Gr. . . B. . . I will tell you that I call myself the *terrible brother* I will even be the *terrible sister* if need be. Belonging in secret to the *Order of the Nopses*,

which is German, my rank permits me to play my cards openly. . . Tell
it to your superiors, for I don't suppose that great secrets have been
confided to a simple [brother] who should find me *very Respectable* (X).
But I am sure that you are more than that. If you have the right to
pronounce the word [. . .] [hieroglyph inserted] (that is to say *Mac-Benac*
and I write it in the Oriental way), if you say *Jachin*, I say *Boaz*, if you
say *Boaz* I say *Jehova*, or even *Machenac* . . . But I know very well that
we are only joking. (*Pléiade*, 1155).

Ross Chambers argues that Blanche's marriage aligned him, for
Nerval, with the double who, in *Aurélia*, is scheduled to marry the
beloved.[8] Bearing this perception in mind, the above paragraph can
be linked to the climactic encounter with the double in the final
dream of Part One of *Aurélia* (which Nerval had only recently
completed): Gérard raises his arm 'to make a sign which appeared
to me to have magical power' (142). This aggressive contest is
converted into a reciprocal gesture of healing in the asylum at the
end of *Aurélia*: 'the spirit figure [Saturninus] placed his hand upon
my forehead, as I had done, the night before, when I had
endeavoured to magnetize my companion' (172). But in the real as
against the symbolic asylum, matters turned out differently. Nerval's
stay at Passy in 1854 reverses the narrative sequence: the letter of
October 17 shows his relations with Blanche in the light of the
occult and latently sexual contest which ends Part One of *Aurélia*.

At a climactic point in the narrative of recovery, Nerval exploded
any normative implications by inserting the radically heterogeneous
lyricism of the 'Mémorables'. This rhapsodic prose sequence seeks to
enact the immediacy of transcendental revelation: 'A star shone
suddenly and revealed the secret of the world of worlds to me.
Hosannah! Peace on earth and glory in heaven!' (174). The
'Mémorables' constitutes a maternally inspired writing of non-
identity: birth and creation are joyful and effortless because they do
not involve the painful labour of producing a substantial entity: 'In
the Himalayas a little flower is born. (. . .) A silver pearl shone in
the sands; a golden pearl sparkled in the sky . . . The world was
created' (173). The inspired writer is fecund rather than potent: 'the
world was created. Chaste loves, divine sighs!'; 'the air quivers, and
light harmoniously bursts the budding flowers [*fleurs naissantes*]. A
sigh, a shiver of love comes from the swollen womb of the earth.'
Breathing and sighing are intimately allied with fecundity. Inspired
language, transcending the concerns of the ego, is selfless. The
various equivocations, doubts and questionings of the confessional

discourse of identity evanesce: the visionary prose consists of a flow-
ing succession of declarative and lyrical statements, untroubled by
either introspective self-examination or temporal succession (they
fluctuate between present and past tenses). The writer is released
from the labour-pains of reproducing an identifiable self through his
autobiographical discourse. Inspired language is diffuse and gentle, 'a
soft foreign tongue,' different in kind from the self-analytical
discourse of identity.

As the studies of Frank Paul Bowman have shown, the imagery of
the 'Mémorables' is embedded in the syncretistic, illuminist and
utopian thought of the period.[9] The message of the Romantic
visionaries, and of the 'Mémorables', concerns 'the utopian and
apocalyptic dream of justice and unity, the spiritualisation of matter
and humanity, the disappearance of the ancient anathema.'[10] The
resurrection of the son coincides with the Second Coming ('glad
tidings') and announces an end of history: 'peace on earth and glory
in heaven.' Celebrating a paradisal transformation of reality, the
texture of the prose further enacts the positive overcoming of identity in language. A relay of song threads together time and space in
an animate texture which is both turned inwards and returned
outwards: 'the choir of stars unfolds itself in infinity; it turns away
and returns upon itself, contracts and expands.' Revealed secrets,
emergence from sheltered grottoes, music and song – these images
subsist in a language which itself opens outwards in a responsive
rhythm – the rhythm of an inspired language which aspires to the
status of revelation.

However, the visionary momentum of the 'Mémorables' is not
sustained:[11] The visionary sequence is abruptly succeeded by dream
narratives: 'I found myself *in spirit* at Saardam, which I visited last
year' (175): Nerval had in fact visited Saardam in 1852. We find
ourselves once more in the presence of an autobiographical narrator,
relating his dreams to his lived experience. Bowman has argued that
these dream narratives are continuous with the visionary sequence,
and carry over its utopian theme.[12] Nevertheless it remains true
that the immediacy and transparency of the visionary prose
sequence is problematised by the return of a voice which no longer
acts as a transparent medium of revelation and is identifiably that
of an autobiographical and psychological subject. Loss of
transparency is confirmed by the discourse which follows: 'I resolved
to fix my dream state and learn its secret' (176). This is a subject
who is by no means certain of the meaning of his dreams and who
now confronts sleep and dream as a threat to the integrity of the

ego: 'Is it not possible to control this attractive and fearful chimera, to rule the spirits of the night which play with our reason?' (176). In seeking to unriddle the enigma of his dreams, Gérard engages in a discourse of psychological introspection. Seeking to come to terms with his own psychological identity, he is aware of being divided between two modes of being ('Sleep takes up a third of our lives'). From the side of the ego he must attempt to re-establish the link between the disjoined spheres: 'Who knows if there is not some link between those two existences and if it is not possible for the soul to re-tie it [de le nouer] now. From that moment on I devoted myself to trying to find the meaning of my dreams' (176-7).

In The interpretation of dreams, Freud admitted the existence of dream-thoughts which defeat analysis: 'there is at least one spot in every dream at which it is unplumbable – a navel, as it were, that is its point of contact with the unknown.'[13] Subsequently, the psychoanalyst Guy Rosolato has proposed that this node or knot serves as the metaphor of a relationship with a maternal dimension which escapes knowing – a relation d'inconnu. Gérard's reference to the problematic link [lien] between the two existences of life and dream (a link which must be retied) can be interpreted in these terms: 'The sleep into which the sleeper plunges can be assimilated to the maternal container for a primordial identification. The navel indicates (. . .) that which is not recognised concerning the originally lived relationship between the child and its mother, but which is daily reproduced in sleep where the desire of the dream is condensed.'[14]

For Rosolato, the hollow of the navel is superimposed on the female fissure [fente] which constitutes the dark abyss of the 'unknown' on which object-relations are founded. In this way (and bearing in mind Gérard's own quest for meaning) he provides us with a means of interpreting the second of the dream-narratives which succeed the visionary sequence:

in front of me there opened an abyss into which there rushed in tumult the frozen waves of the Baltic. It seemed that the whole of the Neva with its blue waters were to be swallowed up in this fissure in the globe. The ships of Cronstadt and Saint Petersburg bobbed at anchor, ready to break away and vanish in the abyss, when a divine radiance from above lighted the scene of this desolation. In the bright beam of light piercing the mist, I saw the rock on which stands the statue of Peter the Great. Above this solid pedestal clouds rose in groups, piling up to the zenith. (176)[15]

It is the rocklike image of the father-emperor who restores stability
to a world threatened by a watery abyss. A similar contrast recurs
in Gérard's subsequent consideration of the problem of dream-
imagery: 'the strangeness of certain pictures, which are like the
grimacing reflections of real objects on a surface of troubled water'
(177). The masculine-paternal identity is re-established over against
an unstable female dimension which is both fascinating and disturbing ('cette chimère attrayante et redoutable'), and which eludes male
knowledge. In this view, it is the unknown fissure of female sexuality
which haunts the psychological subject as that which is not known,
but against which he will react as the assumptions of sanity require
he must: '"Why should I not," I asked myself, "at last force those
mystic gates, armed with all my will-power, and dominate my sensations instead of being subject to them?"' The image, not fortuitously,
is one of rape and domination.

Michel Foucault has proposed that 'the society that emerged in the
nineteenth century – bourgeois, capitalist or industrial society – call
it what you will – did not confront sex with a refusal of recognition.
On the contrary, it put into operation an entire machinery for
producing true discourses concerning it.'[16] Dr Labrunie was, at an
early date, an exponent of this development: 'On brumaire 9, XIV
(1806), he submitted his thesis on "The Dangers of the Deprivation
and Abuse of Venereal Pleasure in Women" (. . .). The chosen
subject – a study of hysterical manifestations in women due to either
a lack or an abuse of sexual relations – announces the direction in
which he will later specialise – female illnesses and gynaecology.'[17]
There is some evidence that Dr Labrunie's son found the prospect
of physical sexuality a disturbing one: Sebillote has underlined the
significance of the statement in Sylvie, 'Seen at close quarters the real
woman revolted our ingenuous souls' (51).[18] Nerval's openly
acknowledged tendency to idealise and spiritualise women can be
understood as a reaction against his father's medical interests.
However in proposing to force apart the gates of dream he is once
more his father's son: it is the psychological subject who finds the
female space of the unknown threatening rather than liberating, and
who now undertakes a quest for knowledge as means of control in
an act of historical reason. If Nerval is nowhere more radical than
in the 'Mémorables', he is nowhere more normative than in the
passages which follow the 'Mémorables' and which reflect on the
problematic relationship between dream and reality. The therapeutic
discourse of identity which results anticipates the project of Freud's
Interpretation of dreams in proposing to investigate the meaning of

dreams in the context of a self-analytical autobiography.

Rosolato proposes that the umbilical knot of the navel is the corporeal metaphor of a relationship with a female sexual orifice, and with the womb as interior container. This female 'unknown' poses a double threat to masculine definitions of reality: it is that fissure which, as absence of the phallus, undermines the solidity of the object-world; equally, it presents the seductive phantasy of a 'regressive' return to the uterus. In this way the doctor, typically, would project the onus of madness onto the female: 'Thus we see converging in an interiorisation which, singularly, makes the psychical apparatus a *container*, possessing therefore a feminine value, everything which escapes the signifying organisation and its totalisation – sexuality represented in femininity itself, madness and the real.'[19] The key term here is 'interiorisation.' In *Aurélia*, dream has represented a spiritual realm which may be 'psychical,' but which is not psychological. On the penultimate page of the text, however, this spiritual dimension is seemingly lost. As it becomes the object of introspection and self-analysis, dream acquires the meaning of an interiorised madness. On the final page of the text, Gérard returns his attention to the figure who, in the asylum, sums up the simultaneous representations of madness and interiorisation – the young madman. Turned in on himself and sustained by a life-support system, Gérard confronts in him an embodiment of self-withdrawal into the interiorised enclosure of the uterus.

Entry into sleep involves a descent into a 'vague underground cavern.' Going to sleep is an 'image of death,' but the cavern also suggests a uterus. The space of the tomb and that of the womb converge in this dangerous transitional moment.

In chapter VIII of Part One of *Aurélia*, Gérard, in the course of a sequence of dream-visions, witnesses the unfolding of an occult world history. Necromancers parthenogenetically reproduce themselves in uterine sepulchres:

> These necromancers, exiled to the ends of the earth, had agreed to transmit their power to one another. Surrounded by women and slaves, each of their sovereigns was assured of being born again in the form of one of his children. Their life lasted a thousand years. When they were about to die, powerful cabalists shut them up in well-guarded tombs where they were fed elixirs and life-giving substances. They preserved the semblance of life for a long time. Then, as the chrysalis spins its cocoon, they fell asleep for forty days to be born again as a little child which was later called to the kingdom. (134–5)

These male wombs are malignant parodies of the female womb:
they do not produce new life but endlessly reproduce the Oedipal
self. In the asylum, Gérard, remembering the necromancers,
exclaims, 'Ah misery! (. . .) we live again in our sons as we have
lived in our fathers' (167). The necromancers are bad versions of
the father-doctor. In the narrative of recovery, the good father
embodies an historically determined reality-principle, but this good
father is inescapably accompanied by a negative double. The bad
father asserts his presence in a fantasmatic perversion of history: the
threat of a pathological loss of reality resides in his continuing
influence.

In *Aurélia*, an open, undefined maternal 'womb' is readily
translated into the material closure of the paternal tomb. In Part
One, Gérard dreams of a woman whose form coalesces with the
landscape of a garden, but this in turn is nightmarishly transformed
into a graveyard:

> gradually the whole garden blended with her own form (. . .). I lost her
> as she became transfigured, for she seemed to vanish in her own immen-
> sity. 'Don't leave me!' I cried. 'For nature dies with you.' (. . .) I threw
> myself on a fragment of ruined wall, at the foot of which lay the bust
> of a woman. I lifted it up and felt convinced it was of *her* . . . I recognized
> the beloved features and as I stared around me I saw that the garden had
> become a graveyard, and I heard voices crying: 'The universe is in
> darkness.' (131)

Subsequently, (in an episode which corresponds to the relapse of
1851) Gérard, visiting a friend, admires the view from a terrace.
While descending a stairway he falls, hurting his chest. He believes
himself mortally wounded and rushes into the centre of a garden:
'I felt happy to be dying this way, at this hour, surrounded by the
trees, trellises, autumn flowers. It was, however, no more than a
swoon' (137). Later, as fever takes hold, he 'remembers' that the view
he had admired overlooked the cemetery where Aurélia is buried.
Again, a garden or landscape is transformed into a cemetery; again
a site saturated with maternal implications is juxtaposed with the
graveyard of the dead beloved. Gérard rushes into the garden as into
the maternal circle which will transform death into rebirth, but this
transition is denied: the open, pastoral space congeals into the
enclosure of the tomb, and Gérard is plunged once more into
delirious dreams. In the climax of this sequence, the dead beloved,
trapped in a material, reified form (represented in the dream as a
sculpted bust) is claimed by the hostile double who rules in the

underworld: 'I imagined that the man they were waiting for was my *double*, and that he was going to marry Aurélia' (142).

In the asylum, the situation of the young madman resumes the episode of the necromancers. '[the necromancers] were fed elixirs and life-giving substances'; '[the young man] was made to swallow liquid and nutritious substances by means of a long rubber tube inserted into his stomach.' Nerval had originally written 'By means of a long tube of rubber inserted into a nostril he was made to swallow a fairly large quantity of semolina and chocolate.'[20] The revision, while highlighting the womb-image, brings the madman's situation into closer rapport with that of the necromancers. Given this rapport, his delusive perception is symbolically accurate: 'I was buried in a certain graveyard.' His trance equates dream and madness just as his state of suspended animation equates womb and tomb: in confronting this figure, Gérard confronts the embodiment of a nexus of concerns which bear directly on his own experiences of sleep, dream and madness. The madman's delusion that he inhabits a tomb expresses, for Gérard, the deadly interiorisation of madness itself as a psychopathological condition. In *Aurélia*, the 'uterine' womb, so far from being a maternal space, is both deathly and paternal. The meanings of the asylum are balanced between this negative condition of stasis and a positive release from enclosure, with the young madman positioned at the point of balance.

In seeking to heal him, Gérard magnetises him, then sings to him. In this way he re-establishes a connection with the maternal-transcendental realm celebrated in the 'Mémorables'. As in the 'Mémorables', song evokes an answering response: 'I had the happiness of seeing that he heard them, and he repeated certain parts of the songs.' Reawakened from the deathly sleep of the paternal tomb, the young man is linked with the resurrected son of the 'Mémorables'.

This renewed maternal influence enables a positive revaluation of the paternal roles – soldier, doctor and gynaecologist[21] – which are redistributed between Gérard and the madman. Gérard is thus able to care for the afflicted young man, where Nerval's father had failed to care for him in his crises. We should, then, conclude that a psychological recovery would reintegrate the spiritual values of the maternal sphere with the stabilising norms of the paternal sphere. Such a recovery would reconcile the spirit world with contemporary historical reality, notably the Crimean war, which is implicated in the imagery of the dream-narratives.[22] Recovered from the fatal divide which polarises the mother and the father, reality itself would then fulfil its utopian potential. The possibility of such an outcome is intimated in the happy conclusion to the 'historical' dream-narrative: the solid statue of Peter the Great, having stabilised the threatening abyss and re-established the historical world, is surrounded by ethereal female forms who bring a message of harmony which is at once visionary and historical:

> In the bright beam of light piercing the mist, I saw the rock on which stands the statue of Peter the Great. Above this solid pedestal clouds rose in groups, piling up to the zenith. They were laden with radiant, heavenly forms, among which could be distinguished the two Catherines and the empress Saint Helen accompanied by the loveliest Princesses of Muscovy and Poland. Their gentle expressions, directed towards France, lessened the distance by means of long crystal telescopes. By that I saw that our country had become the arbiter of the old quarrel of the East, and they were awaiting its solution. My dream ended in the sweet hope that peace would at last be granted us. (176)

Nevertheless this cannot but seem a secondary, compromised version of the visionary radicality of the *Mémorables*. As the maternal and paternal figures return to their ordained roles, and as the ecstatic dream-language returns to a discourse of identity, the celebration of holy madness is suspended. It recedes on an horizon of utopian possibility, becoming a dream from which the sleeper must awaken. With that awakening, the utopian priority cedes to a medical one, the healing of a damaged reality to the healing of a damaged self, represented in the figure of the young madman.

II

Although concluded, *Aurélia* was not quite completed at the time of Nerval's death and the final pages present specific textual problems, most notably the vexed issue of the love letters to Jenny Colon, which the text creates a potential space for.[23] Michel Jeanneret has argued that the remaining problems are evidence of the failure of a critical 'discourse on madness.'[24] We might more reasonably conclude that they result from the fact that Nerval had not quite finished work on his manuscript at the time of his death. Nevertheless his difficulties with the text may have been symptomatic. According to an acquaintance who saw him a few nights before his death, 'he (. . .) spoke all the while of the book he was writing, *le Rêve et la vie*. "I'm desolate," he said sadly. "I've ventured on an idea which I'm losing myself in. I spend hours trying to find my way. I'll never finish. Can you believe I can scarcely write twenty lines a day?"'[25]

Aurélia could not prove to be anything other than a difficult undertaking for Nerval. Writing at a time of continuing instability, he sought not merely to record and analyse his inner experiences and their meaning, but to recreate them imaginatively in a work of literature. As he worked on *Aurélia* throughout 1854, he was aware that the projection of a self-image was itself an ambivalent undertaking. That year Eugène de Mirecourt published a biography of him, *Les contemporains – Gérard de Nerval*. While still resident at the Passy clinic he had posed for a portrait for the frontispiece of the volume. On leaving the clinic in May he undertook his expedition to Germany. At the end of that month, he wrote to George Bell,

> illness has made me so ugly, – melancholy doesn't look after itself. I'm afraid of encountering on display a certain portrait for which I was made to pose when I was ill, under the pretext of a necrological biography. The artist is a talented man. . . [but] *he is too true to life*. Tell everyone that my portrait resembles me, but *posthumously* – or else that Mercury has acquired the features of Sosia and posed in my place. (*Pléiade*, 1115)

In 1841 a peculiar nexus of associations involving madness, biography and death had crystallised when Jules Janin wrote an 'obituary' of Nerval on the occasion of his first breakdown in 1841. The episode was still fresh in Nerval's mind when he reproached Dumas for publicising his madness in 1853 – 'Some years ago I was believed dead and he [Janin] wrote my biography' (*Pléiade*, 149). These associations resurfaced at the end of May 1854, when Nerval received a copy of the de Mirecourt biography. He scribbled various notations on the engraved portrait which provided the frontispiece: they include a rebus which, deciphered, reads *le feu Gérard* – the late Gérard – and also the words *Je suis l'autre*.

The journey to Germany was full of overt significance. In the letter to Bell, the crossing of the Rhine becomes a descent into the underworld: Nerval quotes the aria *Divinités du Styx* from Gluck's *Orphée* (his mother was buried in eastern Germany). The theme of the double was also on his mind. In a letter to Blanche written on June 1st, when he had just finished reading the de Mirecourt biography, he pictures his former self in the clinic: 'I beg you to address (. . .) a speech in my favour to all your ladies, so good for me, and always so indulgent. Explain to them that the pensive being whom they saw trailing along, morose and troubled, in the salon, in the garden, or at your hospitable table, was assuredly not myself.

From the other side of the Rhine, I deny the sycophant who had taken my name, and perhaps my face' (*Pléiade*, 1118). Proclaiming himself recovered, Nerval, employing the strategy of *Aurélia*, reclaims health by projecting illness onto the other, the 'past self.' But the strategy was to backfire: in mid-July he wrote to Blanche informing him that he had suffered a relapse.[26] He returned from Germany in mid-crisis, and by August 8 was once more resident at Passy. Thus, where the final chapter of *Aurélia* narrates the ascent of the autobiographical self from the underworld, real life finds the autobiographer retracing this thematic sequence in reverse. Crossing the Rhine he descends into the underworld; on the ambiguous border territory of Strasbourg he re-encounters versions of the double, with its portents of death; in the 'dreamland' of Germany, he lapses back into delirium. The pattern of inversion is completed by his return to an asylum where he encounters not a positive relationship with 'Saturninus' as madman and spiritual brother, but a version of Oedipal rivalry, with Blanche assuming the seniority of a paterfamilias and himself recast in the role of madman.

In December 1853, Nerval wrote optimistically to Blanche about the memoir of madness on which he had commenced work: it will 'rid my head of all these visions which have so long inhabited it. These unhealthy phantasmagorias will be succeeded by sound notions' (*Pléiade*, 1089). A few days later, he wrote again: 'As soon as I am rid of these worries I will (. . .) leave behind this tendency to write nothing but personal impressions, which results from my turning round in a narrow circle' (*Pléiade*, 1094). The therapeutic nostrum was to prove ineffectual: the letters from Germany show Nerval still turning about in his vicious circle. Writing to his father on June 12, he remarked 'I've done well in keeping my poetical life separate from my real life' (*Pléiade*, 1122). This, in fact, is just what he failed to do, and in turning his inner life into literature he may well have perpetuated his problems. As is the case with Cowper's final poem, 'The Castaway', or a number of Clare's asylum poems, 'literature' proves, after all, not to be a therapeutic medium – on the contrary. In his essay on Hölderlin, Foucault proposed that what confronts us in the nineteenth century is 'the enigmatic identity which permits [language] to speak at the same time of madness and of an artistic work' (Foucault's emphasis).[27] Where Nerval is concerned, the dualism of *vie poétique* and *vie réelle* recalls the title of the work in progress, *Le Rêve et la vie*, and suggests that there is a parallel between literature and the ambiguous domain of dream. 'The *I* under another form continues the task of existence': this might well describe the autobiographical self of the literary confession. If, for Gérard, madness is *l'épanchement de la rêve dans la vie réelle*, then for Nerval in 1854, madness takes the form of an overflowing of *la vie poétique* into *la vie réelle*. The very writing of an autobiography of dream, vision and madness undoes in advance the project of reintegration: the self is thrown into question from the outset, from the very moment of setting pen to paper and creating its own double – 'I under another form.' The process of writing creates its own disturbing effect, so that the projected narrative resolution culminates at a moment of personal irresolution. In *Aurélia*, it is the language of subjective literature itself which implicates the play of madness.

III

Gautier testifies that Nerval's lucidity of expression never deserted him: 'There was no darkening, no aberration, no failure of precision, to betray the wild disorder of his mental faculties. He remained impeccable to the very end.'[28] However, as Gautier clearly understood, the lucidity of Nerval's treatment of obsessional themes in *Aurélia* hardly guards against their power. Rather it elucidates the scope and implications of a madness which cannot be contained by the bounds of a confessional discourse of identity. In his reminiscences of Nerval Gautier offered two variant accounts of the work:

(i) *Aurélia* (. . .) shows cold reason seated at the bedside of hot fever, hallucination analysing itself in a supreme philosophical effort.

(ii) It has been said of *Aurélia* that it is a poem in which madness tells her own story. It would have been even more accurate to describe it as Reason writing the memoirs of Madness at her dictation. The philosopher remains coolly present during the visions of the lunatic.[29]

Aurélia cannot be summarised by a single formula or considered as a single discourse: in the interplay of reason and unreason, neither dominates, equally, neither collapses into the other. Gautier is close here to Nerval's own view, as stated in *A Alexandre Dumas*: 'Some day I will write the history of that "descent into the underworld" and you will see that it has not been entirely devoid of reasoning, even if it has always lacked reason' (*Pléiade*, 158). The relationship of reason and madness in the work is not merely undecidable[30] but irreducibly paradoxical: it presents the unprecedented phenomenon of a metadiscourse of madness.

Baudelaire, in a tribute to Nerval, echoed Gautier: 'A writer of an admirable frankness, of a high intelligence, and *who was always lucid*' (Baudelaire's emphasis).[31] Underlying the remarks of Gautier and Baudelaire is an intuition that Nerval's situation requires new conceptualisations of madness. As it becomes a scene of cultural and literary production, madness acquires a distinctively modern character.[32]

At this point we might conveniently turn to René Girard, who offers a revisionist view of a 'culture of madness' evolving out of Romanticism and into modernism. Discussing Deleuze and Guattari's *Anti-Oedipus*, Girard suggests that when madness becomes the object of critical enquiry, then it will also prove to be the consequence of such an enquiry. As Western culture increasingly adapts itself to an ongoing condition of crisis, then unreason becomes critical, self-reflexive and lucid: 'We must see in the reference to delirium, not an individual aberration, but a predictable aberration of culture itself. It is the destiny of modern culture, of the modern end of all culture in the historical sense, to live all successive moments including delirium in relative lucidity.'[33]

Girard returns to base by laying the blame for this modern apocalypse at the door of Romanticism, and it is through this door that *Aurélia* must be approached. The phenomenon of a creative and subjectively self-reflecting writing produced from within the experience of madness itself testifies that the relationship between writing and madness enters a new stage in the nineteenth century, one which is rooted in Romanticism, but which has consequences for post-Romantic and modern culture.

The notion of Romantic creativity appeals to the necessary madness of an interiorised artistic conception, in order to resacralise the art work in a secular, urban and capitalist civilisation: 'the last madness which will remain to me,' Nerval wrote, 'will probably be that of imagining myself a poet' (*Pléiade*, 159). The madness of the artist, existing beyond the daylight of reason and consciousness, provides an ultimate refuge for the sacred character of the art work, even where this is manifested as (in Foucault's terms) 'a perpetual rupture.'[34] 'The death of God leads to an experience in which nothing may again announce the exteriority of being, and consequently to an experience which is *interior* and *sovereign*.'[35] This experience, according to Foucault, is the precondition of 'a discourse

(. . .) that joins madness *and* an artistic work,'[36] nevertheless it hardly frees the art work from the operation of ideological and market forces. It is precisely the 'pathology' of the artist which now confirms the sovereign value of the art work.

In a secular era, the ordeals of Hölderlin, Clare and Nerval, investing them with something of the sacred character of the holy madman, guarantee the integrity of their visionary texts. Such an exaltation of poetic madness must, of course, be distinguished from the actual experiences undergone by these writers, but these experiences are themselves inflected by contemporary paradigms, not least those of Romanticism. If Clare and Nerval are able to productively express their respective crises in poetic modes of writing, it is because the inner meanings precipitated by these crises, however radically transgressive, are inherently 'poetic' in a period characterised by a divide between a solitary or private subject and an external object world. But it is precisely the 'poetry' of their madness (Nerval walking his lobster in the Palais-Royal) – rather than the text of their mad poetry – which modern culture has digested without visible strain.

Clare, a low-class outsider standing at the privileged threshold of Romanticism, must be granted a special right of appeal against modern cultural appetite. In England the reception of Clare's 'Byronic' poems of 1841 has been very different from that of the visionary Northampton asylum lyrics: if *Don Juan* and *Child Harold* continue to obstinately resist our efforts to consume them, it is because Clare, writing as Lord Byron, is able to direct the intolerable nature of his situation *against* an audience which is no more real than the identity of the poet who writes the poems. Clare well knew that his audience, as constituted by the various advertisements he wrote for the poems, did not in fact exist, or rather, existed only to the extent that he was 'in fact' Lord Byron (among others). The poems remain radical and uncompromised for as long as they stand at the margins of 'literature': the last laugh is on those of us who fail to constitute an audience for them.

Nerval could afford to be more confident in his expectations, and *Aurélia* was written with a real audience very much in mind, one which included his father, his doctor, literary colleagues such as Dumas, and, last but not least, a reading public which he was not inclined to ignore.[37] When Shoshana Felman remarks that 'we are experiencing today an inflation in discourses on madness,'[38] this is a development we might well trace back to *Aurélia*. The real complexity of the work is offset by the sustained lucidity of its writing, but, by another turn of the screw, madness is most effectively communicated through this very lucidity. In writing out the contradictions of subjectivity from within an acute experience of the gap between self-alienation and self-transcendence, Nerval's book is undoubtedly subversive: the inheritance of Dr Labrunie is thoroughly unsettled insofar as that inheritance amounts to an identity. But Nerval could not escape from a larger ideological settlement: in important respects, he did not seek to. If the subjectivism of the work is viewed in historical perspective, then it can be seen that it sells its author's experiences in the cultural marketplace. Alexandre Dumas, starting up a new literary journal, Le Mousquetaire, and inviting Nerval to collaborate, was in no doubt that his friend's predicament would be of interest to readers. He was eager to capitalise on it and in November 1853, he proposed that Nerval (who was in the Passy clinic) write an account of his experiences, under the title 'Three days of madness' for Le Mousquetaire.[39] Certainly, Aurélia, asserting itself (in the 'quality' journal, Revue de Paris) as 'literature' rather than journalism, is a rejoinder rather than a response to Dumas's proposal (as though to underline the point, the text commences with a broadside of legitimising references to Swedenborg, Apuleius and Dante). Nevertheless for Nerval, no less than for Gautier and Dumas, the literary marketplace was an unavoidable fact of life. Gautier (himself worn down by a lifetime of literary journalism) remarked that 'the journals were always open to him, and each article he presented to an editor was welcomed.'[40] Aurélia, while it is not 'Three days of madness', cannot be considered in isolation from this context: for all its 'writerly' complexity, it is a triumph of readerly persuasion.[41] This is sufficiently demonstrated in the commentaries which those two exemplary readers, Gautier and Moreau de Tours, wrote within a few years of each other.

Such factors affect the reception of the work no less than its production. Both Gautier and Moreau responded to a writing of madness which is simultaneously romantic in expression and medical in representation. In this way, Aurélia not only reveals the ideologies which have redefined madness for modernity, it participates in the redefinition. Whatever complexities we encounter as readers, we do not critically distance ourselves from the narrator's voice. Because it so acutely registers the problematics of self-consciousness, this voice seems to speak on our behalf, and to convey what we ourselves recognise, through extremes of alienation and transcendence, pathology and vision, as a tantalisingly intimate articulation of psychical interiority. In *Aurélia*, then, we bear witness to the realisation of a mode of subjectivity which psychoanalysis, surrealism and existentialism have, in the second half of our century, converted into common cultural currency – one which confirms absurdity and anomie on the one hand, dream, desire, and fantasy on the other, as constitutive elements of our 'inner' being – not *against* but *in* the modern world. For the modern reader, there is no shock in *Aurélia* other than the shock of recognition. Because we recognise and accept the intimacy of the narrator's voice, we also recognise it as a version (or at least a potential version) of our own inner voice. Delirium, still dangerous perhaps, but no longer alien or other, has been democratised. As banal instances of this, we might note that the exclusive drug experiences of the French Romantics have become commonplace since the 1960s, and that the emergence of a drug culture at that moment coincided with a vogue for R. D. Laing and 'schizophrenia.' Foucault's inquiry into madness, written in the same period, has stimulated a whole field of academic studies of which this book is yet another instance. Madness, to quote Felman once more, is a word which is 'available to all who wish to utter it.'[42]

As though anticipating such developments, the intimacy of Nerval's discourse in *Aurélia* invites the reader's complicity: 'My imagination gave me infinite delight. In recovering what men call reason, do I have to regret the loss of these joys?' The question both presumes a sympathetic response and insinuates an empathetic one. This provides some measure of how close *Aurélia* is to us. We comprehend the narrator's inner experience, both in its plural complexity and its lucidity, as a portrayal of our own potential condition. In an age when forms of unreason, manifested through subjective interiority (an interiority which literature has played its part in constructing), have become interwoven with the lucid, self-reflecting psychological fabric of our society and culture, *Aurélia* speaks directly to us.

Notes

Introduction

1. Gusdorf, 1984, p. 298.
2. Foucault, 1977, p. 75.
3. Ibid., p. 71.
4. Foucault, 1971, p. xi.
5. 'The highly interiorised stages of stages of consciousness in which the individual is not so immersed unconsciously in communal structures are stages which, it appears, consciousness would never reach without writing' (Ong, 1982, p. 178).
6. See David Vincent, 1981, pp. 36-7.
7. The terms 'interiorisation' (see Ong, note 5 above) and 'internalisation' are used by different critics and theorists to signify approximately the same concept, i.e. a development of subjective inwardness in various forms. Roy Schafer offers the following definition: 'Internalization refers to all those processes by which the subject transforms real or imagined regulatory interactions with his environment, and real or imagined characteristics of his environment, into inner regulations and characteristics' (Schafer, 1968, pp. 44-5). I have usually preferred the term 'interiorisation.'
8. Adorno, 1989, p. 41.
9. Max Horkheimer, cited in Jay, 1973, p. 102.
10. See Habermas, 1974.
11. For a brief account of Otloh and his writings, see Colin Morris, 1972, pp. 79-83.
12. 'The word which sounds externally is the sign of a word which shines within us, and this inner word better deserves the title of "word." What is uttered with the mouth is merely the sound of a word' (in Howie, 1969, p. 333).
13. Cf. Marcuse, 1972, pp. 56-78.
14. Foucault, 1973, p. 555.
15. Ibid., p. 556.
16. Stierle, 1977.
17. Ibid., pp. 425-6.

18. Particular discourses, for all that they impose a line of identity, can never fully manifest this set of norms. There is a residual tension between scheme and manifestation, so that discourse, is 'under its concrete aspect, always at the same time a non-discourse' (p. 427). Ordinarily, however, this residual tension is not a dominant factor, otherwise discourse could not constitute itself as discourse.
19. See Benveniste, 1971, pp. 223–30.
20. Ibid., pp. 206–7.
21. Ibid., p. 218.
22. Ibid., p. 224.
23. Stierle, 1977, p. 435.
24. Ibid., p. 437.
25. Ibid., p. 441.
26. Cf. Benveniste: 'Rimbaud's *Je est un autre* ["I is another"] represents the typical expression of mental "alienation," in which the "I" is dispossessed of its constitutive identity' (1971, p. 199).

Chapter 1

1. The topic of Tasso's madness has been most recently and most fully explored by Bruno Basile in *Poëta melancholicus* (1984). See in particular Chapter 1, to which I am much indebted.
2. Tasso, 1853, pp. 161–2.
3. Cited in Rosen, 1968, p. 145.
4. Tasso, 1853, p. 237.
5. Cited in Rosen, 1968, pp. 146–7.
6. Brand, 1965, p. 22.
7. Ibid., pp. 22–3.
8. Foucault, 1971, p. 286.
9. Tasso, 1958, p. 264.
10. Ibid., pp. 265–6.
11. Tasso, 1853, p. 247.
12. Panofsky, 1971, p. 167.
13. Medcalf, 1981, p. 124. In the absence of independent testimony, the question of whether or not Hoccleve actually did suffer the breakdown he reports has been much debated. Doob (1974) is inclined to be sceptical, but Medcalf makes an altogether more persuasive case for accepting the factual basis of the poems. He notes that circumstantial evidence (records of payments) tallies with Hoccleve's account, and points out that he provides verifiable information on other matters – names of colleagues, for example. As Medcalf notes, there are conventional elements in the poems, but some details (such as the mirror episode discussed below) are 'painful and surely personally reminiscent' (p. 132).
14. Quotations are from Hoccleve, 1970. Line references are given in brackets.

15. See Curtius, 1979, p. 474.
16. Tasso, 1958, p. 266. Petrarch's sonnet begins, 'Alone and thoughtful, I go pacing the most deserted fields with slow, hesitant steps, and I am watchful so as to flee from any place where human traces mark the sand' (tr. George Kay). Basile shows how Tasso relates Petrarch's sonnet to its subtext, a passage in Cicero's *Tusculan disputations*: 'Hence it comes that, when the soul is grieved, others seek out solitude, as Homer says of Bellerophon: "In the Aleian plain he desolate wandered in sorrow, / Eating his heart out alone, and the footsteps of man he avoided."' See Basile, 1984, pp. 36-7.
17. Ibid., p. 264.
18. See Penelope Doob, 1974, p. 31.
19. Adorno, 1989, p. 42.
20. Ibid, p. 42.
21. *Prose diverse*, ed. C. Guasti (Le Monnier, Florence, 1875), I, p. 435. (Cited in Kates, 1983, p. 130, note 13).
22. Bracketed page references for Tasso's poetry are to Tasso, 1952. George Kay's translations of three poems are from *The Penguin Book of Italian Verse*; all other translations are mine.
23. *Rime . . . di nuovo datte in luce con gli argomenti et espositioni de l'istesso autore* (Brescia, 1593), p. 7. (Cited in Basile, 1984, p. 33. n. 32.)
24. Brand, 1965, p. 154.
25. Kates, 1983, pp. 100-1.
26. Curtius, 1979, p. 95.
27. Viau (1590-1626), a French libertine poet, came into conflict with the Jesuits: he was tried and imprisoned for writing blasphemous verses.
28. Barker, 1984, p. 31.
29. Ariès, 1979, p. 395.
30. Foucault, 1977, p. 74.
31. Stone, 1982, pp. 284-5.
32. According to an account given by the poet's nephew to Tasso's friend and biographer, Manso, Tasso at first concealed his identity from his sister (whom he had not seen for many years), disguising himself as a shepherd. He pretended to bring news that her brother was in danger, before revealing himself.
33. Until his death in 1595, Tasso remained difficult and unsettled, dogged by ill health and fits of melancholy. But he also remained lucid and active. See Brand, 1965, pp. 26-32.

Chapter 2

1. All page references for this volume are to *Lucida intervalla: containing divers miscellaneous poems*, ed. Michael V. Deporte, 1979.
2. The biographical summary which follows is indebted to Michael Deporte's Introduction to *Lucida intervalla*.

3. Deporte in Carkesse, 1979, p. ix.
4. See Foucault, 1971, p. 39ff.
5. See Porter, 1987(a), p. 46.
6. Cited in Porter, 1987(a), p. 46. This statement, by Dr Nicholas Robinson, dates from 1729, but it is consistent with the earlier views of Thomas Willis (see Porter, ibid.).
7. Screech, 1985, p. 29. Screech shows how Plato's ambiguous differentiation between 'organic' and 'charismatic' forms of madness persisted in Christian culture through to the Renaissance.
8. Hobbes, 1839, III, p. 62.
9. Ibid., pp. 64-9.
10. Habermas, 1974, p. 49.
11. See Sennett, 1986, p. 47.
12. Doerner, 1981, p. 24.
13. Ibid.
14. Reed (1970) claims, on the basis of dubious calculations, that about seventy-five people per day visited Bethlem in the Elizabethan and Jacobean periods. Patricia Allderidge has convincingly disputed Reed's figures (1985, pp. 17-33). Old Bethlem was certainly open to visits and loomed large in the popular imagination. But there is little evidence that such visits were a popular phenomenon before the reopening on the new Moorfields site in 1676. Conditions in the old Bethlem were squalid and cramped compared with the more open and salubrious design which impressed early visitors to New Bethlem.
15. Sennett, 1986, p. 77.
16. Ibid., pp. 17ff., pp. 109ff.
17. Cited in Porter, 1987(a), p. 122.
18. Ibid., p. 37.
19. Foucault, 1970, p. 51.
20. Porter, 1987(a), p. 38.
21. Flecknoe, 'A short discourse on the English stage', Critical essays of the seventeenth century, edited by Joel E. Springarn, 3 vols, II, Oxford University Press, 1908, p. 95.
22. See Sennett, 1986, pp. 107-22.
23. Ibid., p. 16.
24. Barker, 1984, p. 11.
25. David Riesman, cited by Stone, 1982, pp. 154-5.
26. Cf. Barker: 'At the very moment when the soul reaches out to appropriate the outer world, the very gesture reinforces the division by which it is other than what it seeks to apprehend. The obverse face of the reception of the Diary as a documentary record of the life and times of the Restoration is its status as an inner history' (1984, p. 10).
27. R. Latham in Pepys, The shorter Pepys, ed. R. Latham, Penguin, Harmondsworth, 1988, p. xxxiii.
28. Sage, 1988, p. 76ff.
29. Allen refused to allow scientific experiments to be carried out on

chronically insane patients in his care. See Hunter and Macalpine, 1963, p. 184.

30. In Hunter and Macalpine, 1963, pp. 191-2.
31. Ibid., pp. 124-7.
32. Deporte comments that this treatment 'seems pure parody, but is actually close to the kind of literal-mindedness one encounters in medical treatises of the day' (in Carkesse, 1979, p. vii).
33. See Foucault, 1970.
34. Porter 1987(a), p. 140.
35. Ibid., p. 126.
36. Ibid.
37. Ibid.
38. Porter, 1987(b), p. 169.
39. Cf. Gilbert and Gubar, 1979, pp. 67-70.
40. See Showalter, 1987, p. 8.

Chapter 3

1. Delany, 1969, p. 56.
2. John Rogers, cited in Watkins, 1972, p. 20.
3. On the 'typicality' of Grace abounding, see Tindall, 1934, p. 22ff.
4. Quinlan, 1953, pp. 34-5.
5. Erikson, 1959, p. 12.
6. Ibid., p. 188. Cf. p. 189: 'Luther accepted for his life work the unconquered frontier of tragic conscience (. . .) "Conscience is that inner ground where we and God have to learn to live with each other as man and wife."'
7. Hill, 1989, p. 68.
8. Eisenstein, 1979, pp. 374-5.
9. Ong, 1967, pp. 283-4.
10. See Chartrier, 1989, p. 118. On the Protestant concern with reaching the common man through the printed word, see Eisenstein, 1979, p. 361ff.
11. Cf. Ong, 1967, p. 282: 'The typographically conditioned Protestant assertion of the power of the word reinforces oral-aural attitudes in the Bible. It also alters them by insisting much more explicitly on the power of the word than does the early Church. This was the Protestant way of coping with the tendency of print, subconsciously sensed, to weaken the feeling that words themselves possess power.'
12. Hill, 1975, pp. 171-2.
13. Delany, 1969, p. 82.
14. Hill, 1975, p. 171.
15. Erikson, 1959, p. 13.
16. Bracketed page references are to Bunyan, 1962.
17. Cf. Carlton: 'Those who broke with the "legalistic" faith of Rome or the

Church of England felt that they had obtained a truly spiritual religion, but they paid a heavy price for their freedom: the loss of objective religious authority' (1984, p. 20).

18. Erikson, 1959, p. 13.
19. Cf. Marcuse, 1972, pp. 56–78.
20. Bunyan, 1962, p. 146, note 163. For an account of Bacon's *Fearful estate* and its impact on seventeenth-century English Puritans, see A. W. Brink, Introduction to Trosse, 1974, pp. 17–19.
21. Brink in Trosse, 1974, p. 28.
22. Hill, 1975, p. 182. Cf. Sawday, 1990.
23. Greenblatt, 1980.
24. Webber, 1968, p. 8.
25. Cited in Bunyan, 1962, p. xii.
26. 'Bunyan's social position was paradoxical and unstable. He was an outcast from the world in some ways, but in other ways had a real "property" and interest in it. He was a despised itinerant manual worker, excluded from land-ownership, exposed to the rigours of the open road as he travelled and the violence of property-owners if he deviated; yet he was also a householder and artisan, descended from yeomen and small traders. His status was higher than that of the common labourer and (. . .) he dissociated himself indignantly from the homeless poor' (Turner, 1980, p. 97).
27. Cf. Turner: 'he conceived the World in political and economic terms, as a hostile hierarchy of wealth and power founded on *place* – social position and landed estates. He saw place as property.' (Ibid.).
28. Montaigne, 1958, p. 736. On Montaigne's melancholy, see Screech, 1983.
29. Sage, 1988, p. 76.
30. Cited in ibid.
31. Ibid., pp. 76–7.
32. 'Jack Lindsay suggested that Bunyan's obsession relates to his family's sales of land in the sixteenth and early seventeenth centuries, their birthright whose loss had necessitated the wandering life of tinkers' (Hill, 1988, p. 69).
33. 'If we ask ourselves what it is that gives the character of strangeness to the substitutive formation and the symptom in schizophrenia, we eventually come to realize that it is the predominance of what has to do with words over what has to do with things' (Freud, 1957, p. 200).
34. Ferdinand de Saussure's formal analysis of the signifying processes of language proposed two interacting categories: a vertical or paradigmatic axis of selection and substitution and a horizontal or syntagmatic axis of combination. Jakobson proposed that these classificatory axes function as magnetic poles: actual verbal utterances tend to gravitate to one or the other. Both axes necessarily function in all utterances, but one may be dominant, the other subordinate. He analysed these two poles in terms of metaphor and metonym (metaphor embodies substitution,

metonym combination), and went on to suggest that these contrasting modes provided formal descriptions of various genres – as for example lyric poetry and realist prose.
35. See Jakobson, 1963, pp. 64–5.
36. *Jubilate agno*, fragment B2, "For", line 306.
37. Cited in Sage, 1988, pp. 240–1, note 11.
38. On the link between Bunyan's 'concrete' terms and metaphors on the one hand, and allegory on the other, see Sharrock, 1948, pp. 109–10.
39. For relevant discussions of passivity of voice and position in Bunyan, see Webber, 1968, pp. 28, 47ff.; Carlton, 1984, pp. 18–19.
40. Parenthetical page references are to Trosse, 1974.
41. Carlton draws attention to the characteristic use of 'disclaiming locutions' in Puritan spiritual writing – 'the act of narratively implying that one is not the agent of one's own actions.' He continues, 'How did the Puritans persuade themselves that some of their own thoughts were *not* their own but were divinely willed events? By using disclaiming locutions' (1984, pp. 19, 21).
42. Sage, 1988, pp. 240–1, note 11.
43. Ibid., p. 88.
44. Brink, in Trosse, 1974, p. 139.
45. Elias, 1978, p. 150.
46. Ibid., pp. 190–1.
47. Chartrier, 1989, pp. 16–19.
48. Cf. Eisenstein, 1979, pp. 430–2.
49. Stone, 1982, p. 109.
50. Hill, 1986, p. 490.

Chapter 4

1. All bracketed references for Cowper's prose writings are to the King–Ryskamp edition of the letters and the prose (1979–85): Roman numerals indicate volume number. I have, however, departed from King and Ryskamp in preferring to retain the title under which Cowper's memoir was published in the nineteenth century. In 1770, or shortly after, Cowper wrote an account of his brother's deathbed conversion which he entitled *Adelphi*: this he seemingly appended to the memoir. Cowper's own manuscript versions have not been located, but King and Ryskamp follow a recently discovered ms transcription made by the wife of his friend and relative Martin Madan: both narratives are given there under the joint title of *Adelphi*, and it is this overall title which King and Ryskamp adopt. This may indeed have been Cowper's intended title but in the absence of definitive evidence the matter is open to debate, and I have felt that the functional title of *Memoir* is more appropriate.
2. Rousseau, 1954, p. 17.

3. Habermas, 1974, p. 51.
4. Cited (by Brink) in Trosse, 1974, p. 138.
5. Stone, 1982, p. 284.
6. Ibid., p. 285.
7. Sennett, 1986, pp. 99–122.
8. Ibid., p. 94.
9. Ariès, 1979, p. 390.
10. Both Ariès and Stone date 'affective' models of family relationships from the eighteenth century. This has been much disputed: evidence has been collected to show that early seventeenth-century parents were no less capable of loving their children than those of the mid-eighteenth century. However a comparison of the autobiographical writings of Trosse and Cowper provides evidence which would support the Ariès/Stone thesis. Mrs Trosse no doubt loved her infant son, yet this did not prevent her from conforming to the social and cultural patterns of the day and sending the baby out to a wet-nurse – with nearly fatal consequences. For a further discussion of these issues, see chapter 5, p. 114.
11. King, 1986, p. 53.
12. Cf. ibid., p. 84.
13. Barthes, 1977, p. 142.
14. Cited in Engell, 1981, p. 71.
15. See Laplanche and Pontalis, 1985, pp. 480–1.
16. Quinlan, 1953, p. 43, footnote.
17. See ibid., pp. 42–3; also Ryskamp, 1959, pp. 139–44.
18. Quinlan concludes, 'In the absence of additional evidence (. . .) it is safer to assume that the misfortunate man was some other client of the doctor' (1953, p. 43). Ryskamp is more stoutly unconvinced: 'The probabilities (. . .) are almost nil' (p. 144). He takes up Quinlan's implied connection between castration on the one hand and testimony of Cowper's physical abnormality on the other, but dismisses it on the (not incontestable) ground that '[Mrs Unwin and John Newton] are not likely to have described such a condition as androgynous or hermaphroditic' (1959, p. 144, footnote).

Chapter 5

1. Rousseau, 1964, pp. 557–8.
2. Gusdorf, 1976, p. 341.
3. King, 1986, pp. 63–4.
4. 'He had a Terrible Dream in which "a Word" was spoken. What the dream was he does not tell us, though from various references to it and to his malady we know its import. *Actum est de te, periisti* – "It is all over with thee, thou hast perished," was the thought ever uppermost in Cowper's mind. It is not impossible that this was the very "Word". (. . .)

but whether it was or not, the meaning must have been the same' (Wright, 1892, p. 206).

5. Cf. Priestman, 1983, pp. 21-2.
6. 'I am conscious (. . .) of having laboured much in the arranging of my matter, and of having given to the several parts of every book of the Task (. . .) that sort of slight connection which poetry demands.' (III, 196).
7. All parenthetical references to *The Task* indicate book (Arabic numerals) and line numbers.
8. See Davidoff and Hall, 1987, p. 162ff.
9. Feingold, 1978, p. 123.
10. Perkin, 1985, p. 281.
11. See Fox, 1982.
12. Digby, 1985, p. 55.
13. Doerner, 1981, p. 60.
14. Digby, 1985, p. 53.
15. Ibid., p. 55.
16. See Foucault, 1971, pp. 246-7; 250.
17. Priestman, 1983, p. 54.
18. See Barrell, 1972, p. 12. Cf. Newey, 1982, p. 103ff.
19. Hume, 1978, p. 252.
20. 'The identity, which we ascribe to the mind of man, is only a fictitious one' (Hume, 1978, p. 259).
21. Ibid., p. 260.
22. Cited in Rybczynski, 1988, p. 36.
23. Cf. Bruce Redmond's discussion of Cowper's trip to Sussex in 1792: 'The expansive wooded downs of Sussex, converted by his fearful imagination into forests and mountains, only aggravate the inner turmoil that the gentle, small-scale topography of Buckinghamshire has been instrumental in controlling' (1986, p. 57).
24. Southey, 1835, p. 109.
25. Doerner, 1981, p. 58.
26. Godlee, 1985, pp. 81-2.
27. Cited ibid., p. 81.
28. Beattie, 1970, p. 78.
29. Cf. King, 1986, pp. 142-3.
30. Beattie, describing the associative mechanism of 'preconscious' reverie in terms of similarity, contiguity and contrast, might be said to anticipate Freud's formal account of the dreamwork.
31. Johnson, 1971, p. 114.
32. Ibid.
33. Ibid.
34. I, 308. Cf. King, 1986, pp. 138-9, 144, 235, 240.
35. King points out that Cowper, reading Beattie's poem *The Minstrel*, would have followed the bard Edwin's learning of 'a via media between "fancy" and "philosophy"' (1986, p. 140).

36. 'Whenever Cowper speaks of the hearth, the symbolic implications of its cheer are never far below the surface (. . .). Outside the diminutive domestic context (. . .), the same flames are transformed into a terrifying symbol of Cowper's worst fears: "Dream'd that in a state of the most insupportable misery I look'd through the window of a strange room being all alone, and saw preparations making for my execution. That it was but about 4 days distant, and that then I was destined to suffer everlasting martyrdom in the fire" (IV, 237). By taming a force that might otherwise rage out of control, the hearth illustrates one cogent reason for Cowper's devotion to the small-scale' (Redmond, 1986, p. 55).

37. Rybczynski, 1988, p. 118.

38. Hill, 1969, p. 220.

39. Stone, 1982, p. 180.

40. At the time of Morley Unwin's death, Cowper wrote, 'I shall still, by God's leave, continue with Mrs Unwin, whose Behaviour to me has always been that of a mother to a son' (I, 171).

41. Stone, 1982, p. 285.

42. See Porter, 1987(a), pp. 223–4.

43. Foucault, 1971, p. 253.

44. Following Hoosag Gregory, Lilian Feder notes an episode recounted in the *Memoirs* wherein Cowper tells how his father asked to hear his young son's arguments against a pamphlet which justified suicide, but then listened to them in silence, leaving the boy to understand that his father 'sided with the author against me.' This is an episode which returned to haunt Cowper: when driven to attempt suicide himself, he asked strangers he met to justify suicide. Feder comments, 'he has obviously recreated the circumstances of the childhood incident, posing to casual acquaintances the question that his father had once asked him (. . .) his repetition of the childhood episode suggests (. . .) that he felt his father placed little value on life, that he saw human existence – and thus the boy himself – as worthless (. . .). His rage at his father's remoteness could not be expressed; it could only be turned on himself, intensifying a sense of worthlessness by then well-established.' Feder goes on to suggest that Cowper projected onto his God his suppressed rage over his mother's early death and his father's 'remoteness' (1980, p. 181ff).

45. Ibid., p. 191.

46. Foucault, 1980, p. 59.

47. Newey, 1982, pp. 274–5.

48. Ibid., p. 276.

Chapter 6

1. No fair copy of a completed autobiography has been found, and John and Anne Tibble have doubted that Clare managed to finish work on

this project. See their Introduction to the *Prose* (Clare, 1951), pp. 1–2.

2. The following abbreviations are used in bracketed references to Clare's writings:

JCAW   *John Clare's autobiographical writings* (Clare, 1983).
JC   *John Clare* (Clare, 1984a).
LPJC   *Later poems of John Clare* (Clare, 1984b).
Letters   *John Clare: selected letters* (Clare, 1988).
MC   *The midsummer cushion* (Clare, 1979).
PJC   *The poetry of John Clare*, Vol. I, (Clare, 1935).
Prose   *The prose of John Clare* (Clare, 1951).

3. Cited in E. Storey, 1982, p. 291.
4. Ibid., p. 295.
5. Vincent, 1981, p. 182.
6. Ibid., p. 183.
7. Barrell, 1972, pp. 110–12.
8. 'I wish to acknowledge that whatsoever merit this ["The Nightmare"] and "The Dream" may be thought to possess they owe it in part to the *English opium eater*, as they were written after (though actual dreams) that interesting production.' (PJC, p. 408).
9. Pearce, 1989, p. 140.
10. See Deacon, 1983.
11. Cf. Tim Chilcott on 'Remembrances': 'word no longer authenticates world. Both in actuality and memory, the particular facts of experience can be eroded until they become, for all intents and purposes, a vacuum' (1985, p. 112).
12. Cf. Edward Strickland: 'Clare's avoidance of the occasions of the sublime is a defensive refusal to succumb to a potentially catastrophic vulnerability' (1987, p. 155).
13. See E. Pawson, *Transport and economy: the turnpike roads of eighteenth century Britain*, Academic Press, London and New York, 1977, p. 310.
14. Powell, 1964, p. 8.
15. Cited in E. Storey, 1982, p. 261.
16. Pearce, 1987, pp. 120ff.
17. Cited in Delepierre, 1860, p. 13.
18. Clare, 1990, p. 371, note to p. 220.
19. Scull, 1982, pp. 72–3.
20. Delepierre, 1860, p. 13.
21. Ibid.
22. See Scull, 1985.
23. Delepierre, 1860, pp. 13–14.
24. Foucault, 1971, p. 246.
25. Cited in M. Storey, 1973, p. 248.
26. Chilcott, 1985, p. 155.
27. Ibid., p. 154.
28. Ibid., p. 155.
29. Cited in J. W. and Anne Tibble, 1972, p. 373.

30. Chilcott in fact makes this point, remarking that 'Don Juan is a work that constantly seeks to enact its own fictiveness' (p. 152).

31. See MacPherson, 1964.

32. In 1763, The Seasons was the subject of a trial which clarified the Copyright Act of 1709. The period of copyright was extended in 1814.

33. Cited in Vincent, 1981, p. 182.

34. Ibid.

35. Cf. Pearce, 1989, p. 143.

36. Chilcott, 1985, p. 175.

37. Michel Foucault would argue that the modern phenomenon of 'literature' perpetuates instability: 'Literature becomes progressively more differentiated from the discourse of ideas, and encloses itself within a radical intransitivity (. . .). [It] becomes merely a manifestation of a language which has no other law than that of affirming – in opposition to all other forms of discourse – its own precipitous existence; and so there is nothing for it to do but curve back in a perpetual return upon itself, as if its discourse could have no other content than the expression of its own form; it addresses itself to itself as a writing subjectivity, or seeks to reapprehend the essence of all literature in the movement that brought it into being' (1970, p. 300). This view is absurdly limited (it seems to take 'literature' as an epiphenomenon of Mallarmé's poetics), nevertheless I would argue for its relevance to Clare's Child Harold.

38. Strickland, 1982, p. 11.

39. Cf. Pearce: 'the speaker virtually asserts and undermines Mary's presence (and his ability to create that presence) in the same breath. She exists; she does not exist' (1987, p. 264).

40. Cf. Chilcott, 1985, p. 160.

41. Cited in M. Storey, 1973, p. 14.

42. See Barrell, 1972, p. 130.

43. Strickland, describing Robinson and Powell's two-volume edition of the Later poems (Clare, 1984b), notes that it 'makes clear the anomalous nature of the famous visionary lyrics, which appear in a radically different light grouped together on a few pages of an anthology rather than surrounded by eleven hundred pages of Clare's late verse' (1987, p. 141). Nevertheless there are enough of the visionary lyrics to constitute a highly significant group. Strickland's description of them as 'a few flashes of vision' is a strategic evasion.

44. Strickland, 1982, p. 3.

45. Ibid., p. 4.

46. To my knowledge, Clare possessed no model for these lines. The Elizabethan 'Elegy' by Chidiock Tichbourne (supposedly written the night before his execution) employs the world-upside-down topos, and is one of the few English poems which resembles Clare's sublime lyrics of the 1840s:

> I sought my death, and found it in my womb;
> I looked for life, and saw it was a shade;
> I trod the earth, and knew it was my tomb;
> And now I die, and now I was but made;

Clare wrote imitations of Elizabethan and Jacobean lyric poetry, which he knew well, but it is not very likely that he was influenced by this poem.

47. 'What lies in the will of the maiden?' (Bloom, 1971, p. 452). Bloom's question has been taken up by both Strickland and Chilcott.
48. Cf. Chilcott: 'She exists more as another aspect of the solipsistic self, a kind of reflexive projection of its despair, than as a separate identifiable presence' (1985, p. 202).
49. Strickland, 1982, p. 7.
50. Ibid., p. 14.
51. Ibid.

Chapter 7

1. Gusdorf, 1984, p. 289.
2. Gautier, 1970, p. 148.
3. In Richer, 1970, pp. 261–2.
4. See Porter, 1987(a), p. 174ff.
5. Bracketed page references for *Aurélia* and *Sylvie* are to *Selected writings of Gérard de Nerval* (1958). I have silently amended Geoffrey Wagner's translation at some points, where a degree of literalism is called for. All bracketed references specified as *Pléiade* are to Vol. I of the *Oeuvres* (Nerval, 1960). Translations are my own unless otherwise indicated.
6. See Hunter and Macalpine, 1963, p. 731.
7. Doerner, 1981, p. 147.
8. Bowman, 1979.
9. Bowman, 1988, p. 37. See also Lokke, 1987, p. 60. Both Lokke and Bowman rely on Foucault for their accounts of Pinel and Esquirol's hostility to religious forms of thought: for a more detailed and nuanced account of this issue (but one which does not basically contradict Foucault) see Goldstein, 1987, pp. 197-230.
10. Information on this topic is due to the researches of Michel Jeanneret. See Jeanneret, 1980.
11. Ibid., p. 67.
12. in Richer, 1970, p. 102.
13. Porter, 1979, p. 17. Cf. Jeanneret, 1980, p. 71.
14. See Jeanneret, 1980, pp. 64–5; 69. See also Corbin, 1990, p. 514.
15. Cited in Porter, 1979, p. 19.
16. Bousquet, 1964, p. 52.
17. Ibid. Bousquet, it should be noted, rejects the notion that dreams are the product of unconscious psychical processes. All dreams, he argues,

are provoked on the borderline between sleeping and waking: they consist of a few key words or images which are elaborated into image-sequences or narratives and remembered as dreams. It follows for him that dreams are culturally determined and can be considered from an historical vantage point. Current clinical research into sleep and dream does not confirm Bousquet's position: tests suggest that the sense of duration in dreams corresponds to the real time elapsed in sleep (see J. Empson, 1989, *Sleep and dreaming*, Faber & Faber, London, pp. 51–7). No less problematic, in my view, is Bousquet's argument that literary or invented dreams are no less valid than 'true dreams' in expressing the dream-set of a particular period: 'Any given period dreams exactly as it tells us it dreams (. . .). Inasmuch as a period has left us the dream of Athalie, it is because it dreamed thus' (p. 51). These problems by no means demolish the value or interest of Bousquet's project. Alain Corbin, who reviews Bousquet's work, avoids theoretical justifications and definitions, simply suggesting that 'dreams have a history' (1990, p. 518).

18. Bousquet, 1964, p. 257.
19. Ibid., p. 234.
20. Ibid., p. 237.
21. Ibid.
22. In using the term 'illusion,' Nerval may be alluding to Esquirol, who wrote, 'Illusions, so frequent among the insane, deceive them respecting the qualities, relations and causes of the impressions actually received, and cause them to form false judgements respecting their internal and external sensations. Their reason does not rectify the error (. . .)' (Cited in Hunter and Macalpine, 1963, p. 734).
23. Jeanneret, 1980, p. 71.
24. Ross Chambers, tracing the relationship between psychiatric and literary-symbolistic modes of discourse in *Aurélia*, concludes that 'Without ever having been exactly denied, medical authority will have been subverted from the inside, invested by a kind of authority deriving from another tradition, that of the descent into the underworld' (Chambers, 1983, p. 79). This, in my view, assumes an over-neat differentiation between the two modes of discourse.
25. The gates are prefigured when Aeneas, seeking out the Cumaean Sibyl prior to his descent into the underworld, comes to a temple built by Daedalus: he and his companions are detained by sculpted representations of the Daedalus story, the maze prominent among them. See Róheim, 1969, pp. 279, 287.
26. Knight, 1936, pp. 59–60.
27. For a relevant interpretation of the theme of the labyrinth in Nerval, see Chambers, 1969, ch. 5. For a review of the topic of melancholy, see Zielonka, 1986.
28. Gérard's hallucination of an eclipsed, disordered cosmos anticipates Nietzsche's famous madman in *The gay science*: 'What were we doing

when we unchained this earth from its sun? Whither is it moving now?
Whither are we moving? Away from all suns? Are we not plunging
continually? Backward, sideward, forward in all directions? Is there still
any up or down? Are we not straying through an infinite nothing?'
(1974, p. 181). The affinity may derive from a shared debt to Jean-Paul's
Dreams.

29. Nerval, 1972, p. 23.
30. See Laszlo, 1981, p. 41.
31. Goldstein, 1987, p. 99. I am very much indebted to Goldstein's research
    here.
32. Ibid., p. 100.
33. Ibid., p. 99.
34. Cited ibid., p. 72.
35. Ibid., pp. 72–3.
36. See ibid., p. 76.
37. Ibid., p. 85.
38. Nerval, 1965, p. 140.
39. Cf. Jeanneret: 'Revelation must fulfill two determining functions: offer
    to the protagonist a key with which to decipher his apparently discon-
    tinuous or absurd experiences; render to language its efficacy by
    guaranteeing it a transcendental model' (1978, p. 202).
40. See Jeanneret, 1980, p. 64. On the contest between 'physiology' and
    'psychology' in nineteenth-century French psychiatry, see Goldstein,
    1987, p. 242ff.
41. See Gusdorf, 1984, p. 257ff.
42. Chambers, 1969, p. 358.
43. Corbin, 1990, p. 514.
44. See Nerval, 1965, p. 65, note c. (Deschamps, translator of Dante's
    Divine comedy, was also an inmate of Dr Blanche's *maison de santé*.)
45. In Richer, 1970, pp. 252–3.
46. L.-H. Sebillotte argued that Nerval's life and work were determined
    both by a fixation on the lost mother and a refusal to identify with an
    unconscious image of a *père sadique*. (Sebillotte, 1948, p. 236ff). See also
    Mauron, 1949; Richer, 1955.
47. Sartre, 1963, p. 61.
48. Nerval arguably identifies with the father hero in *El Desdichado* – 'Je suis
    (. . .) le veuf' ('I am the widower'). In this reading, the dead beloved is
    Mme Labrunie, while the hero's traversal of the Acheron as river of
    death refers back to the father's crossing of the Bérésina.
49. Richer, 1955, p. 62.
50. See Sebillotte, 1948, pp. 128–9.
51. Gilbert, 1979, p. 10.
52. See Chambers, 1969, p. 364.
53. Ibid., pp. 358–9.

Chapter 8

1. Cf. Benjamin, 1973, pp. 167–9.
2. Cf. Marx on the fetishisation of the commodity: 'It is as clear as noon-day, that man, by his industry, changes the forms of materials furnished by Nature, in such a way as to make them useful to him. The form of wood, for instance, is altered by making a table out of it. Yet, for all that, the table continues to be that common every day thing, wood. But so soon as it steps forth as a commodity, it is changed into something transcendent. It not only stands with its feet on the ground, but, in rela-tion to all other commodities, it stands on its head, and evolves out of its wooden head grotesque ideas, far more wonderful than "table-turning"' (*Capital*, 4 vols, Vol. I, London, Lawrence & Wishart, 1974, p. 76).
3. Petitfils, 1986, p. 316.
4. Kofman, 1979, pp. 44–5.
5. Freud, 1955, XVII, p. 245.
6. Ibid., p. 244.
7. Petitfils, 1986, p. 311.
8. Chambers, 1969, p. 358.
9. See Bowman, 1984, 1986.
10. Bowman, 1979, p. 86.
11. Cf. Jeanneret: 'Other dreams (. . .) follow on – Saardam, Vienna – whose signification is far from being clear: their symbolism, less definitely coded, does not deliver (. . .) a reassuring or univocal message. Above all, the revelation of cosmic harmony seems to deteriorate (. . .). From the mystical conviction at the start of the 'Mémorables', the *récit* returns to an uncertain discourse' (1978, pp. 221–2).
12. Bowman contests Jeanneret's argument that the dream-narratives are problematic (See Jeanneret, 1978, p. 221ff; Bowman, 1986, pp. 169, 177). He effectively answers some of Jeanneret's points, but not all of them.
13. Freud, 1976, p. 186.
14. Rosolato, 1978, p. 257.
15. Cf. Rosolato: 'it [the navel] appears as marked centre of the body, all the more so in that its lack of function makes it only a formal mark. It thus participates in all the symbolism of the centre (. . .) end point of spirals, limit and flanks of the abyss, of the whirlwind, centre of the spherical vortex and of the whirling ring, it further sustains the reversal of the spiral (as in E. Poe's *Descent into the maelstrom*)' (1978, pp. 257–8).
16. Foucault, 1980, p. 69.
17. Petitfils, 1986, p. 14.
18. See Sebillotte, 1948, pp. 217–18.
19. Rosolato, 1978, p. 271. The 'real' which Rosolato refers to here is not to be confused with notions of reality. Rosolato follows Jacques Lacan, who (following a remark of Freud's) proposes that *le réel* is that which

remains unknowable for the subject.

20. See Nerval, 1960, p. 1273, note to p. 407. Other factors link the young madman with the necromancers. Immediately on entering the asylum, Gérard believes it contains underground chambers, comparable to those which house the necromancers: in the asylum he recalls the necromar ers: '"Thus," I went on, consulting my memory of the ancient world, "that necromancers dominated entire peoples"' (167).

21. Gérard delivers the young madman from his womblike state of suspended animation by bringing him to the point of drinking some water, thus cutting the umbilical cord of the intravenous feeding tube. Reciprocally, Saturninus in Gérard's asylum dream, delivers Gérard (through a side door) from the tower: 'these countless stairs which wore you out so (...) are the bonds [liens] of old illusions (...)' (172).

22. See Bowman, 1986, for a full discussion of Nerval's concern with the Crimean situation.

23. 'These yellowed characters, these faded drafts, half-crumpled letters, these are the treasures of my only love... Let me read them again... Many of them are missing, others torn or scratched out; here is what I find ...' (170). (Nerval did not in fact transcribe the letters at this point.)

24. Jeanneret, 1978, p. 221.

25. In Richer, 1970, p. 336.

26. It has been suggested that this followed a visit to his mother's grave at Glogau. See Petitfils, 1986, p. 332.

27. Foucault, 1977, 84.

28. Gautier, 1970, p. 148.

29. (i): in Richer, 1970, p. 14; (ii): Gautier, 1970, pp. 157-8 (translation modified).

30. Cf. recent analyses of the madness-cure polarity in *Aurélia* by Shoshana Felman and Ross Chambers. Felman writes, 'The structure of *Aurélia* is based upon an unresolvable tension between (...) two contradictory discursive tensions in the work: the mode of hallucinatory inflation and the mode of critical deflation' (1985, p. 76). Chambers argues that 'The narrative of cure does not go without a certain form of textual 'madness' (1983, p. 84). Michel Jeanneret (1978) balances this polarity differently in his reading of *Aurélia*, finding that a 'discourse of madness' contaminates a critical 'discourse on madness.' In my view, much of this debate was pre-empted more than a century ago by Gautier.

31. The passage, as translated by P. Charvet, can be found in Baudelaire, *Selected writings on art and artists* (Penguin, Harmondsworth, 1972, p. 174). However it is given here in Richard Howard's more literal translation, taken from Michel Butor, *Histoire extraordinaire*, trans. Richard Howard, Jonathan Cape, 1969, p. 165.

32. Baudelaire, in both of the writings where he discusses Nerval, associates him with Poe (see the 1856 Poe essay, 'Edgar Allan Poe, his life and

works', and 'Hégésippe Moreau' in *L'Art romantique*). Baudelaire saw Poe as a quintessentially modern writer, arguing that his inebriation and delirium were 'a mnemonic means, a method of work' (*Selected writings on art and artists*, p. 184).

33. Girard, 1978, p. 118.
34. Foucault, 1977, p. 85.
35. Ibid., p. 32.
36. Ibid., p. 85.
37. See *Promenades et souvenirs*, written close in time to *Aurélia*: 'As for memoirs, one never knows if the public cares much about them – nevertheless I am one of the writers whose life is intimately linked with the works which have made them known (. . .). May we be forgiven for these transports of personality, we who live under the gaze of everyone, and who, whether glorious or lost, can no longer attain the benefit of obscurity' (*Pléiade*, 139).
38. Felman, 1985, p. 13.
39. In a note to Dumas dated November 1853, Nerval wrote, 'You asked me for three articles on three days of my life which you yourself have entitled *THREE DAYS OF MADNESS* and which I will call *three days of reason*' (*Pléiade*, 1075).
40. In Richer, 1970, p. 23.
41. See Roland Barthes, *S/Z*, trans. Richard Miller, Jonathan Cape, London, 1975, pp. 4–5.
42. Felman, 1985, p. 13.

Bibliography

Adorno, Theodore, 1989, *Kierkegaard: construction of an aesthetic*, translated and edited by Robert Hullot-Kentnor, University of Minnesota Press, Minneapolis.

Allderidge, Patricia, 1985, 'Bedlam: fact or fantasy?', in *The anatomy of madness*, edited by W. F. Bynum, Roy Porter and Michael Shepherd, 3 vols, II, pp. 897–904, Tavistock, London.

Ariès, Philippe, 1979, *Centuries of childhood*, Penguin, Harmondsworth.

Barker, Francis, 1984, *The tremulous private body: essays on subjection*, Methuen, London and New York.

Barrell, John, 1972, *The idea of landscape and the sense of place 1730–1840: an approach to the poetry of John Clare*, Cambridge University Press, Cambridge.

Barthes, Roland, 1977, *Image-music-text*, essays selected and translated by Stephen Heath, Fontana/Collins, Glasgow.

Basile, Bruno, 1984, *Poëta melancholicus*, Pacini, Pisa.

Beattie, James, 1970, *Dissertations moral and critical*, Friedrich Fromann Verlag, Stuttgart–Bad Canstatt.

Benjamin, Walter, 1973, *Charles Baudelaire: A lyric poet in an era of high capitalism*, translated by Harry Zohn, NLB, London.

Benveniste, Emile, 1971, *Problems in general linguistics*, translated by Mary Elizabeth Meek, University of Miami Press, Florida.

Bloom, Harold, 1971, *The visionary company*, Cornell University Press, Ithaca, New York.

Bousquet, Jacques, 1964, *Les thèmes du rêve dans la littérature romantique: essai sur la naissance et l'évolution des images*, Didier, Paris.

Bowman, Frank Paul, 1979, 'Une lecture politique de la folie réligieuse ou "théomanie"', *Romantisme*, 24, 75–87.

——— 1984, 'Illuminism, utopia, mythology' in *The French romantics*, ed. D. Charlton, 2 vols, I, Cambridge University Press, pp. 76–112.

——— 1986, '"Mémorables" d'*Aurélia*, signification et situation générique', *French Forum*, 11 (2), 169–81.

——— 1988, 'La marginalité en religion', *Romantisme*, 59, 31–40.

Brand, C. P., 1965, *Torquato Tasso: a study of the poet and his contribution to English literature*, Cambridge University Press, Cambridge.

Brink, A. W., see Trosse, 1974.

Bunyan, John, 1962, *Grace abounding to the chief of sinners*, edited by Roger Sharrock, Oxford University Press, Oxford.

Carkesse, James, 1979, *Lucida intervalla: containing divers miscellaneous poems*, edited with an introduction by Michael V. Deporte, Augustan Reprint Society Nos 195–6, University of California Press, Los Angeles.

Carlton, Peter J., 1984, 'Bunyan: language, convention, authority', *English Literary History*, 51, 17–32.

Chambers, Ross, 1969, *Nerval et la poétique du voyage*, Corti, Paris.

—— 1983, 'Récits d'aliénés, récits aliénés: Nerval et John Perceval', *Poétique*, 14, 72–90.

Chartrier, Roger, (editor), 1989, *A history of private life*, general editors, Philippe Ariès and Georges Duby, 4 vols, III, *Passions of the Renaissance*, translated by Arthur Goldhammer, The Belknap Press of Harvard University Press, Cambridge, Massachusetts and London.

Chilcott, Tim, 1985, *'A real world & doubting mind': a critical study of the poetry of John Clare*, Hull University Press.

Clare, John, 1935, *The poetry of John Clare*, edited by J.W. Tibble, 2 vols, Dent, London and New York.

—— 1951, *The prose of John Clare*, edited by J.W. and Anne Tibble, Routledge & Kegan Paul, London.

—— 1979, *The midsummer cushion*, edited by Anne Tibble and R.K.R. Thornton, MIDNAG-Carcanet, Ashington.

—— 1983, *John Clare's autobiographical writings*, edited by Eric Robinson, Oxford University Press, Oxford.

—— 1984a, *John Clare*, edited by Eric Robinson and David Powell, Oxford University Press, Oxford.

—— 1984b, *The later poems of John Clare*, edited by Eric Robinson and David Powell, 2 vols, I, Oxford University Press, Oxford.

—— 1988, *John Clare: selected letters*, edited by Mark Storey, Oxford University Press, Oxford.

—— 1990, *John Clare: selected poetry*, edited with an introduction and notes by Geoffrey Summerfield, Penguin, Harmondsworth.

Corbin, Alain, 1990, 'Backstage', in *A history of private life*, 4 vols, general editors, Philippe Ariès and Georges Duby, IV, *From the fires of Revolution to the Great War*, edited by Michelle Perrot, translated by Arthur Goldhammer, The Belknap Press of Harvard University Press, Cambridge, Massachusetts and London, pp. 451–667.

Cowper, William, 1835, *Works, with a life of the author*, edited, with biography, by Robert Southey, 11 vols, I, Baldwin and Cradock, London.

—— 1979–1985, *The letters and prose writings of William Cowper*, 5 vols, edited by James King and Charles Ryskamp, Oxford University Press, Oxford.

Curtius, Ernst Robert, 1979, *European literature and the Latin Middle Ages*, translated by Willard R. Trask, Routledge & Kegan Paul, London.

Davidoff, Leonore, and Hall, Catherine, 1987, *Family fortunes: men and women of the English middle class*, Hutchinson, London.

Deacon, George, 1983, *John Clare and the folk tradition*, Sinclair Browne, London.

Delany, Paul, 1969, *British autobiography in the seventeenth century*, Routledge & Kegan Paul, London.

Delepierre, Octave, 1860, *Histoire littéraire des fous*, Trübner, London.

Deporte, Michael V., see Carkesse, 1979.

Digby, Anne, 1985, 'Moral treatment at the retreat', in *The anatomy of madness*, 3 vols, II, edited by W.F. Bynum, Roy Porter and Michael Shepherd, Tavistock, London, pp. 52-72.

Doerner, Klaus, 1981, *Madmen and the bourgeoisie: a social history of insanity and psychiatry*, translated by J. Neugroschel and J. Steinberg, Basil Blackwell, Oxford.

Doob, Penelope 1974, *Nebuchadnezzar's children: conventions of madness in middle English literature*, Yale University Press, New Haven.

Eisenstein, Elizabeth L., 1979, *The printing press as an agent of change: communications and cultural transformations in early-modern Europe*, 2 vols, I, Cambridge University Press, Cambridge.

Elias, Norbert, 1978, *The civilizing process*, vol. I. *The history of manners*, translated by Edmund Jephcott, Basil Blackwell, Oxford.

Engell, James, 1981, *The creative imagination: enlightenment to romanticism*, Harvard University Press, Cambridge, Massachusetts and London.

Erikson, Erik H., 1959, *Young man Luther: a study in psychoanalysis and history*, Faber, London.

Feder, Lilian, 1980, *Madness in literature*, Princeton University Press, Princeton, New Jersey.

Feingold, Richard, 1978, *Nature and society: later eighteenth century uses of the pastoral and the georgic*, Harvester Press, Hassocks.

Felman, Shoshana, 1985, *Writing and madness (literature/philosophy/psychoanalysis)*, translated by Martha Noel Evans with the author, Cornell University Press, Ithaca, New York.

Foucault, Michel, 1970, *The order of things: an archeology of the human sciences*, translated by Alan Sheridan, Tavistock, London.

────── 1971, *Madness and civilization: a history of insanity in the age of reason*, translated by Richard Howard, Tavistock Social Science Paperback, London.

────── 1973 *Histoire de la folie a l'âge classique*, Gallimard (Collection Tel), Paris.

────── 1977, *Language, counter-memory, practice: selected essays and interviews*, edited by Donald F. Bouchard, translated by Donald F. Bouchard and Sherry Simon, Cornell University Press, Ithaca, New York.

────── 1980, *The history of sexuality, Vol 1: an introduction*, translated by Robert Hurley, Vintage Books, New York.

Fox, Christopher, 1982, 'Locke and the Scriblerians', *Eighteenth Century Studies*, 16, 1-25.

Freud, Sigmund, 1955, 'The "uncanny"', in *The standard edition of the complete psychological works of Sigmund Freud*, translated and edited by James Strachey, 24 vols, XVII, Hogarth Press, London, pp. 217-56.

――― 1957, 'The unconscious', in *The standard edition*, translated and edited by James Strachey, 24 vols, XIV, Hogarth Press, London, pp. 159-215.

――― 1976, *The interpretation of dreams*, translated by James Strachey, edited by James Strachey with Alan Tyson, Penguin, Harmondsworth.

Gautier, Théophile, 1970, *My fantoms*, edited and translated by Richard Holmes, Quartet Books, London.

Gilbert, Clare, 1979, *Nerval's double: a structural study*, University, Mississippi.

Gilbert, Sandra and Gubar, Susan 1979, *The madwoman in the attic: the woman writer and the nineteenth century imagination*, Yale University Press, New Haven.

Girard, René, 1978, *'To double business bound'*, Johns Hopkins University Press, Baltimore and London.

Godlee, Fiona, 1985, 'Aspects of non-conformity: Quakers and the lunatic fringe', in *The anatomy of madness*, edited by W.F. Bynum, Roy Porter and Michael Shepherd, 3 vols, II, pp. 73-85.

Goldstein, Jan, 1987, *Console or classify: the French psychiatric profession in the nineteenth century*, Cambridge University Press, Cambridge.

Greenblatt, Stephen, 1980, *Renaissance self-fashioning: from More to Shakespeare*, University of Chicago Press, Chicago and London.

Gusdorf, Georges, 1976, *Naissance de la conscience romantique au siècle des lumières*, Payot, Paris.

――― 1984, *L'homme romantique*, Payot, Paris.

Habermas, Jürgen, 1974, 'The public sphere: an encyclopedia article (1964)', translated by Sara Lennox and Frank Lennox, *New German Critique*, 1 (3), 49-55.

Hill, Christopher, 1969, *The century of revolution, 1603-1714*, Sphere Books, London.

――― 1975, *The world turned upside down: radical ideas during the English Revolution*, Penguin, Harmondsworth.

――― 1986, *Society and puritanism in pre-revolutionary England*, Penguin, Harmondsworth.

――― 1988, *A turbulent, seditious, and factious people: John Bunyan and his church*, Oxford University Press, Oxford.

Hobbes, Thomas, 1839, *The English Works of Hobbes*, 11 vols, III, edited by Sir William Molesworth Bart, John Bohn, London.

Hoccleve, Thomas, 1970, *Hoccleve's works: the minor poems*, edited by F. J. Furnivall and I. Gollancz, revised by Jerome Mitchell and A. I. Doyle, EEts, es 61 and 73, Oxford University Press, Oxford.

Howie, George (editor), 1969, *St Augustine: on education*, edited and translated, with an introduction and notes, by George Howie, Henry Regnery, Chicago.

Hume, David, 1978, *A treatise of human nature*, Oxford University Press, Oxford.

Hunter, Richard and Macalpine, Ida, 1963, *Three hundred years of psychiatry, 1535-1860: a history presented in selected English texts*, Oxford University Press, London.

Jakobson, Roman, 1963, *Essais de linguistique générale*, Editions de Minuit, Paris.

Jay, Martin, 1973, *The dialectical imagination: a history of the Frankfurt School and the Institute of Social Research, 1923-50*, Heinemann, London.

Jeanneret, Michel, 1978, *La lettre perdue: écriture et folie dans l'oeuvre de Nerval*, Flammarion, Paris.

―――― 1980, 'La folie est un rêve: Nerval et le docteur Moreau de Tours', *Romantisme* 27, 59-74.

Johnson, Samuel, 1971, *The history of Rasselas*, Oxford University Press, London.

Kates, Judith, 1983, *Tasso and Milton: the problems of Christian epic*, Bracknell University Press, Lewisburg; Associated Universities Press, Toronto and London.

King, James, 1986, *William Cowper: a biography*, Duke University Press, Durham, North Carolina.

Knight, W. F. Jackson, 1936, *The Cumaean gates*, Oxford University Press, Oxford.

Kofman, Sarah, 1979, *Nerval: le charme de la répétition: lecture de 'Sylvie'*, Age d'Homme, Lausanne.

Laplanche, J. and Pontalis, J.-B., 1985, *The language of psychoanalysis*, translated by Donald Nicholson-Smith, Hogarth Press, London.

Laszlo, Pierre, 1981, 'El Desdichado - 38', *Romantisme*, 33, 35-57.

Lokke, Kari, 1987, *Gérard de Nerval: the poet as social visionary*, French Forum Monographs 66, Lexington, Kentucky.

MacLennan, G., 1983, 'Nerval's "Aurélia" and the writing of subjective crisis', unpublished Ph.D. thesis, University of East Anglia.

MacPherson, C.B., 1964, *The political theory of possessive individualism: Hobbes to Locke*, Oxford University Press, Oxford and London.

Marcuse, Herbert, 1972, *From Luther to Popper*, NLB, London.

Mauron, Charles, 1949, 'Nerval et la psychocritique', *Cahiers du Sud*, 293, 76-97.

Medcalf, Stephen, 1981, 'Inner and outer', in *The later middle ages*, edited by Stephen Medcalf, Methuen, London, pp. 108-71.

Montaigne, Michel de, 1958, *Complete works of Montaigne*, translated by Donald F. Frame, Hamish Hamilton, London.

Morris, Colin, 1972, *The discovery of the individual, 1050-1200*, SPCK, London.

Nerval, Gérard de, 1958, *Selected writings of Gérard de Nerval*, translated with a critical introduction by Geoffrey Wagner, Peter Owen, London.

―――― 1960, *Oeuvres de Gérard de Nerval*, edited by Albert Béguin and Jean Richer, 2 vols, I, Gallimard, Bibliothèque de la Pléiade, Paris.

―――― 1965, *Aurélia, ou le rêve et la vie. Lettres d'amour*, edited, with commentary, by Jean Richer, with the collaboration of François Constans et al., Minard, Paris.

——— 1972, *Journey to the Orient*, translated by Norman Glass, Peter Owen, London.

Newey, Vincent, 1982, *Cowper's poetry: a critical study and reassessment*, Liverpool University Press, Liverpool.

Nietzsche, Friedrich, 1974, *The gay science*, translated, with commentary, by Walter Kaufmann, Vintage Books, New York.

Ong, Walter J., 1967, *The presence of the word*, Yale University Press, New Haven and London.

——— 1982, *Orality and literacy: the technologizing of the word*, Methuen, London.

Panofsky, Erwin, 1971, *The life and art of Albrecht Dürer*, Princeton University Press, Princeton, New Jersey.

Pearce, Lynn, 1987, 'John Clare and Mikhail Bakhtin. The dialogic principle: readings from John Clare's unpublished manuscripts', unpublished Ph.D thesis, University of Birmingham.

——— 1989, 'John Clare's "Child Harold": a polyphonic reading', *Criticism*, 31(2), 139–57.

Pepys, Samuel, 1970–83, *The diary of Samuel Pepys: a new and complete transcription*, 11 vols, edited by R. Latham, and W. Matthews, G. Bell & Sons, London.

Perkin, Harold, 1985, *Origins of modern English society*, Ark, London.

Petitfils, Pierre, 1986, *Nerval*, Julliard, Paris.

Porter, Lawrence M., 1979, *The literary dream in French romanticism: a psycho-analytic interpretation*, Wayne State University Press, Detroit, Michigan.

Porter, Roy, 1987(a), *Mind-forged manacles: a history of madness in England from the Restoration to the Regency*, Athlone Press, London.

——— 1987(b), *A social history of madness: stories of the insane*, Weidenfeld & Nicholson, London.

Powell, David, 1964, *Catalogue of the John Clare collection in the Northampton public library*, compiled by David Powell, County Borough of Northampton Public Libraries, Museums and Art Galleries Committee.

Priestman, Martin, 1983, *Cowper's 'Task': structure and influence*, Cambridge University Press, Cambridge.

Quinlan, Maurice, 1953, *William Cowper, a critical life*, University of Minnesota Press, Minneapolis.

Redmond, Bruce, 1986, *The converse of the pen: acts of intimacy in 18th century familiar letters*, University of Chicago Press, Chicago and London.

Reed, Robert, 1970, *Bedlam on the Jacobean stage*, Octagon, New York.

Richer, Jean, 1955, 'Nerval devant la psychanalyse', *Cahiers de L'Association Internationale des Etudes Françaises*, 7, 51–64.

——— 1970, *Nerval par les témoins de sa vie*, textes réunies et présentés par Jean Richer, Minard, Paris.

Róheim, Géza, 1969, *The gates of dream*, International Universities Press, New York.

Rosen, George, 1968, *Madness in society: chapters in the historical sociology of mental illness*, Routledge & Kegan Paul, London.

Rosolato, Guy, 1978, *La relation d'inconnu*, Gallimard, Paris.

Rousseau, Jean-Jacques, 1954, *Confessions*, translated by J.M. Cohen, Penguin, Harmondsworth.

—— 1964, *Oeuvres complètes*, edited by Bernard Gaguebin and Marcel Raymond, 4 vols, II, Gallimard, Bibliothèque de la Pléiade, Paris.

Rybczynski, Witold, 1988, *Home: a short history of an idea*, Heinemann, London.

Ryskamp, Charles, 1959, *William Cowper of the Inner Temple, Esq. A study of his life and works to the year 1768*, Cambridge University Press, Cambridge.

Sage, Victor, 1988, *Horror fiction in the Protestant tradition*, Macmillan, London.

Sartre, Jean-Paul, 1963, *The problem of method*, translated, with an introduction, by Hazel E. Barnes, Methuen, London.

Sawday, Jonathan, 1990, '"Mysteriously divided": civil war, madness and the divided self', in *Literature and the English Civil War*, edited by Thomas Healey and Jonathan Sawday, Cambridge University Press, Cambridge, pp. 125–43.

Schafer, Roy, 1968, *Aspects of internalization*, International Universities Press, New York.

Screech, M. A., 1983, *Montaigne and melancholy*, Duckworth, London.

—— 1985, 'Good madness in Christendom', in *The anatomy of madness* edited by W. F. Bynum, Roy Porter and Michael Shepherd, 3 vols, I, pp. 25–39, Tavistock, London.

Scull, Andrew, 1982, *Museums of madness: the social organization of insanity in nineteenth-century England*, Penguin, Harmondsworth.

—— 1985, 'A Victorian alienist: John Conolly, FRCP, DCL (1794–1866)', in *The anatomy of madness* edited by W.F. Bynum, Roy Porter and Michael Shepherd, 3 vols, I, pp. 103–50, Tavistock, London.

Sebillotte, L.-H., 1948, *Le secret de Gérard de Nerval*, Corti, Paris.

Sennett, Richard, 1986, *The fall of public man*, Faber & Faber, London.

Sharrock, Roger, 1948, 'Spiritual autobiography in *The pilgrim's progress*', *Review of English Studies*, 24, 102–20.

Showalter, Elaine, 1987, *The female malady: women, madness and English culture, 1830-1980*, Virago, London.

Southey, Robert, see Cowper, 1835.

Stierle, Karlheinz, 1977, 'Identité du discours et transgression lyrique', *Poétique*, 8, 422–41.

Stone, Lawrence, 1982, *The family, sex and marriage in England 1500-1800*, abridged edition, Penguin (Peregrine), Harmondsworth.

Storey, Edward, 1982, *A right to song: the life of John Clare*, Methuen, London.

Storey, Mark, 1973, *Clare: the critical heritage*, Routledge & Kegan Paul, London.

Strickland, Edward, 1982, 'Conventions and their subversion' in John Clare's "An invite to eternity", *Criticism*, 24 (1), 1–15.

―――― 1987, 'John Clare and the sublime', *Criticism*, 29 (2), 141–61.

Tasso, Torquato, 1853, *Lettere*, edited by C. Guasti, 1853, 5 vols, II, Le Monnier, Florence.

―――― 1952, *Poesie*, edited by Francesco Flora, Riccardo Ricciardi, Milan and Naples

―――― 1958. *Dialoghi* 2 vols, II, edited by E. Raimondi, G.C. Sansoni, Florence.

Tibble, J. W. and Anne, 1972, *John Clare, a life*, Michael Joseph, London.

Tindall, Willam York, 1934, *John Bunyan, mechanic preacher*, Columbia University Press, New York.

Trosse, George, 1974, *The life of the Reverend Mr George Trosse*, edited with an introduction by A. W. Brink, McGill-Queen's University Press, Montreal and London.

Turner, David, 1980, 'Bunyan's sense of place', in *The pilgrim's progress: critical and historical views*, edited by Vincent Newey, Liverpool University Press, Liverpool, pp. 91–110.

Vincent, David, 1981, *Bread, knowledge and freedom: a study of nineteenth century working class autobiography*, Europa Publications, London.

Watkins, Owen C., 1972, *The puritan experience*, Routledge & Kegan Paul, London.

Webber, Joan, 1968, *The eloquent 'I': style and self in seventeenth century prose*, Wisconsin University Press, Madison and London.

Wright, Thomas, 1892, *The life of William Cowper*, T. Fisher Unwin, London.

Zielonka, A, 1986, 'L'Expérience de la mélancolie et la joie chez Nerval', in *Le Rêve et la vie: 'Aurélia', 'Sylvie' et 'Les chimères' de Gérard de Nerval*, Société des Etudes Romantiques, Actes du colloque du 19 janvier, 1986, C.D.U et Sedes réunies, Paris, pp. 17–31.

Index